The Sexual Fix

The Sexual Fix

Stephen Heath

Schocken Books • New York

First American edition published by Schocken Books 1984
10 9 8 7 6 5 4 3 2 1   84 85 86 87
Copyright ©Stephen Heath 1982
All rights reserved
Published by agreement with The Macmillan Press Ltd, London

Library of Congress Cataloging in Publication Data

Heath, Stephen.
  The sexual fix.

  Includes bibliographical references.
  1. Sex.   2. Sex customs—United States.   I. Title.
HQ21.H386   1983   306.7   83-2967

Manufactured in Hong Kong
ISBN 0-8052-3860-3

Contents

Acknowledgements

In order to make what follows as easily readable as possible, notes and references have been kept to a minimum within the main body of the text; full details of the sources of quotations may be found in the Notes section at the end of the book. It might be added that the temporary anonymity of some of the quotations in the text is not without advantages: in most of these cases (and notably as regards passages cited from works of popular sexology) it is the generally representative nature of the quotation that is important, not its particular authorship.

The author and publishers wish to thank the following, who have kindly given permission for the use of copyright material:

Allison & Busby Ltd, for an extract from *Flesh* by Brigid Brophy.

Arlington Books Publishers Ltd, for an extract from *Octavia* by Jilly Cooper.

Faber & Faber Ltd and Harcourt Brace Jovanovich Inc., for 'Hysteria' in *Collected Poems 1909–1962* by T. S. Eliot.

Granada Publishing Ltd and Alfred A. Knopf Inc., for an extract from *Flying* by Kate Millett.

Laurence Pollinger Ltd on behalf of the Estate of the late Mrs Frieda Lawrence Ravagli and Viking Penguin Inc., for extracts from D. H. Lawrence's *Lady Chatterley's Lover* and *Aaron's Rod* (copyright 1922 by Thomas Selzer Inc., renewed 1950 by Frieda Lawrence).

The Sterling Lord Agency Inc. on behalf of Erica Jong, for an extract from *How to Save Your Own Life*, copyright © 1977, published by Holt Rinehart & Winston Inc.

I

'a sex–bomb is exactly what you are!'

New Man & Woman (an encyclopedia 'for
better loving relationships' in 52 weekly
parts), 1980

Don't be afraid. You are certainly normal. Everyone is. You have
problems. Everyone does. 'If you're not sure what your erogenous
zones are, much less where they are and what to do once you've
found them, you're not alone.' Don't worry. 'We are all persecuted
sexual perverts.' Sex is like a stormy voyage into seas to be con-
quered, an initiation into the depths of your being, an encounter
with the real you. There's a lot to learn, it won't be easy, the going
may be hard: 'it is sometimes very difficult and painful to confront
one's own sexuality'. You must have the courage. Nothing is gained
without effort and this, after all, is your whole life at stake. 'So let's
go to work.'

Your sexual body is 'a magnificent work of art'. Of course. But
then it is also 'a terribly complicated, intricate mechanism, as
complex as a computer'. Don't take it for granted, do some maintenance on it, 'refuel in bed', make sure the machinery is always
ticking over, remember the key 'Orgasm Message': *'Your sexual
equipment has to last you a lifetime, so keep it in good repair.'* If you're a
woman, you're in luck, anywhere you like you can be toning up
your pubococcygeus, that 'fabulous love muscle': 'contract, hold,
relax'; 'once you get your PC in terrific shape, don't slide back or
you'll undo all your good work'. If you're a man, things are not quite
as obvious or convenient but you can always practise your hand at
'squeeze technique' and keep abreast of the latest developments in
'genital pleasuring'. Some repairs will be too big for you to manage
on your own (you can't expect to do it all yourself!). A friend might
be able to help a little and your doctor could give reassurance, but
what you really need is specialist advice, proper treatment. The ideal
would be a stay in a well-established institute (the very best are in the

United States) where you can be put through a programme with 'assigned tasks' or 'sexual exercises' (remember, no one said this was going to be easy). Yes, it can be expensive, and it's regrettable that 'those who ask for aid are but a tiny fraction of those who could benefit'. Still, there are books, many many books, you can give yourself a 'self-help course in sex therapy'. Clearly you want to *Treat Yourself to Sex*, so get a *Good Sex Guide* and try to achieve *The Joy of Sex* (but don't rest on your laurels, there is *More Joy of Sex* too). You must claim *Your Right to Sex Happiness*, even if this will involve you in coming to terms with *The Obstacles to Sexual Happiness* (reward for your effort will be in knowing *How Sex Can Keep You Slim*). The goal, naturally, is *Total Loving*. And by the way, *God Says Yes to Sexuality*.

So how are you getting on as a 'fully orgasmic adult'? A man, you are most likely suffering from 'impotence' (or shall we say 'erectile insufficiency'?), primary, secondary or selective (you might, less nobly, be a 'precocious ejaculator'). A woman, you are most likely 'frigid' (and don't fool yourself, 'you *are* frigid if you can achieve orgasm through clitoral stimulation, but bomb out during coitus'). You, the woman, in fact are what sexology (the modern study and treatment of sexuality) is all about, 'the orgasmic attainment of the female' being a very favourite topic. So much so that there are several sexological points of view on the question and you may find yourself classed merely as 'pre-orgasmic', not frigid, quite capable, just needing to be led, gently yet firmly, towards the true orgasmic satisfaction. Anyway, despite the sorry world of 'melting erections and absent climaxes' in which the sexologist is called upon to labour, all cannot fail to be naturally happy in the end: 'the natural state of affairs is good sexual functioning'. Thus there really is no cause for worry, the equipment is made to go right and we are all of us normal – don't be afraid, you too can and will make it.

We have, it seems, been 'catapulted out of the sexual dark ages into a glittering age of sexual enlightenment and pleasure'. The present essay is about the process of that 'catapulting' and the terms of our 'sexual enlightenment'. Its main argument is simple and polemical, and might be summarized as follows: sexuality is without the importance ascribed to it in our contemporary society (Western capitalist); it is without that importance because it does not exist as such, because there is no such thing as sexuality; what we have experienced and are experiencing is the fabrication of a 'sexuality', the construction of something called 'sexuality' through a set of representations – images, discourses, ways of picturing and describing – that propose and confirm, that make up this sexuality to which we are then referred and held in our lives, a whole *sexual fix* precisely; the much-vaunted 'liberation' of sexuality, our triumphant emergence from the 'dark ages', is thus not a liberation but a myth, an ideology, the definition of a new mode of conformity (that can be understood, moreover, in relation to the capitalist system, the production of a commodity 'sexuality').

If the argument is put in this way, however, its contradictions should equally be stressed at the outset, these being part of its development. To say that liberation is the definition of a new mode of conformity has to be accompanied by the recognition nevertheless of what has been in many respects a truly liberating progress: we do, clearly, live in a dramatically improved sexual freedom when compared with our Victorian ancestors; from the introduction of and the provision of access to effective forms of contraception to the general availability of sexual information (in which sexology has indeed been important) there is a range of factors that do make for a genuine liberation. To say that sexuality does not exist as such is simultaneously not at all to deny the reality of the sexual in human life and the force and variousness of its experience; on the contrary, it is the beginning of an attempt to displace the particular and limiting representation of it that we know today as 'sexuality'. To say that sexuality is without the importance currently ascribed to it cannot be to forget the truly radical importance of certain forms of direct fundamental concern with actual human sexual experience; in feminist and gay movements, for example, these themselves questioning at so many points the given conception and utilization of 'sexuality' in our society.

Such contradictions are a matter not just of the present essay's argument, but also of its situation. It is written in the wake of 'the sexual revolution', in the context of the massive publicization of sexuality (the establishment of 'sexuality' as a public interest, its all-pervasiveness through the media and beyond as issue and topic), and is written against, in criticism of, that notion of a revolution, the terms of that sexuality and its publicization, while at the same time trying to retain and suggest the radical implications of a concern with human sexual experience, the significance and the necessity of that concern, indeed of that reality. Who is prepared to say today that 'sexuality' is a limited and limiting account of individual realization? And how is it to be said as part of a progressive social and political argument? We live in a society in which we are continually told of and assigned to our 'right' to sexuality, 'the new understanding which sees enjoyable sex as a right, not a privilege, of human beings' (as it is stated on the very first page of *Treat Yourself to Sex*). What can we do but be dutifully grateful? Yet this imperative sexual demo-cracy sustains a quite definite status quo: a delimited sphere of free circulation and exchange to which individuals are ordered as indi-viduals, their authentic being and fulfilment represented to them as that sexuality, a kind of natural and absolute possession outside of any social, economic, political context. 'The only rights we have are over our own body.' Exactly. We are all bodies, separate bodies, our rights begin and end there as the right to the sexuality we are offered and to which we are commanded freely to conform (the democracy is in the command, addressed to everyone, not in any reality, in which the sexual is never some simply given individual birthright from nature but always involved in the specific terms of the social organization). Certainly, this 'permissiveness' (permission is an expression of authority, what we are allowed) has been subject to criticism. 'Festivals of Light' and cant moralizers such as David Holbrook crying corruption through a haze of oppressive mysticism ('sex is the realm of experience in which we enter most deeply into "female element being"') are only too ready with attacks in the interests of the establishment of a new (old) moral order (itself based on appeal to a natural, good, warm, depths-of-our-humanity sexu-ality to which we need to return; no surprise that Mary Whitehouse is the author of a book entitled *Whatever Happened to Sex?*). The gamble – and the contradictory situation – of this essay is as to whether it is possible to begin a critique of contemporary sexuality and to urge the conformity of the contemporary notion of liberation *from the other side*, from a position that is not anti-sex and pro-repression but for change in the social relations of subjectivity, of our existence as related individuals – a change that today's construction and valuation of 'sexuality' can be seen to oppose.

This essay is above all a description and a critique of this construction and valuation. Its main areas of discussion are thus: the historical movement from the terms of the 'dark ages' to those of modern 'enlightenment'; the development of the conception of sexuality and the role played in that development by Freudian psychoanalysis and the growth of sexology; the discourse of sexology and the general representation and currency of sexuality today; the possibilities of an alternative understanding of sexuality and the relations of the latter to questions of meaning and language and representation; the double binds and contradictions and problems of the sexual now, something of an ethics of engaging human sexual experience. Within and across the areas, a variety of matters and materials will be raised and used, from Victorian medicine to literary criticism, from Krafft-Ebing to Jilly Cooper. The focus is representation: the setting up and out, the production and depiction and fixing of our 'sexuality'.

Let it be emphasized that this essay is partial (which is not to imply any lack of attention to the correctness of the arguments and evidence presented): 'partial' in that it is an *essay*, that no attempt is made to provide a full and exhaustive account of all matters raised (the history of sexology would fill many volumes, as would the history and inordinately complex detail of psychoanalysis); 'partial' too in that this is a critical and polemical work, that it is written as an *involvement* in a contemporary situation (in which, for example, there is no longer any need to defend 'sexual liberation' in those terms). What is in question here is the functioning of 'sexuality' today; the focus, once again, is the representation of that – a focus that is at once wide and narrow: many things will be omitted, which does not mean that they are here forgotten.

II

'It was a moment when a woman's soul is more incarnate than at
any other time; when the most spiritual beauty bespeaks itself
flesh; and sex takes the outside place in the presentation.'

Thomas Hardy, *Tess of the d'Urbervilles* (1891)

'Sexuality' is a nineteenth-century word. The great Oxford *New
English Dictionary on Historical Principles* (usually referred to as the
OED) cites a passage dating from 1800 for its first appearance, but
this is the word used in a straightforward and limited sense of the
(biological, zoological) statement of the fact of sex, of a sexual
reproduction in plants, insects, animal life: 'the quality of being
sexual or having sex', as the OED puts it. It is with the second sense
of 'sexuality' recognized by the OED that we find ourselves near to,
at the beginnings of, our general modern usage and understanding:
'Possession of sexual powers, or capability of sexual feelings.' As
will become clear later, the OED's example-quotation here is particularly apt as an expression of the historical context and problem of
the word's appearance: a sentence from the *Clinical Lectures on the
Diseases of Women* by the distinguished physician James Matthews
Duncan, published in 1889: 'In removing the ovaries, you do not
necessarily destroy sexuality in a woman.' 'Sexuality' comes in a
medical discourse and involves the question of 'a woman', Duncan's
sentence suggesting more than it says and in that area of suggestion
opening the way and signalling the need for the subsequent development of our conception of sexuality (we read the sentence now after
that development, in the light of that conception, while Duncan
could intend no more than a strictly clinical meaning, the physical
capacity for sexual feeling; but then the phrase 'sexual feeling' itself is
still an uncertain acknowledgement of something more, something
known but not conceived, not conceptualized, not explicable in the
clinical terms). The OED also gives a third, rather vague sense,
'recognition of . . . what is sexual', with a quotation from a novel by
Charles Kingsley, *Yeast*, published in 1848 and containing reference

to an 'honest thorough-going sexuality'. In many ways, this has a more modern, everyday ring than the Duncan use of the word and its source in a novel is not without significance in this respect – the importance of the novel for the generalization of the representation of sexuality will be a theme of the present essay. At the same time, it should be said that Kingsley, remembered popularly today as the author of *The Water Babies*, was an enthusiast of natural history. 'Sexuality' would have been available to him from that field of study and enters *Yeast* within the possibilities of the simple, first OED meaning.

'Sexuality' includes 'sex' and one or two aspects of the extension of the latter must also be mentioned. The word 'sex', referring to 'either of the two divisions of organic beings distinguished as male and female respectively', has a long history; thus the theologian John Wycliffe can talk in 1382 of 'maal sex and femaal'. Of interest in the range of this sense of the word is the emergence, on the basis of the differentiation of assigned characteristics and behaviours ('the gentler sex' complements 'the sterner sex'), of a use of 'sex' absolutely, 'the sex', to designate women. The OED has an example from 1589, 'a matter somewhat in honour touching the Sex' (meaning a matter that concerns women), and another, much later and now more explicit as to what is finally at stake, from 1792, 'the sex of Venice are undoubtedly of a distinguished beauty'. Women are 'the sex': fair, gentle, apart, different from the world of men; they are defined by their sex which is the condition of their difference, and hence very quickly they *are* sex, defined entirely within and as that. The other major sense of the word 'sex' is its use not to refer to this or that sex but rather to talk of the very fact of the distinction between male and female in general, of what the OED with some awkwardness calls 'the sum of those differences in the structure and function of the reproductive organs on the ground of which beings are distinguished as male and female, and of the other physiological differences consequent on these'. The initial quotation given, startlingly enough after such a definition, is from an early seventeenth-century poem by John Donne entitled 'The Primrose': 'For should my true-love less than woman be,/She were scarce anything; and then, should she/Be more than woman, she would get above/All thought of sex, and think to move/My heart to study her, and not to love;/Both these were monsters . . .' (note the monstrousness of a woman who were to get above all thought of the sexual). The real currency and exploitation of the word under this sense, however, dates from the nineteenth and twentieth centuries and allows us to envisage an area of our lives – the area referred to as 'sex' – that involves not just the physiological, but a whole number of varied elements and ideas and values. From about 1910 on, there is then a rapid and popularizing introduction of cognitive and derivative 'sex' terms: 'sex-life' (1919, *Daily Mail Year Book*, 'the mysteries of life, and especially of sex-life should be unfolded to young people wholesomely but clearly'); 'sex-appeal', a new version of 'the sex' (1927, *Sunday Express*, 'she has a large endowment of the "plus" quality of femininity, the unexplainable but unmistakable flair called "sex-appeal" '); 'sexy' (1928, *Daily Express*, 'it is much more dangerous to enter into a conversation of this sexy sort with foolish, meddling people'); and so on. D. H. Lawrence, whose novel *Sons and Lovers* of 1913 is quoted by the OED as source for the appearance of 'sex-instinct' and who contributed articles on contemporary sexuality to papers such as the *Daily Express* and the *Evening News*, provides in his writings of the nineteen-twenties a kind of compendium of 'sex' and its new terms (thus, for example, in the first draft of *Lady Chatterley's Lover*, written in 1926/7, we find 'the sex relation', 'the sex warmth', 'the sex glamour', . . .). From here we move easily to a notion of sex as a commodity, an entity that one can love or hate, that can be true or false (already in Lawrence), and that, in our contemporary usage, one can *have* ('I had sex with her last night').

There is one other related term that needs consideration, 'sexology', 'the scientific study of sex and of the relations between the sexes'. The OED quotes learned sources in the nineteen-twenties for 'sexological' (1920), 'sexology' (1927) and 'sexologist' (1929). In fact, however, 'sexology' has an earlier appearance in English in the form of 'sexualogy' in the work of Karl Pearson in the eighteen-eighties. Pearson was Professor of Applied Mathematics and Mechanics at University College London, with specialist interest in statistics and statistical methods of investigation. He was also, in a characteristic late nineteenth-century British combination, a socialist freethinker and a firm proponent of eugenics (eugenics was a supposed science for the improvement of the human race through procedures of controlled breeding, 'selection in reproduction', with only the 'abler races' and their 'higher specimens' being permitted to have children). It is as eugenist that Pearson comes to sexualogy in a

paper on 'The Woman's Question', printed for private circulation in
1885 (again this proximity at every moment of 'sex', 'sexuality' and
women, 'the woman'). The direct context is anti-feminist, an argument with the terms of feminist struggles for emancipation. Emancipation is a question not for women but for society to decide and
that decision must have regard to the larger question of reproduction. Feminists should face sex problems 'with sexualogical and
historical knowledge': 'We have first to settle what is the physical
capacity of woman, what would be the effect of her emancipation on
her function of race-reproduction, before we can talk about her
"rights", which are, after all, only a vague description of what may
be the fittest position for her, the sphere of her maximum usefulness
in the developed society of the future.' In the fight for and definition
of emancipation, the feminists deny their natural function; since the
feminists are the better, more intelligent females of the population,
the result can only be eugenic disaster – the withdrawal from
'race-reproduction' of exactly those women who ought most to be
bearing children and the consequent deterioration of the human
stock (the extreme expression of all this is C. W. Saleeby's *Woman
and Womanhood. A Search for Principles*, 1912, which urges a 'Eugenic
Feminism' dependent on women recognizing their reality as 'mammals'). Paradoxically, Pearson can argue quite strongly elsewhere,
in essays such as 'Socialism and Sex' (1887), for 'the complete
emancipation of our sisters'; yet this is always finally within the
limits of social efficiency, of 'maximum usefulness', the argument
against 'emotional' feminists who fail to grasp the vital issue of the
proper control of reproduction. Hence the need to 'lay the founda-
tions of a real science of sexualogy' and this initial appearance of
sexology as anti-feminist strategy is worth noting for what
follows.★

This brief historical consideration of words allows us to empha-

★ The contradictions and sheer confusion of the debate at the close of the
nineteenth century should be borne in mind. A large section of the socialist
movement in Britain was bitterly hostile to campaigns for freedom of birth control
and quite unsympathetic to feminist struggles. Birth control could be regarded
simply as a capitalist ploy against the increasing strength of the proletariat, with the
limitation of family size a false issue designed to avoid the true one of the
redistribution of wealth; while the idea of woman as 'sacred mother' was all too
common, with feminism an individualistic and retrograde diversion from the
progress towards socialist change. The leading socialist artist and thinker William
Morris in his widely-read utopian novel *News From Nowhere* (1891) is quite typical
in this respect. The visitor to the future new society questions an old man as to the
changes that have taken place:

'But I want to return to the position of women amongst you. You have studied

size at once that sexuality is a recent phenomenon. At the risk of stating the obvious, let us be clear that what such an emphasis involves is not, of course, any notion that somehow there was no sexual activity prior to the nineteenth century nor that that activity was not an object of interest and discussion and reflection, represented as a significant part of human experience. It involves simply the recognition that historically a new kind of awareness is developed, engaging a specific conception and systematization of that activity and its experience which are realized and changed and formed in response to the new awareness, the fact of the representation given. There is a maxim of the French moralist La Rochefoucauld to the effect that people would never fall in love if they had not heard tell of love. The maxim could be adapted and adopted for the sexual inasmuch as activity and experience are never outside of cultural forms, definitions, orders (the idea that the sexual is some naked and primordial realm of individual human being is itself a fully cultural representation). 'Sexuality' is the term of our conception and systematization, specific and historical, how we represent the sexual – 'sex' – as an entity, with 'sexology' its study. Sexuality, human experience of the sexual, is as old as language, as old as human being; 'sexuality' particular construction of that experience, goes back little more than a hundred years. One of the difficulties we face is the slide under the same word between these two references: we need the word 'sexuality' in the first sense, but we cannot say or write it today without bringing with it the assumptions, the representation, of the second. It is with the demonstration of those assumptions and that representation that we are here concerned.

The word 'sexuality' appears then for us in 1889 in a set of *Clinical Lectures on the Diseases of Women*. There is an appropriateness in this

---

the "emancipation of women" business of the nineteenth century: don't you remember that some of the "superior" women wanted to emancipate the more intelligent part of their sex from the bearing of children?'

The old man grew quite serious again. Said he: 'I *do* remember about that strange piece of baseless folly, the result, like all other follies of the period, of the hideous class tyranny which then obtained. What do we think of it now? you would say. My friend, that is a question easy to answer. How could it possibly be but that maternity should be highly honoured amongst us? Surely it is a matter of course that the natural and necessary pains which the mother must go through form a bond of union between man and woman . . . .'

Morris can then indulge in a little eugenics: 'English and Jutish blood' is 'on the whole . . . predominant' in the new society and has been much 'improved'.

reference on two counts. First, the date (the latter part of the nineteenth century, not the particular year; the dating of words and their different senses can usually anyway only ever be approximate) registers the historical moment and context of the new awareness, of the pressure making for that awareness in respect of 'matters of sex' (a phrase used by Karl Pearson in 1887). The context is that of a society in which the form of the family, at least as regards the dominant middle class that serves as the overall standard for recognized public morality and social values, is heavily patriarchal, organized as a little world round the strict authority and power of the father; in which there is an intense economic and philosophical-ideological stress on the individual (the individual as a basic constituent of the market and its political order) that can go along with and in ways support ideals of private individual fulfilment in love and affection, individual experience and feeling (this continuing the valuation of the personal and the association of marriage with love that had been steadily progressing in the middle and upper classes in the eighteenth century and in relation to which the Victorian patriarchal family stands as an old and regressive family type); in which there is a situation of achieved industrialization and urbanization (the industrial revolution and the growth of cities) bringing a certain individual mobility (the social and geographical circulation of individuals, movements from country to city, new patterns of work, railway transport, the speed and anonymous flow of the city) and giving rise again to stress on the individual, individual existence and possible satisfaction outside of traditional frameworks of kinship and community, and to a massive development of prostitution, now known as a full-scale social problem (the medical journal *The Lancet* estimated in 1857 that there were some 80,000 prostitutes in London for a total population of the capital of 2,362,000); in which middle-class women, excluded by the morality of the Victorian family and the constraining image of 'the gentler sex' from the public sphere of work,* are condemned outside marriage to the marketing of their

---

* Hence the peculiarly Victorian development of an investment of sexual pleasure in the *sensation* of class difference: 'slumming' with working-class women, dressing up your lady-wife to look like a servant-girl. The classic example is provided by Arthur Munby, a London barrister who collected and commissioned photographs of 'labouring women' and who described the innumerable women he met and interviewed in his voluminous diaries and notebooks. Munby had a long relationship with a maid-of-all-work named Hannah Cullwick whom he finally married in 1873, keeping the marriage entirely secret and requiring Hannah to alternate between the roles of servant and lady. The relationship depended on

'female skills' as governesses to small children or to the slide into poverty or prostitution, and within marriage to a life of enforced idleness and the cultivation of feminine sensitivity with its host of ailments and nervous disorders; in which there is a spectacular growth in the commercial publication of reading matter – newspapers, magazines, novels – dealing with every aspect of family life and individual affection and emotion.

Second, the medical source for the appearance of 'sexuality' is indicative of the problem in that appearance. The term appears but has no content, no conception, no theory; it points precisely to a problem, to something needing to be understood, not to any understanding. In 1905 Freud publishes his *Three Essays on the Theory of Sexuality*; such a title is impossible in the Victorian nineteenth century for which it could be a question only of essays on 'the reproductive function' or 'the generative organs' (a number of works of the period have these formulae in their titles). On the one hand, the sexual, inasmuch as it can be envisaged, is a medical topic, kept within the strict limits of reproduction, bounded by the ethics of a profession extremely careful of its social reputation (as witness, for instance, the almost total silence of doctors of the time on the subject of birth control and its methods; when in 1885 an English doctor, H. A. Allbutt, dares to publish a work on contraception, *The Wife's Handbook*, it is to find himself immediately struck off the Medical Register for 'infamous conduct in a professional respect'). On the other hand, there is a pressure of the sexual, a problem, an awareness of something that is now difficult and that can only – that must – be understood as medical, contained ideologically and institutionally (in the practice of doctors, for example) within medical representations, as illness, disorder, disturbance of the individual. Hence the characteristic and extensive medicalization of the sexual, of sexuality – which thus simultaneously emerges as a word, a notion, to mark the doubt, the problem, the new awareness.

Munby's erotic perception of 'nobility' and 'degradation' and their ritual exploitation. Hannah, the servant in whom upper-middle-class Munby sees 'a noble and gentle woman', is to be raised to 'spiritual beauty' by means of 'toil and servile labour'. Sessions are arranged in which Hannah is photographed as this or that type of working woman or posed as a half-naked, blackened chimney-sweep with Munby towering over her; in which she is humiliated before Munby's eyes and for him by the photographer who treats her as socially inferior, pushes her roughly into position, rubs dirt on her for greater realism: 'She obeyed him as a thing of course, and [I] saw him blacken and besmear her. . . . It made my blood tingle: but it made me bow in spirit more than ever, before so divine an abnegation of self.'

The common Victorian term for a climax of sexual pleasure, the equivalent of today's 'to come', is 'to spend'. 'I spent', the running theme of the most detailed sexual memoirs of the century, Walter's *My Secret Life*. 'I spent': sperm and money. The physiological economy of the body has its reflection in the commerce of bodies, the prostitution of women for the expense of men. In a drastic condensation of this mirroring play of expenditures, Walter at one point recounts the fascinated pleasure he gained from filling a prostitute's vagina with silver shillings, eighty in all ('adding shilling after shilling, and making her walk after each addition to the load'). It would be wrong to regard this relation of sex and expense as something unprecedented and exclusively Victorian: 'spending' has a much longer history as a sexual term (ideas of 'spending one's seed'): *Aristotles Master-Piece*, a compilation of sex-lore originating in the sixteenth century, shows concern with rates of expenditure and offers a wealth of advice; while the notorious bawd Pris Fotheringham stood on her head and had half-crowns thrown into her as an 'attraction' in a London brothel *circa* 1660. It remains the case, however, that the nineteenth century sees a systematic tightening and development of the idea of the body as a kind of precarious economy, the site and the unit of a delicate balance of forces requiring regulation and steady rhythms of exchange.

In previous ages, that is, there had at least existed the possibility of speaking sexual experience in terms distinct from regulation and the finality of an economic exchange, in terms that stray and run over in pleasure: not 'spending' but 'bliss', 'bliss on bliss' as Milton puts it in his epic *Paradise Lost*, describing Adam and Eve 'imparadised in one another's arms'. The seventeeth-century poet Thomas Carew lengthily details the process of discovering his partner in love-making, in a poem entitled 'A Rapture':

> And, where the beauteous region doth divide
> Into two milky ways, my lips shall slide
> Down those smooth alleys, wearing as I go
> A tract for lovers on the printed snow;
> Thence climbing o'er the swelling Apennine
> Retire into thy grove of eglantine,
> Where I will all those ravished sweets distil
> Through love's alembic, and with chemic skill
> From the mixed mass one sovereign balm derive,
> Then bring that great elixir to thy hive.

There is a progression, from the woman's breasts over her belly down to her sex, but equally a ramifying time of moments of images and delights that makes the progression a part, not the whole, of the experience. The lips 'slide' (earlier a kiss is 'wandering') and the rapture is excessive, without measure, wearing paths and climbing mountains. There is no regulation of expense; rather, an idea of abundance and plenty, without loss, a supreme chemical transmutation, the creation of something infinitely vital that can be given, offered – to the lover and to the reader in the poem. That Carew is writing within a poetic convention, drawing from a stock of images and conceits, is the point: this is an available discourse of sexual experience, a certain given *ease*.

Even the convention of Romantic love, to take a further example, provides something of such a discourse. That convention is established in the late eighteenth and early nineteenth centuries; in particular in J.W. von Goethe's enormously influential *The Sorrows of Young Werther*, an account of the passionate love of a young man for a woman who is the fiancée and then the wife of his best friend, ending in the young man's suicide (a suicide imitated by young men in a number of European countries). It is then, in fact, carried over in a weakened form into the Victorian period, the marginal and isolating passion transposed into a version of the expected love between husband and wife, and through to today, despite and along with 'the sexual revolution', as the power of the 'love story' (Erich Segal's best-selling novel of that title is the striking modern instance of the protracted life of the transposed convention – a perfect young couple, a brief idyll of married happiness, the death of the wife, the husband's narrative, the latter a kind of vague memory of the letters left by Werther in which he sets out his passion and sufferings and which make up the bulk of the narrative of Goethe's book). In many ways, the convention of Romantic love avoids and displaces sexual experience: Werther's is an impossible love for himself in the image of Charlotte, his loved-one, she as his image, not the desire for any relationship; he is in love with love and there is no physical jealousy of the husband-friend, only a love that exists in excess, that can have no place, hence the resolution of suicide. Yet it catches up nevertheless an intensity beyond the calculation of any economy, is a possible discourse of rapture, the prodigious commotion of a passion and not the problem of a regulation.

For it is this that is the crux in the Victorian nineteenth century, this *problem* of the sexual, of *'sexuality'* as the sexual is now beginning to be named and realized and pulled into a hesitant focus. It is not that the Victorians, as is so often said, repress the topic of sexuality; it is, on the contrary, that they produce it, that with them the sexual becomes a problem which thus needs to be faced – thought about and investigated, explained and theorized, with medicine having the prime responsibility for this social task: over to the doctors, the sanctioned custodians of the body in their recently acquired professional respectability, to furnish the treatises on the reproductive function or the reports on prostitution. For the individual the sexual is then received as *doubt*. In 1763 the libertine John Wilkes, in his *Essay on Woman*, summed up human existence in the following laconic couplet: 'life can little else supply/But just a few good fucks and then we die.' Such a stance is impossible for the Victorians, not because of 'immorality' or 'bad language' (there was plenty of both) but because Wilkes's cynicism excludes the individual and excludes doubt: it is *clear* in the sense that Wilkes's contemporary the Marquis de Sade is clear and the Walter of *My Secret Life* is not. De Sade runs through 'fucks', perversions, a gamut of sexual acts on the grounds of a convinced and decided materialism: there is no purpose or meaning in the world; religion, morality, family, and so on collapse before the fact of 'Nature', of which the sexual is a part to be used for pleasure and power and, philosophically, to destroy human illusions. Walter runs through women, encounter after encounter, in order to know, to try to be sure, to grasp an elusive certainty and resolve the question of his identity as a man; the sexual is the problematic foundation of human being, the site and the trouble of existence as an individual. We have entered the age of sexuality.

What has been described above is from a perspective that is exclusively male. The position – the idea – of women is doubtful, inasmuch as she, 'the woman', is the ultimate point, the reference, of the male doubt. Men spend, women have no sexual reality other than as the reflection and confirmation of this expenditure; they have their being in the expense of the man and their pleasure, if it exists, must be exactly equivalent to and determined by his: 'she spent with me', another leitmotif of *My Secret Life* (hence too a common belief in a matching cervical ejaculation, the woman just like the man). *If it exists*, for the dominant representation is that women have no sexual reaction, which is thus a male 'feeling'; women *must not be* sexual, which would upset the order, the balance, the stability of social and family relations. Dr William Acton, the pre-eminent British specialist in sexual matters and an international authority on prostitution, put it well in his book *The Functions and Disorders of the Reproductive Organs* in 1857: 'most women, happily for them, are not very much troubled with sexual feeling of any kind'; 'what is the habitual condition of the man is the exception with the woman'. In a later edition, the wording became 'most women, happily for society . . .'. The slide, from 'for them' to 'society', is a slip of the tongue of truth.

Sex is a balance, in the individual for the maintenance of the social, and the balance is precarious, an impossible tourniquet of countermanding directions. A realm of the sexual is acknowledged, for men: hidden from the family, it is the condition of the necessity of prostitution, with efforts made to bring the latter under state and medical control as a recognized social service (Britain lags behind the state brothels of other European countries but the Contagious Diseases Acts, 1864–9, effectively admit a need for prostitution and seek to put it on a healthy basis by instituting the compulsory medical examination of any woman on the streets suspected of being a prostitute). Women have no place in that realm, their reality is motherhood; Acton again: 'the best mothers, wives and managers of households know little or nothing of sexual indulgences. Love of home, children and domestic duties, are the only passions they feel . . .' It is as just that image of the best that Victoria reigns; the Poet Laureate Tennyson gets it right in his poem 'To the Queen' written in 1851, the year of the Crystal Palace Great Exhibition: 'A thousand claims to reverence closed/In her as Mother, Wife, and Queen'; the image is full, flawless, an ideal closure of identity, the woman as perfect One. And yet, as Acton himself indicates with his 'most women' and 'the best', it is known that sexual feeling is an experience of women as well as of men. It is simultaneously known and not known, denied: contained in a representation as 'sickness', a potential nervous state of women, the female sex; or projected out into a division between two classes of women, the most best and the some worst, the virtuous and the vicious, the angel in the house and the dark shadow of the bestial whore.

Coventry Patmore, author of a sequence of sonnets on man and love entitled precisely *The Angel in the House,* has a poem which can serve to give something of a summary expression of all this. Its title is 'Unthrift'. *Thrift* is the supreme Victorian middle-class virtue: moderation, wise frugality, good housekeeping, the proper use of money and energy, ordered and regular expenditure; *unthrift* is thus waste, excess, ruinous expenditure, everything that is most immoral, a profound social disturbance: imagine a female sexual pleasure without end or finality . . . Up to the woman then to act with measure, to hold to and confirm her position in the general economy:

> Ah, wasteful woman, she who may
>   On her sweet self set her own price,
> Knowing man cannot choose but pay,
>   How has she cheapen'd paradise:
> How given for nought her priceless gift,
>   How spoil'd the bread and spill'd the wine,
> Which, spent with due, respective thrift,
>   Had made brutes men, and men divine.

The object of men, the woman is given as cause: she can make a man divine in her image or, dissipating 'her priceless gift', reverse the last line of Patmore's poem and turn him to a brute. Woman is the fault of man's sexual trouble, of sexuality, and must expect to be punished at any and every moment – on the one hand, the tolerance, if not encouragement, of the necessary prostitution; on the other, the vengeful rejection of 'the fallen woman', the angel tumbled from grace.

   We are left with this: the recognition of a male sexuality but with no conception of 'sexuality' other than as the regulation of the physiology of the body through expenditure, spending, discharge; the denial of a female sexuality, with the sexual entirely limited to the function of reproduction; the real pressure nevertheless of an excess over and above these two representations, which in turn then needs to be dealt with, cast into limiting representations that can support and maintain the first two. The latter task is what is in play in the nineteenth-century medicalization of the sexual which operates according to two large overall modes of understanding, for the man and the woman respectively: *hypochondria* and *hysteria*.

III

'Debate in Congregation on proposed admission of women to some of the Honour Schools. I had no idea of speaking, but did say a few words – to the effect that it was a question for *doctors*. . . .'

C. L. Dodgson, diary entry (1884)

For us today hypochondria is a state of over-anxiety about one's health. Clinically, there is debate as to whether any distinct syndrome of hypochondria, or hypochondriasis, really exists, as to whether it cannot always be broken down into other syndromes (so that it would never be adequate as a diagnosis in any particular case). Authorities who allow the distinctiveness of hypochondria identify three major elements in its clinical pattern: 'The first is a preoccupation with bodily symptoms, the second is a fear of such symptoms, and the third is a conviction that disease is present despite the lack of objective evidence and, usually, despite the completion of all appropriate examinations and investigations.' Historically, hypochondria has received any number of definitions and explanations, from initial association with disorder of the digestive tract to eventual association with any state of melancholy (the context in which James Boswell could sign himself 'The Hypochondriack' in a series of essays for *The London Magazine* commencing in 1777). A constant and important part of this history, moreover, is the discussion of hypochondria along with hysteria, whether to emphasize their similarities or their differences. The Oxford physician Thomas Sydenham begins his epistolary treatise on 'hysteric diseases' in 1681 with a consideration of hypochondria, stressing both 'the great similitude' and 'the difference between the two diseases'; Robert Whytt, another physician and a distinguished experimental physiologist, writing in 1765, had it that 'upon the whole . . . the symptoms of the hysteric disease in women, seem only to differ from those of the hypochondriac in men, in so far as the former, sometimes, proceed from the *uterus*, and are, on account of the more

delicate frame of the sex, more frequent and often more violent than
the symptoms of the hypochondriac affection in men'. That last
quotation brings out both the parallel discussion and the sexual
differentiation involved. As we come to the nineteenth century there
is something of a generally available consensus that 'hypochondria
usually affects males, hysteria only women'.

'The difficult class of hypochondriac patients'; thus Acton, significantly in the course of his *Functions and Disorders of the Reproductive
Organs*. The hypochondriac is an important and common fact for
Victorian medicine and medical practice, is a difficult case, bound up
with the sexual. In hypochondria the Victorian physician recognizes
and poses the nervous trouble of sexual feeling. 'Nervous' was
beginning its career as a fashionable term in the latter half of the
previous century; the same Robert Whytt cited above had already
defensively acknowledged a popular conviction that 'physicians
have bestowed the character of *nervous* on those disorders whose
nature and causes they were ignorant of' and gone on 'to try to wipe
off this reproach'. What Victorian medicine massively institutes is
the relation of the nervous to the sexual as cause in a kind of general
condition of man: man is involved in sexuality, sexuality is at the
root of, *is* nervous disorder. Given the sexual feeling to which the
male human is subject, every man is, potentially if not actually,
hypochondriac; the specifically Victorian problem-awareness of the
sexual produces by definition the fact of 'the difficult class of
hypochondriac patients'. *By definition* since there is no conception of
the sexual, leaving aside the species and social function of reproduction, other than as trouble, disorder, an ever-threatening disturbance of the regulation of the economy of the body – and of society
with it. Hence anxiety is everywhere, and *rightly so*, for the sexual in
this conception truly is a danger to individual – and thereby social –
health. It is the age that is hypochondriac, as much as the individuals.
There is then, inevitably, a veritable compulsion to discover diseases
which cause the anxiety, to give the nervous the foundation and
substance of a 'real' illness and contain the sexual in that. We can thus
observe the production of diseases which – nothing to do with the
actual diseases of the period (the typhus fever of the slums of the new
industrial cities, for example) – are strictly *Victorian*. No doubt the
most striking of these is *spermatorrhoea*.

Though it is perhaps in France that the term and the idea are introduced into medical thought (by a surgeon named Claude-François Lallemand in a monograph published in two parts in 1836 and 1842), it is in Britain that spermatorrhoea has its full development as the illness-answer to the sexual questions of hypochondria, and this above all as a result of the formidable activity of Dr John Laws Milton, an indefatigable fighter in what he himself refers to as 'the battle of spermatorrhoea'. Laws Milton, a noted skin specialist, describes the illness in a series of articles which, from a preliminary report in *The Lancet* in 1854, have become by 1887 the twelfth edition of a treatise of more than two hundred pages, *On the Pathology and Treatment of Spermatorrhoea*. The tone of the work is often that of a crusade and Laws Milton is alternately triumphant and gloomy: 'the battle of spermatorrhoea has been fought and won . . . we may feel sure that it can never again be blotted out from the curriculum of surgical teaching'; but, 'the present state of opinion about spermatorrhoea, both in the profession and among the public, is not satisfactory . . . and there does not seem much prospect of improvement'.

So what is spermatorrhoea? Quite simply, spermatorrhoea is the male disease of 'involuntary seminal emissions', and more particularly nocturnal emissions. As Laws Milton puts it, 'seminal emissions are a real, serious, and sometimes obstinate disease'. Stringent maxims are in order: 'in men who have reached the age of three and four and twenty, everything beyond one emission a month requires attention'; 'lads never really feel better for emissions, they often feel decidedly worse'. Those in the medical profession who hold that 'an emission once a week or so can do no harm' hold to 'a very dangerous tenet', and it is exactly against such careless ignorance that the battle needs to be fought. Spermatorrhoea is no laughing matter but a widespread affliction: 'I am putting no imaginary case, I merely describe what I have heard scores of times.' Young men are wandering the streets in desperate search for physicians who 'will grapple thoroughly with the disorder', the symptoms of which are breathlessness, anxiety, bad digestion, brain fevers and local irritations (coupled with masturbation, voluntary as well as involuntary emissions, spermatorrhoea can lead to 'epilepsy, phthisis, insanity, paralysis, and death'). Remedies are worthy of the disease (the point, of course, is to eliminate the emissions): besides the improvements to be expected from applying cold water, sleeping on the floor, doing one's military service and consuming claret (but 'it is useless to expect any medical action from less than a bottle a day'), Laws Milton occasionally practises cauterization (i.e. burning) of the skin tissues of the penis but especially recommends one or two appliances to be worn during sleep: the 'urethral ring', a spiked metal circle that pierces the tumescent member, or the 'electric alarum', a 'most-ingenious instrument' that administers shocks to the penis at the slightest stirrings of an erection . . .

The determining factor here is not in the first instance any design of repression but the approach to the sexual as an impossible economy of physiological balance. There are forms of emission that are 'natural', others that are 'unnatural': for the former, emission as a result of 'connexion', heterosexual genital intercourse; for the latter, all other emissions, voluntary masturbation, involuntary wet dream, or whatever. Emission via connexion is an absolute necessity, fundamental to adult health (Laws Milton is an indignant opponent of abstinence, which can only lead to impotence or worse), *but* – the turn of the screw of the impossible – a normal, 'natural' sex life cannot protect a man from the evils of spermatorrhoea, has no incidence on the illness: *'connexion has no power of curing spermatorrhoea'*. Suppose a patient goes to one of those carelessly ignorant physicians (for such, alas, there are) who tells him that his complaint is merely nervous and recommends sexual intercourse. What will happen? 'He will go on substituting one form of emission for another, till the first period of continence warns him, by a return of discharges, that he is no nearer a cure than he was.' Exactly. *Nothing* can cure spermatorrhoea, and certainly not sexual relations, which only conceal the stealthy advance of the disease lurking in the very system of the body. Marriage, a regular sex life, is finally the worst course of action imaginable, an appalling source of delusion: 'the frame still continues to be exhausted; the genital organs and nervous system generally are still harassed by the incessant tax, and the patient is all the while laying the foundation of impotence'.

It is with that somewhat surprising conclusion – sexual intercourse is itself the royal road to impotence – that we touch on the effective mechanism of this Victorian illness, its image of the body caught up entirely in the terms of physiological regulation. Men need to 'evacuate', to 'empty themselves' (remember that Laws Milton is equally against sexual abstinence, another road to impotence; rates of the advisable frequency of evacuation are now an important topic of medical debate), but the satisfaction of this need is also the crisis of a loss, a dissipation of vital force, something of a failure in thrift. Hence the perpetual difficulty – and the anxiety – of regulation, of balancing expenditure, the hopeless deadlock of spermatorrhoea, which can thus play its part in the representation of sexuality. There is no idea of sexuality, no libido, no desire, but there are signs, traces, pointers to a 'sexuality' that cannot be recognized – cannot figure in the clinical picture – other than as the symptoms of a doubtful body: a body which is guilty, since involved in sexuality after all, and not guilty, since after all sexuality is affliction, suffering. Spermatorrhoea provides hypochondria with the justification of a basis in a *genuine* cause for anxiety; it relieves the patient by offering him the coherence of a 'real' disease. We can then note that, in its recruitment, this disease is a class disease, found mostly in 'barristers, medical men, authors, tutors, clergymen', in young middle-class men who must spend long years in making a career before they can think of being able to afford the responsibilities of marriage and who are all the while under the scrutiny of an extreme public sexual morality but also under the pressure of the medically acknowledged need for evacuation and yet at the same time for restraint. Spermatorrhoea says all that: an impossible sexuality.

This sexuality, male problem and medical concern, extends into other areas of Victorian writing, is the constant representation. Two instances will serve here as illustration.

In 1869 and 1875 two pornographic works by a certain John Davenport were published in London. Their titles respectively were: *Aphrodisiacs and Anti-aphrodisiacs (Three Essays on the Powers of Reproduction)* and *Curiositates Eroticae Physiologiae (Tabooed Subjects Freely Treated)*. Each of the titles is as though split into two modes: on the one hand, the reference to a whole pseudo-erudite tradition of sexual lore and titillation, a wealth of arcane learning, '*recherché* and festivous anecdotes'; on the other, the Victorian moment, the spermatorrhoeic bind, 'three essays on the powers of reproduction' (worthy of Acton), 'tabooed subjects freely treated' (a credit to the mass of moralizing 'hygiene manuals', *Plain Words to Young Men on an Avoided Subject* and so on). The contemporary eroticism, that is, is quickly and easily medical, in line with the physiological conception of the sexual that it encounters, develops and repeats. Davenport stresses this: his curiosities are 'eroticae *physiologiae*', the books depend on 'interesting *physiological information*'. The run of the section-headings for the various chapters plunges us into the same world – the same economy – as that of Laws Milton: 'Ch. I . . . Number of *ictus* per *noctem* [how many times a night] – old Parr [a celebrated case of male longevity] – the love tariff fixed by the Rabbis to prevent the waste of semen among God's chosen people . . .'; 'Ch. III . . . Evils of too great an evacuation of the semen – A French epitaph – A tendency to epilepsy caused by too great an evacuation of the seminal fluid, described in several cases . . .'*

Circa 1890, *My Secret Life* is privately printed in a handful of copies: eleven little volumes, more than four thousand pages, author anonymous. Walter, the narrator-hero of these memoirs, of this secret life, a middle-class gentleman of relatively easy means, is as though racked by a compulsion to sexual organs, by an obsession for knowledge. What does Walter want? To be sure, certain. His story is that of a kind of dedicated investigation cast in the mould of the science of the age, a succession of observations and practical experiments (prostitutes become live anatomical wall-charts as Walter visits a brothel with a surgeon friend for a lecture on the distinguishing signs of virginity) which, once again, culminate in 'essays on reproduction' (Walter gathers his findings into one set of remarks on the male organs, another on the female organs, yet another on coition). The climax of Walter's many amorous adventures is not so much intercourse itself as the examination of the genitals of his partners which follows (according to his own calculations, at the

---

* The medicalizing pornographic mixture perhaps has its most direct and popular public expression in the 'anatomical exhibitions' which enter the fairgrounds of the later nineteenth century. What is new is not, of course, the showing of 'freaks' or 'monstrosities' but the assumption of seriousness, the ambition of a systematic presentation, the strong assertion of social purpose and benefit: in short, the whole medical context and image, and then the emergence of the sexual within this. The most famous of these exhibitions is the 'Musée Spitzner', a museum of anatomy created by Dr Pierre Spitzner in Paris in 1865. Doubtless Spitzner had no claim to the title of doctor but that title is an absolutely necessary part of the exhibition, of its meaning. The museum toured European countries, England included, finally settling in Belgium where its success continued well into our century. 'Museum'? An amazing collection of preserved curiosities and painted wax models of bodies and organs bloated or withered by this or that disease, examples of some medical demonstration: two hands, wrists cuffed and jacketed, hold down a woman's body, while two more cut into her womb; penises and vaginas, row after row, in every state and shape of deformity . . . It still exists in Brussels.

time of writing Walter has thus inspected some fourteen hundred vaginas, 'this supreme feminine article'*). What does Walter want to know? The female sex, 'the woman', to be sure of *her*; that is, of himself, of his identity as man. Thus the compulsive cycle: encounter, act, verification; endlessly repeated, woman after woman. Thus the interminable doubt: the need to try *every* woman, *all* women, in order to have from them the certainty of the sex, the assurance of Woman, complete and enclosed, finally known and secured in that knowledge; and this the most 'objectively' – medically, physiologically – possible (at the end of Walter, a few years later, is Jack the Ripper, the Whitechapel murderer, dissecting his prostitute victims, removing vagina and womb with all the professional skill of . . . a medical man). And yes, of course, good Victorian, Walter suffers from spermatorrhoea, notes with anxiety his nocturnal emissions.

Woman's function is reproduction. Sexually, she is man's object and falls under his order and authority. In herself, she is outside of the sexual, has no specific sexual being, is untouched by sexual feeling. Yet the reality is troublesome, disturbing, slips out of true with this given creed. What is to be done with this contradiction? How is a sexual being of women to be acknowledged nevertheless while sustaining the image of its non-existence? The answer lies in its recognition as disorder: out of order, it can only be the manifestation of something wrong, an illness. Condemned to sexuality, man is prone to all sorts of consequential nervous and physical afflictions, is in the difficult class of hypochondriac patients; if possessed by sexuality, woman is close to danger, violently overtaken, liable to fits and spasms, is in the realm of hysteria – for it is as this that hysteria now operates: as the sexual representation of women. In a letter to John Stuart Mill in 1870 on the 'Woman's Suffrage Question', Charles Kingsley writes: 'we must steer clear of the hysteric element, which I define as the fancy and emotions unduly excited by suppressed sexual excitement'.

---

* Sexology is somehow not very far away in all this and it is really no surprise to find Walter welcomed today, with that characteristic imperturbably inadvertent sexological humour, as a pioneering worker in the field, warmly commended by sexologists Eberhard and Phyllis Kronhausen for 'his positive and appreciative attitude towards the female genitals'.

It is worth simply emphasizing straightaway that the Victorian nineteenth century sees the widespread dissemination of the notion of hysteria, its public generalization; the word itself coming increasingly readily to hand as an all-purpose term to characterize any 'female' behaviour. Consider, for example, the following passages drawn from a single novel, Wilkie Collins's *The Moonstone*, 1868, a detective mystery story told by several different narrators:

> I was ready enough, in the girl's own interest, to have a little talk with Rosanna in private. But the needful opportunity failed to present itself. She only came down-stairs again at tea-time. When she did appear, she was flighty and excited, had what they call an hysterical attack, took a dose of sal-volatile by my lady's order, and was sent back to her bed.   (male narrator)

> 'If you won't take me before the magistrate, draw out a declaration of your innocence on paper, and I will sign it. Do as I tell you, Godfrey, or I'll write it to the newspapers – I'll go out, and cry it in the streets!'
> We will not say this was the language of remorse – we will say it was the language of hysterics. Indulgent, Mr Godfrey pacified her by taking a sheet of paper, and drawing out the declaration. She signed it in a feverish hurry.   (female narrator)

> I was so painfully uncertain whether it was my first duty to close my eyes, or to stop my ears, that I did neither. I attribute my still being able to hold the curtain in the right position for looking and listening, entirely to suppressed hysterics. In suppressed hysterics, it is admitted, even by the doctors, that one must hold something.   (female narrator)

> The hysterical passion swelled in her bosom – her quickened convulsive breathing almost beat on my face, as she held me back at the door.
> 'Why did you come here?' she persisted, desperately.   (male narrator)

> *Then*, I knew that I had saved him; and then I own I broke down. I laid the poor fellow's wasted hand back on the bed, and burst out crying. An hysterical relief, Mr Blake – nothing more! Physiology says, and says truly, that some men are born with female constitutions – and I am one of them!   (male narrator)

Anything excessive, however slightly, anything wayward in respect of the given conventions of expected behaviour, is the sign of the

female (bearing witness if shown by a man to a 'female constitution'), is the mark of woman's difference, which difference is exactly
defined as her difference *from* man – and the given conventions
include the expectation of difference, of hysterical behaviour:
women are expected to be women. Women faint, lose their senses,
burst into tears, are desperate and feverish: female behaviour. Man's
identity depends on it, he needs the *opposite* sex as guarantee of his.
But then in return there is the risk in the opposite, the other; man's
being is fringed with darkness, the menace and unknown of the
female. Hysteria tamed: women are flighty and excited, humour
them, pacify them, this is a regular part of the domestic scene;
hysteria threat; something may be turning very nasty under the
swelling bosom and the beat of the convulsive breathing, something
that one would like to keep precisely at a distance in its classification
as hysteria – and not finish like Wilkie Collins himself, peering into
dark corners of the house where, he fancied, 'a green woman with
tusk teeth' lay in wait for him.*

The idea of hysteria has a very long history (an ancient Egyptian
papyrus of *circa* 1900 BC already comes close to it with certain details
of specific morbid states in women). Today, there are many
authorities for whom that history is over (rather as hypochondria is

---

* The classic literary statement of this threat is a brief prose passage felt worthy of
preservation in T. S. Eliot's *Collected Poems 1909–1962*, first published in a volume
in 1917 and entitled 'Hysteria':

> As she laughed I was aware of becoming involved in her laughter and
> being part of it, until her teeth were only accidental stars with a talent for
> squad-drill. I was drawn in by short gasps, inhaled at each momentary
> recovery, lost finally in the dark caverns of her throat, bruised by the ripple
> of unseen muscles. An elderly waiter with trembling hands was hurriedly
> spreading a pink and white checked cloth over the rusty green iron table,
> saying: 'If the lady and gentleman wish to take their tea in the garden, if the
> lady and gentleman wish to take their tea in the garden . . .' I decided that if
> the shaking of her breasts could be stopped, some of the fragments of the
> afternoon might be collected, and I concentrated my attention with careful
> subtlety to this end.

Everything is there: from the gasping breath and the shaking breasts to the attempt
to compose and hold the secure male observing distance, the relative security of her
seen as hysteric; with, in between, the fear of being sucked in, fragmented, bruised
– dark caverns, teeth, the ripple of unseen muscles.

seen by many as having lost any value as a diagnosis): hysteria has been dissolved as a clinical entity and the great hysterical attacks described in previous medical literature – and now moreover rare – accepted as the manifestation of what was in fact temporal lobe epilepsy; 'failure to recognize the convulsions of temporal lobe epilepsy for what they were for over four thousand years led, among other false trails, to the strange concept of "hysteria", allegedly a mental condition causing the patient to imitate convulsions and other neurological signs and symptoms which in turn led to many strange psychiatric theories still with us though their original rationale has been long forgotten'. Others, however, believe that hysteria is and should remain a valid substantive diagnosis, that it continues to be 'a vigorous entity or set of entities, even if somewhat pleomorphic'. 'Pleomorphic' is a way of saying that 'the symptoms of hysteria are enormously varied', of acknowledging that 'the range of phenomena encompassed in the concept of hysteria is enormous'. Given which, it will be readily understood why no summary definition of hysteria will be attempted here; our interest is in one or two conceptions and uses of hysteria as representation. Suffice it to cite the somewhat bland definition produced by the Brain Injuries Committee of the Medical Research Council in 1941 (the date is not by chance: the two World Wars gave rise to a wide variety of hysterical manifestations): 'Hysteria: a condition in which mental and physical symptoms, not of organic origin, are produced and maintained by motives never fully conscious directed at some real or fancied gain to be derived from such symptoms.' It will be noted that this definition makes no reference to the sexual or to sexuality (as well it would not if hysteria is being seen as a condition with a multitude of possible causes, including, for example, the shocks of war).

Yet it is on the sexual that hysteria turns in its history as representation. The term 'hysteria' derives from the Greek word *hystera* meaning 'uterus', 'womb'. It was the name for the ancient Greeks of a convulsive order in women attributed to the displacement of the uterus (fits were preceded by what were subjectively described by the women sufferers as feelings of an internal rising up and a consequent suffocation in the chest and the throat, the beginning of Collins's 'the hysterical passion swelled in her bosom'). The philosopher Plato, in a dialogue known as the *Timaeus*, gives a good account of this 'wandering womb' idea, relating it to frustration of the function of reproduction: 'the matrix or womb in women, which is a living creature within them which longs to bear children. And if it is left unfertilized long beyond the normal time, it causes extreme unrest, strays about the body, blocks the channels of the breath and causes in consequence acute distress and disorders of all kinds.' Cure would thus depend on getting the uterus back into place and one method for this was the use of violently ill-smelling substances inhaled through the nose, driving the uterus back down the body – the origin of smelling salts (the 'sal-volatile' administered to the maid Rosanna in the first of the Collins passages).

With the coming of the anatomical dissection of the human body and the accompanying movement away from unquestioning allegiance to the opinions of the classical medical authorities (Galen, Hippocrates), this old idea of hysteria was inevitably undermined: visibly the womb was not a free-moving agent able to wander up and down the body as it pleased. The link between hysteria and the uterus was not, however, abandoned. The womb may not move about but it may still directly influence the brain, provoking convulsions. For the physician Edward Jorden, writing in 1603, hysteria is 'an effect of the Mother or wombe wherein the principal parts of the bodie by consent do suffer diversely according to the diversitie of the causes and diseases wherewith the matrix is offended'. In other words, something of a 'mutual compassion' holds between the different parts of the body which suffer in sympathy with the matrix or womb. This sympathetic suffering is set in motion by noxious vapours which ascend from the womb to the brain (whence 'the vapours' as the term for a depression of mind, for being out of spirits; a term that has a general history, applied to any depression and to either sex, and a particular – and interlinked – one, used in connection with women and with hysteria in the background; 'the Vapours to which those of the other Sex are so often subject', writes the eighteenth-century essayist Addison).

The real break with the relation of hysteria and uterus is made in the seventeenth century with the development of a notion of hysteria as a disorder of the mind itself, as what we would now call a psychosomatic illness. This allows, among other things, for the possibility of its existence in men as well as in women (as long as the uterus was in one way or another the cause of hysteria, the latter could clearly have no male incidence). In fact, however, the subsequent history is not simple and progressive but messy and contradictory. The strength of the idea of hysteria as a female condition continues and reference is still made to the uterus. When hysteria is admitted in men, it is understood nevertheless as a female affliction, to which women are characteristically prone for a variety of reasons connected with their reproductive function (retention of menstruation, for example) and because their weaker brains and nerves make them anyway peculiarly subject to excitation and violent passion.

This messiness and contradictoriness is the reality and the force of hysteria in the nineteenth century. One has, together: the separation of hysteria from the uterus and the recognition of its symptoms and manifestations in men (Charles Kingsley can refer with no problem in 1870 to 'hysteria, male and female'); a powerful revival of the uterine explanation and an emphasis on hysteria as consequent on irritation of the female reproductive organs (hence numerous operations to remove the uterus, fallopian tubes, ovaries of perfectly healthy women); the emergence of new theories that seriously attempt a clinical definition of hysteria as an entity and develop the notion of it as psychosomatic, a physical disorder resulting from psychological disturbance (a major work in this connection is Dr Robert Brudenell Carter's *On the Pathology and Treatment of Hysteria* published in 1853; for Carter, 'emotion is a force adequate to the production of very serious disorders of the human frame'); the general availability of hysteria as a description of the 'female', behaviour, constitution, temperament, and so on (as witness the Wilkie Collins passages); an idea of a relation between hysteria and the sexual that, variously conceived and with differing degrees of explicitness, runs across all of these and is always 'in the air' (the uterine theory stresses the reproductive function, Kingsley talks of 'suppressed sexual excitement', Carter regards 'the sexual passion' as the most violent of the possible emotional triggers, and so on); last, but hardly least, a widespread presence of the disorder itself (since women are looked upon as by nature hysterical, the number of cases will be large – and everything is set up to produce them).

The reality and the *force* of hysteria. . . . The confusion is socially expedient and effective. What a lecture published in *The Lancet* in 1891 calls 'that protean disease, hysteria, which lurks under so many strange shapes' can appear – can be detected – almost anywhere and anyhow, brought into service in whatever way is needed. It names and dispenses with a whole realm of the 'emotional', any reaction that falls outside the convention of the 'reasonable', and it talks about and contains the relation of women and sexuality, and it is always there with a history and a context of medical seriousness and credit that underlies and guarantees its general extension, supporting and maintaining the basic representation: of women as *the female sex*.

For that is the point: women are determined by the fact of being female, by their sex, in other words by their reproductive organs; and they are thus subject to a host of symptoms and disturbances and ailments, of which hysteria – in its sense of a violent, convulsive attack, 'insanity' – is the extreme. Women are now fully gynaecological, the growth clientele for a medical profession bent on establishing social respectability and profitability. When Sir David Hamilton, a male midwife, was knighted in 1703, there was ribald mockery of 'the first cunt-knight that e'er was seen'; in the nineteenth century pregnancy has become a serious illness, requiring strict professional (male) attention and supervision and offering a lucrative and highly respected field of medical specialization. The level of ignorance was stunningly high – ovulation, for example, was quite generally believed by the medical profession to occur at the same time as menstruation – but operations such as clitoridectomy, removal of the clitoris, and ovariotomy, removal of the ovaries, were regularly performed for a range of supposed conditions, hysteria included. Introduction of the speculum, the instrument for the examination of the interior of the vagina, was heavily resisted in the name of the protection of feminine modesty and 'the character of Englishwomen'. Even when allowed, it could not be used with unmarried women, virgins, since to do so would run the risk of arousing sexual feeling – the very sexual feeling which women, the best wives and mothers, were elsewhere said to lack.

Mention was made earlier of the 'pleomorphic', enormously varied nature of hysteria, as also of contemporary doubts as to its existence as a clinical entity. In its history, hysteria has been regarded as a physical disorder, a psychosomatic one, with mental stress producing organic effects, and a psychological one, with physical symptoms but no organic basis. Today, it has been variously dissolved,

conflated with temporal lobe epilepsy, left as a psychological disturbance and considered as involving both mental and organic factors:
'notwithstanding the substantial importance of psychological factors in promoting the disorder, there is a link in some patients with
cerebral organic dysfunction', concludes Dr Harold Merskey in a
recent textbook, *The Analysis of Hysteria*. There is emphasis on
psychological motive, as the Brain Injuries Committee's definition
made clear: the symptoms carry some intention, 'not fully conscious'; some gain for the patient is at stake (escape from a difficult
situation, for example). There is recognition too that the pattern of
hysterical symptoms, the form taken by the manifestation of hysteria, may well be determined by medical fashion itself (in the
Victorian nineteenth century, that is, medical expectation and social
representation, the latter deriving from and contributing to the
former, set the terms for hysteria which its manifestations then
followed – one had the hysteria one was expected to have, after the
manner of hysterics). Finally, as noted before, there is little reference
to the sexual, which has lost its importance in the medical understanding of hysteria; the index to Merskey's textbook contains just
one reference under the heading 'Sexual basis for hysteria'.

This summary, however, has omitted the most famous work
done in connection with hysteria, work carried through in the late
nineteenth century and crucial in the movement from the 'dark ages'
to the new 'enlightenment' – the work of Charcot and Freud. It is
this that must now be considered, involving as it does both the
nineteenth-century representation of the sexual and a certain development from that, the establishment of the conception of 'sexuality' and its modern 'discovery'.

IV

'He [a fellow psychoanalyst] seems to have taken up with some woman again. Such practice is a deterrent from theory. When I have totally overcome my libido (in the common sense), I shall undertake to write a "Love-life of Mankind".'

Sigmund Freud, letter to Jung (1907)

Jean-Martin Charcot was a French neurologist and physician-in-charge at the Salpêtrière, a vast Paris hospital devoted to disorders of the brain and nervous diseases. It would be difficult to overestimate Charcot's international reputation and by the 1880s, at the height of his fame, medical men from all over the world flocked to attend his lectures and demonstrations, among them the young Sigmund Freud.

The Salpêtrière was filled with patients afflicted with a multitude of apparently diverse and incurable complaints; many of its wards were little more than a kind of dumping-ground, providing shelter and custodianship rather than offering any hope of therapeutic success or even of diagnosis. Charcot directed his energies towards these people, the material for a massive study of a largely unknown field of medicine, working on the understanding and classification of non-organic nervous diseases; and in particular, in the late 1870s and 1880s, on the phenomenon – or phenomena – of hysteria, the latter by this time in some discredit as a serious object of medical research precisely because of its general extension and the notion of it as a natural weakness of women, not a *real* illness.

For Charcot hysteria was a psychological disorder with physical symptoms and possible physical changes; ideas can promote symptoms and, furthermore, the idea informing the symptom will determine the mode of its physical realization (thus, in hysterical paralysis, the area paralyzed will often correspond not to any scientifically recognized neuroanatomical unity but to popular conceptions of the different 'parts of the body'). Hysteria has no organic basis, in the sense, for example, of being caused in some way by the female reproductive system; and it is to be found in men as well as women (in a ratio of one male case to every twenty female cases) and also in children, the reference to children being an argument against any sexual aetiology or causality of the disorder (hysteria occurs in children, there is no sexual life before puberty, therefore hysteria cannot have a sexual cause . . . Freud will follow exactly this argument and its denial of infantile sexuality in his early work on hysteria). At the same time, there is a physical and constitutional background to the development of hysteria as a result of hereditary degeneration: people are prone to hysteria because of some characteristic enfeeblement of the brain passed on to them from their parents and ancestors.

This stark outline, however, gives nothing of the feel and sheer dramatic brilliance of Charcot's work, of the lectures and demonstrations in which other elements and themes come jostling back, make startling reappearances. Hysteria is multiform, protean, unruly: anything, apparently, goes. Charcot wants to classify, to bring this hopelessly uncertain disease into order, present it as an entity, give it a clinical picture, its *tableau clinique*. Now you have confusion, now you see coherence. Spellbindingly, Charcot identifies a major hysterical fit, the '*grande hystérie*', describing it as patterned in phases which culminate in a position known as '*arc en cercle*', the hysteric's body held taut in a curved arc. He establishes special stigmata, '*stigmates*', symptoms occurring in the interval stages between fits, such as narrowed vision, anaesthesia or lack of feeling in a part of the body or down one side, ovarian tenderness . . . The circle turns. 'Stigmata'? A memory of the *stigma diaboli*, the marks of the devil of the European witch trials of the seventeenth century: women running wild, signs – such as insensitivity in an arm or a leg – proving their demonic possession. 'Ovarian tenderness'? Any Victorian doctor would agree, no problem, and the ovaries can be removed, simple: hysteria is about *that*. '*Grande hystérie*', '*arc en cercle*'? The elements of a fantastic spectacle of women.

Not the only elements, for we must add hypnosis and the careful staging. Hypnosis was medically disreputable, with its popular past of association with fairground and charlatan, the quack and the immoral. In England, forty years earlier, Dr John Elliotson of University College Hospital had provoked uproar and scandal with his hypnotic experiments; and sensational pamphlets were quick to promise full revelations of 'the strange practices of Dr Elliotson on the bodies of his female patients'. Exactly. But then Charcot was a

great man, the very top of the medical profession, and his reputation
will allow him to involve himself in such a dubious area. That he did
was because of the striking similarities between the effects produced
under hypnosis and the symptoms of hysteria: the same kinds of
behaviour could be observed and hysterical patients often seemed to
lapse into spontaneous somnambulistic states as though hypnotized.
So much so that Charcot came to regard hysteria as a necessary factor
in hypnotic success: only those who were hysterically inclined were
truly amenable to hypnosis, the latter thus being a phenomenon
dependent on an innate predisposition, the bringing out of a hysterical reality in the individual. Notwithstanding this stress on predisposition and the physical, hereditary background, however, a further result of the linking together of hysteria and hypnosis was to
emphasize the power of ideas in the symptoms and manifestations
of the former; as hypnotics act in accordance with suggestions, so
hysterics act in accordance with some psychological determination.
Charcot would show, as an enthusiastic Freud was to put it, that
such manifestations as hysterical paralyses were 'the result of ideas
which had dominated the patient's brain at moments of a special
disposition'.

Let us now remember the staging. For hypnosis was not just part
of the theory and discussion of hysteria, it was also part of its
demonstration. In the famed Tuesday lectures, Charcot, with the
help of his assistants, would demonstrate in the patients under
hypnosis the repetition of the phases of the '*grande hystérie*', the major
attack. It was pure theatre, and the audiences grew, and grew far
beyond the confines of the medical profession, 'authors, journalists,
leading actors and actresses, fashionable demi-mondaines'. The
pictures and engravings of the period capture the scene: the audience
rapt in attention, the assistants, the master, and then the young
woman, in the pose of a convulsion, head thrown back, body arched
forward, she fixed for the gaze, the offered object of the lesson, the
term of the demonstration.

It was too perfect. The same patients were used time after time,
like so many actresses. Expectation of what should happen was high
and what was wanted was more or less well known to these women,
Charcot anyway giving a verbal commentary on the various phases
throughout the performance. To emphasize the power of ideas was
one thing, to stress hypnosis as an actualization of hysteria, of an
innate hysterical predisposition, quite another – and indeed was to

forget that power of ideas. New understanding of hypnosis as itself a
state induced by suggestion, and not a state dependent on a hysterical
structure which subsequently allows suggestions to be made, put
paid to credibility in these demonstrations of a natural expression of
hysteria. Patients, who were entirely dependent on Charcot and the
Salpêtrière, knew hysteria and went with the pattern. Some, indeed,
were rehearsed beforehand by the zealous assistants eager to please
the master. One woman, Blanche Wittmann, could 'do' the major
attack so well that she became known as the 'Queen of Hysterics' and
later confessed that, even 'under hypnosis', she had always been
perfectly conscious of her act.

Charcot set a pattern and a fashion; hysteria followed, an artifact
of prevailing medical expectation and social representation and of
the relationship between patient and doctor. Today, Merskey, a
former physician in psychological medicine in a specialist London
institution, can report having seen '*arc en cercle*' just once in his entire
professional career, and cite a colleague whose score is only twice in
forty-five years.

At the centre of the picture is the woman. Hysteria is dissociated
from the womb but we come back nevertheless to the female sex.

Care was taken by Charcot's assistants at the Salpêtrière to ensure
a photographic record of the cases presented in the demonstrations.
Published in a three-volume 'iconography' this record consists of
photographs of women alone, no men; plates interspersed within the
text of the clinical details, Charcot's running commentary. Often
there is a portrait of the particular woman as she is at rest, the 'normal
physiognomy', much like any other late-nineteenth-century portrait
photograph; then the phases of the attack, the pattern, the order of
hysteria so dear to Charcot in his endeavours to bring it into the
coherence of a clinical entity; very occasionally nurses intrude, by
the side of the patient, determinedly fixing the camera, but generally
it is the single woman, with now and then an effect of 'beauty' – a
young girl composed on her bed, something of the Pre-Raphaelite
Millais's painting *Ophelia*; 'terminal stage of the attack' reads the
accompanying caption, but there is no trace of disturbance, 'in her
the delirium sometimes takes on a religious character'. The interest
for Charcot, as for the compilers of the record, is in the phases, the

stages, the step by step unfolding of the attack, and above all here in
the 'passionate attitudes' struck in response to hallucinations experienced during the period of delirium. The photographs are arranged
in sequences, a still silent film, a catalogue of gestures; the attitudes
presented and named in their succession – 'threat', 'appeal', 'amorous supplication', 'eroticism', 'ecstasy' . . .

There is no sexual aetiology of hysteria. But all the same . . .
Women are recorded in a scenario that moves from 'threat' through
'amorous supplication' to 'ecstasy'. In the demonstrations hypnotized patients had their convulsions triggered off by pressure applied
to 'hysterical zones', the ovaries especially were pressed and
kneaded. The very use of hypnosis set a sexual scene, the master
dominating the woman pliant to his every command; years later,
with hindsight, Freud was to comment to Jung that 'it is obvious that
anyone who makes use of hypnotism will not discover sexuality. It is
used up, so to speak, in the hypnotic process.' Freud was also to
recall overhearing Charcot one day heatedly acknowledging the
importance of 'the genital thing', adding that the master would
probably have denied making any such statement. Hysteria and the
sexual? Everything turns on the idea of sexuality being envisaged,
imagined, grasped for here. There is no sexual aetiology if sexual is
to mean some cause in the reproductive organs. But then there are
traces, signs, marks of sexual preoccupation, something is at stake in
hysteria – in its manifestation, its conception, its representation.
Charcot opposes a sexual aetiology in the first sense and then
reinscribes the sexual, those traces, throughout his work and practice. And across all this, carried in this reinscription, is something
else again: the sexuality, that is somehow implicated in ideas, in
patterns and movements of meaning, in the play of the history of the
individual being, in excess of 'organs' or of any 'function' (reproductive or other), something that is not conceived in this nineteenth-
century hysteria but that is there none the less, something perhaps to
be *heard*.

What is missing in the Salpêtrière photographs is indeed the voice,
missing too in the demonstrations themselves. The patients are
allowed speech, but within the limits of a kind of deafness, as though
nothing could be gained from listening, or as though it could only be
out of order, a distraction from the presentation in hand. The picture
counts, built up by Charcot's commentary, illustrated by this or that
exhibited woman, not the words, the unlikely chatter, the noise of

particular individuals. When a patient cries out, 'Mummy!', Charcot comments: 'You see how hysterics shout. Much ado about nothing. Epilepsy, which is much more serious, is much quieter.' When another is said by her mother to talk of 'someone with a beard, man or woman', the response is 'whether man or woman is not without importance, but let us slide over that mystery'. Charcot sees, Freud will hear. Perhaps the whole of psychoanalysis is in that shift. Seeing is believing: Charcot's greatest error, he becomes a spectator, he believes what he sees, gives demonstrations, publishes photographs; hearing is doubting: Freud's – difficult and hesitant – move, all the cinema is banished, no photographs, opposition to the various proposals for filming psychoanalysis, only a private room, the patient immobile on the couch, a voice starting and stopping and drifting and cutting across itself with new stories, difficult questions, lapses and erasures.

It is possible from here, from this shift, to develop a conception of sexuality in which the latter is not taken as a thing or an entity but is grasped instead as a disposition of human experience turning on the problem of the *individual* within the species function of reproduction, in which precisely the individual is unimportant, *excessive*. That disposition of human experience involves the constituent relations of the sexual in meaning and language, in the determinations of the psychical: sexuality as a history of the individual in those relations, a process that is never foreordained – we are not given as identities – or terminated – we are never accomplished as identities, totally set. Psychoanalysis develops such a conception, or provides the grounds for doing so, but equally runs in quite different directions, produces quite contrary descriptions. The work of Freud alone, its founder, is immense in volume and worked out into hundreds of ideas and schemes which are constantly being refined, modified and changed. Only three aspects will concern us here: the possibility of the conception of sexuality just mentioned; the importance of Freud and psychoanalysis for the current conception and functioning of 'sexuality'; the historical role of Freud and psychoanalysis in the emergence of that conception. It is the latter aspect which is of immediate interest in the story of hysteria.

Freud attended Charcot's lectures at the Salpêtrière over a period of just under five months between October 1885 and February 1886

(Freud was at this time 29, qualified as a doctor but without an established post or practice, engaged to be married, very much at the start of a career); he offered his services as German translator for Charcot's latest book, achieved a certain acquaintanceship with the great man, and was generally overwhelmed (his first son would be named after Charcot, Jean-Martin Freud): Charcot had proved, Freud later wrote, 'the genuineness of hysterical phenomena and their conformity to laws'. Back home in Vienna, Freud gave a paper to the Viennese Society of Physicians outlining Charcot's work and teachings and including reference to male hysteria. Though Freud in subsequent autobiographical writings was to develop a highly charged account of this event and the opposition he encountered ('an old surgeon actually broke out with the exclamation: "But, my dear sir, how can you talk such nonsense? *Hysteron* means the uterus. So how can a man be hysterical?"'), it seems that, in fact, the paper was politely and rather routinely received; Charcot's ideas were well known, several of those present had themselves recorded cases of hysteria in male patients (the 'old surgeon' would have been very much an exception in the Society), and, more than Freud then realized, Charcot's methods and conclusions were damagingly open to criticism.

Freud at this point was holding firmly to Charcot's separation of hysteria from any sexual cause and maintaining a balanced position on the question as to whether body or mind was the determining ground of the disorder, allowing for both physiological and psychological factors in any explanation. In the medical practice he had opened on his return, Freud used established methods of treatment such as hydrotherapy and electrotherapy (therapy employing water and electricity), massage and rest cures. Dissatisfied with the results obtained, he began, in the latter part of 1887, to use hypnosis.

It was not the influence of Charcot that led to this use of hypnosis in Freud's practice (hypnosis was important for Charcot in the demonstration and theory of hysteria rather than in its treatment) but that of a Viennese colleague, Josef Breuer, the other decisive figure in Freud's confrontation with hysteria. Some years prior to Freud's visit to Paris and the Salpêtrière, Breuer had treated a hysteric, Anna O., who had fallen into spontaneous hypnotic states during which she would narrate ideas and stories troubling her and then awake calmed, 'comfortable'. Profiting from this 'auto-hypnosis' and himself additionally hypnotizing her, Breuer went through with her, day after day, the history of each of her symptoms, having her 'talk out' each one until she reached the moment of its first appearance when it would disappear – 'when this had been described the symptom was permanently removed'. Breuer called the treatment the 'cathartic method', from the Greek *catharsis*, purgation; Anna O. called it 'the talking cure', since the therapeutic effect was gained through words, verbalization, bringing things into speech. It was in this perspective that Freud turned to hypnosis: under hypnosis, patients were to be induced to remember the circumstances surrounding the onset of their symptoms. The cathartic method was taken over with enthusiasm and gave Freud some real therapeutic success, duplicating the results obtained by Breuer. The outcome was a jointly authored volume of *Studies on Hysteria*, published in 1895, in which Breuer and Freud each set out case histories of patients treated and contributed a more general, theoretical chapter.

The major stress of the *Studies* is that '*hysterics suffer mainly from reminiscences*', which are bound up with unconscious psychical traumas or shocks. In and through the symptoms, the hysteric is unconsciously remembering some painful previous experience. Even as the volume was being prepared, however, Freud was pushing away from the simple assumptions and procedures of the cathartic method. Hypnosis proved difficult to apply in every case (Anna O. had been a peculiarly susceptible patient and had, after all, started by hypnotizing herself) and Freud was not a very skilled practitioner. He began to deal with his patients without hypnosis, putting pressure on their foreheads with his hand and urging them to bring into consciousness the memories of which, somewhere else in their minds, they must have knowledge. A 'free association' technique was also developed in which patients were encouraged to say whatever came into their heads, irregardless of any rational ordering of a discourse but simply in response to the flow of ideas and words as they crossed the mind, setting going chains of elements – of associations – that might eventually lead into the hidden material. Hypnosis, moreover, could remove individual symptoms, but this was hardly equivalent to a real cure: the interplay of forces provoking the hysteria could remain intact, often issuing in new symptoms as the old ones were taken away or in the subsequent relapse of the patient. The task was to get at what was blocking the coming into consciousness of the memories, the reminiscences involved: '*by means of my psychical work*', wrote Freud, '*I had to overcome a psychical force in the patients which was opposed to the pathogenic ideas* [the ideas determining the illness] *becoming conscious (being remembered)'*. One encountered in hysteria, as Freud quickly saw and said, a *defence* or *repression*.

But why should this be? What is the distressing area in the lives of these patients which is subject to repression, against which defence is built up? Freud's answer was sexuality, the individual's 'sexual life', the source of the 'incompatible ideas', all the material unacceptable to consciousness. Thus Freud reinstates a sexual causation of hysteria; but psychological, not organic; or rather, given his nineteenth-century scientific training and intellectual situation, Freud regarded the sexual as able to provide psychology with a physiological and biological base. The therapeutic technique and understanding is purely psychological but the sexual aetiology of hysteria links mind and matter, roots the psychological in the organic – since 'no one will be inclined to deny the sexual function the character of an organic function'. No psychology without sexuality, with the latter, as Freud later puts it to a recalcitrant Jung, 'the indispensable "organic foundation" without which a medical man can only feel ill at ease in the life of the psyche'; sexuality gives the energy for the emotional investment ('affect') and discharge ('abreaction') in play in hysteria (and, as the theory progresses, in the other nervous disorders and in human psychical functioning generally), the energy that Freud will subsequently characterize as 'libido':

'Sexual motive forces' are 'an indispensable premiss' in explaining hysteria. How are these motive forces to be understood? The cathartic method, chimney-sweeping, the talking cure have to do with some trauma in the patient's past. So what is at stake in this original traumatic event and, again, why the defence and repression, why the hysteria?

Freud's first answer was devastatingly simple: the original traumatic event is seduction as a child by an adult. The experience is passive, the child submits to the adult, and is soon forgotten, the child makes little or nothing of it, being at this stage in a 'presexual' state and lacking in sexual feeling. The traumatic effect comes afterwards, works by 'deferred action' when the beginnings of sexual feeling at puberty revive the forgotten memory, now endowed with a new force and significance: 'It is not the experiences themselves which act traumatically, but their revival as a *memory* after the subject has entered on sexual maturity.' The trauma, as it were, is in the memory and it is this that leads to defence and repression. If these fail, there is a 'return of the repressed': the memory comes through, converted into symptoms, 'compromise-formations' that both express and hide it, that stand between unconscious and conscious. It should be noted, moreover, that this 'seduction theory' was extended by Freud to other conditions – the psychoneuroses – besides hysteria: specific forms of childhood sexual encounter lead to specific disorders in adult life.

Freud's patients do indeed tell stories of seductions, analysis runs into such memories, the cases become so many vivid family histories. Yet the seduction theory suggests a dramatically high level of parental perversion. Can all these stories be true? Can all hysterics have been thus seduced? Freud's own brothers and sisters show hysterical tendencies: can his father have been involved in childhood seduction? Freud starts to analyze himself and this self-analysis brings up difficult memories, problematic sexual impulses, a mass of libidinal material from his past. Suppose these stories of seductions were *fantasies*, deriving not from any real event (though such events may well occur in some cases) but from the individual's own sexual activity and history. Suppose that there were no 'presexual' stage but, on the contrary, an 'infantile sexuality', that the child was implicated in sexual feeling from the outset. In 1897 Freud was beginning to be clear as to the truth of these suppositions; by the end of the year, the seduction theory was in ruins and effectively abandoned. 'I have learned to explain', he wrote in 1905 in what was more or less his first explicit published indication of his change of view, 'a number of phantasies [= fantasies] of seduction as attempts at fending off memories of the subject's *own* sexual activity (infantile masturbation). When this point has been clarified, the "traumatic" element in the sexual experiences of childhood lost its importance and what was left was the realization that infantile sexual activity (whether spontaneous or provoked) prescribes the direction that will be taken by later sexual life after maturity. The same clarification . . . also made it necessary to modify my view of the mechanism of hysterical symptoms. They were no longer to be regarded as direct derivatives of the repressed memories of childhood experiences; but between the symptoms and the childish impressions there were inserted the patient's *phantasies* (or imaginary memories), mostly produced during the years of puberty. . . .'

We emerge from a world of 'scenes' and an external violence of sexual imposition – all those seducers, all those 'trouble makers' – into one of a whole imagination of sexuality, the process of the individual's own history, full of meanings and ideas and movements and shifts, a constant activity of the sexual from beginning to end of a life, of human individual being.

The cathartic method sought to get rid of something, to purge; the psychoanalytic method, the method of the *psychoanalysis* that Freud introduces, becomes a true talking cure: the patient speaks, the analyst listens, interprets, helps towards meaning.* The sexual, sexual behaviour, is within the terms of the history of the individual, is never abstract from meaning, from patterns of significance for an unconscious as well as a conscious part of the mind. Cure is about grasping those terms of the history, understanding the behaviour in those patterns it makes and sustains. The conception of sexuality has changed; or rather, it has now finally become radically possible.

When Charcot talks of everything coming down to 'the genital thing', when Breuer, walking with Freud and after meeting the husband of one of his patients, suddenly comments that these cases are always to do with secrets of 'the marriage-bed', when a distinguished Viennese professor of gynaecology, Rudolf Chrobak, sharing a case with Freud, declares that 'the sole prescription for such a malady' is 'normal penis, repeated doses', we are in the nineteenth-century economy of the sexual, a balance to be maintained and ensured, something to do with organs, physiology, bodily functions, something one knows about and simultaneously knows – and want to know – nothing of; Freud hears these three men making such remarks yet 'two of them later denied having done so . . . the third

* It seems that Freud's actual practice, initially at least, was more aggressive: patients had their attention led back to repressed sexual ideas 'in spite of all their protestations'. Class, too, determined practice in this respect: 'servant-girls', Freud explains to Jung in 1907, are barely worth consideration and the analyst can tell them their story without needing to listen: 'Fortunately for our therapy, we have previously learned so much from other cases that we can tell these persons their story without having to wait for their contribution. They are willing to confirm what we tell them, but we can learn nothing from them.'

[Charcot] would have probably done the same'. And the nineteenth century, it should be stressed, is lasting a long time: the remarks would not be denied today (far from it) but they are still made, the same remarks, the same premises of sexuality. When Freud pulls towards fantasy and meaning, we are in a new conception, no longer organs, the sexual act, normal penis, genital finality: sexuality now as complex history and structure and patterning of desire.

But let us not lose sight of Freud. This new conception is available and is developed in psychoanalysis but the latter equally continues and develops other emphases. To the end Freud retains his ambition to anchor the psychological in the organic. In 1925, for example, he can produce formulations which would come close to amounting in practice to an abandonment of psychotherapy for chemotherapy, treatment by chemical substances, looking forward to an account of the sexual that will 'assign chemical processes to it and . . . attribute sexual excitement to the presence of some particular, though at present unknown substance'.* More importantly here, working with the new conception of sexuality, Freud is concerned just as much as before to establish its lawful nature, to demonstrate a regular organization of human sexual being. Such a project is not necessarily in contradiction with the conception of sexuality as an interminable and open individual process, neither given nor finished but it can also lead to a fixed and thing-like 'entity' conception, bringing with it as such heavily normative descriptions – this is sexuality and this is the way it is.

What Freud outlines and then constantly fills in over the years of his work is a narrative of the development of human individuals from the polymorphously perverse sexual activity of the infant (all over the place, no inhibitions) through to the genital organization of normal adult sexual life (including for the woman, for example, the transition from 'clitoral orgasm' to the 'maturity' of 'vaginal orgasm') in which sexual instinct or drive is subordinated to the reproductive function, 'becomes, so to say, "altruistic"'. Along the path of this development lie: the progress from auto-erotism (infantile sexual satisfaction obtained without reference to an external

---

* Modern research has in a way identified such a substance, the hormone *androgen* (there are, in fact, several different but related hormones qualifying as androgens), proposed indeed as 'the libido hormone in both sexes'. This does not change, however, the psychological implication of the sexual in each individual, the fact of an individual history, and the possibility of understanding sexuality in respect of that, the understanding begun by psychoanalysis.

object or to a unified image of one's own body) through narcissism (erotic investment in one's own unified image) to choice of an external object; the movement across stages of sexual pleasure (oral, anal, genital); the entry into and resolution of the Oedipus complex (a structure of desire and hostility in respect of the father and mother); the repression of the sexual in the latency period between infancy and puberty; the conflict at puberty, which sees the organic development of the body for sexual activity, between the repression and the reawakened sexual drives. Infantile sexuality thus becomes the basis in the individual's development for the organization of adult sexuality, the latter being a limited, impoverished version of the former, a kind of successful – normal – neurosis. Any 'aberration from normal sexuality' can therefore be seen as 'an instance of developmental inhibition and infantilism' – something went wrong in the regular development.

No doubt we have come a long way from the nineteenth-century medicalization of sexual experience and its account of the latter's 'disorders'. Freud's *Three Essays on the Theory of Sexuality* in 1905 does mark an original approach and understanding, precisely a theory of sexuality. Yet it is important also to include Freud in the nineteenth century, at the close of which, in the last fifteen years, he initiates psychoanalysis.

Hysteria is decisive for such an inclusion. In those last fifteen years two things can be cited at once as fundamental in the initiation of psychoanalysis. First, Freud's self-analysis, begun in 1897 and culminating in *The Interpretation of Dreams* published in late 1899: the demonstration of the existence of an unconscious area of mental activity that is nevertheless fully engaged in thought, in meaning; dreams have meaning, say a great deal in relation to the history of the individual beyond his or her conscious control and intention, dreams as 'the royal road to the unconscious' and to a whole new description of the mental apparatus, of the mind. Second, the confrontation with hysteria and in it with the force of the sexual. The two fit together: the self-analysis confirms the importance and the particular reality of the sexual, the fact of an individual history from infancy to the present with difficulties and inhibitions and impulses, and moves towards an idea of the mind, conscious and unconscious, that helps

understanding of the defence and repression, the mechanisms, found
in hysteria. The sexual and the unconscious: 1895, *Studies on
Hysteria*; 1899, dated 1900, *The Interpretation of Dreams*; 1905, *Three
Essays on the Theory of Sexuality*. Psychoanalysis *exists* in this movement: hysteria, an account of the functioning of the mental apparatus, sexuality.

In the beginning was the woman, the hysteric: Anna O., Emmy
von N., Lucy R., Katherina – , Elisabeth von R.; the *Studies on
Hysteria* are all of women. One starts there, these women who force
against the bounds of sense, the established orders of meaning, with
their symptoms, their cries, their words. Something troubling: the
woman, the sexual, the problem that hysteria serves to name and
place. Yes, we have jettisoned the old equation of women and
hysteria, but still . . . . Remember Plato, as Freud does in his
Autobiographical Study of 1925: 'I was going back to the very beginnings of medicine and following up a thought of Plato's.' The same
returns, continues: 'all women play on the uterus', writes a present-
day psychoanalyst, Michèle Montrelay, repeating a basic tenet of
Victorian medical thinking. From the outset, women as the woman
represent sexuality for psychoanalysis; the old story, the nineteenth
century, law and order: how to get women properly in position, deal
with the problem they *are* – and that men will be too if the fixed
terms of difference and identity should slip. In 1898 Freud wrote to
his friend Wilhelm Fliess, author of a book computing the regularity
and influence on psychic character of women's menstrual periods, to
congratulate him on the birth of a son, saluting him in a poem
penned for the occasion as one who 'has stemmed the power of the
female sex so that it bears its share of obedience to the law'. And if
psychoanalysis itself were not exactly occupied in that role, if the
sexuality it proposed were not exactly a huge construction of and
tribute to the law? The law of sexual identity.

What does psychoanalysis hear in hysteria? A problem of sexual
identity in phallic terms: the hysteric is unsure as to being woman or
man, 'the hysterical position – having or not having the phallus' (a
recent formulation by analyst Irène Diamantis). She is in trouble
with her position as a woman, simultaneously resisting and accepting the given signs, the given order; like the patient of Freud's who
'pressed her dress up against her body with one hand (as the
woman), while she tried to tear it off with the other (as the man)'.

Listening to the woman as hysteric, psychoanalysis opens up and closes off sexuality, with the point of closure precisely 'sexual identity', 'sexual difference', the fixed terms: the man, the woman, 'as the man', 'as the woman', the one and the other. Hence, symptomatically, the curious lag of psychoanalysis felt by Freud with regard to 'femininity': the initial problem, women are still at the end, as Freud ponders 'female sexuality' in the 1930s, the great enigma, 'the dark continent'. Curious just because of that beginning with hysteria, the cures with women, attention focused there. But then not so curious, since hysteria was designed to produce the very idea of a problem, the perspective of the woman as a kind of disturbing embodiment of some doubtful and threatening – 'dark' – sexual essence. In every sense psychoanalysis answered to the nineteenth-century hysteria it took as its first and decisive object. What works is identity, genital organization, the phallus, *that* differ-ence, 'the polar character of sexuality', having or not, variations from there, with the woman as other to the man, *his* difference, less and more, falling short and beyond; she lacks the phallus, is less, but since she is therefore different, she is also more, excessive, beyond him, an enigma. Start from the hysteric, the trouble of identity, then focus centrally on the terms of identity with the man, the male, as measure, as standard ('we have been in the habit of taking as the subject of our investigations the male child'), then, finally, come back to the woman as as yet, as always, unknown ('we need not feel ashamed') – the programme of Freudian psychoanalysis, with the lag produced by the logic, women can only be 'the woman', different *from*, and sexuality is the arena and the conception of that order.

For centuries, however, hysteria has indicated a failure of the order, a refusal to take the place assigned, to be the difference, the woman – to support the position of 'the man', so powerful and oppressive for both sexes. To explain hysteria by 'the problem of sexual identity' is to miss and to contain the struggle it represents, the resistance it marks *against* that assumption of identity, is to refind hysteria as a nature of women/woman (one may find hysteria in men but it remains, says Freud, a 'feminine' disorder – or, as the Wilkie Collins character put it a few years earlier, 'some men are born with female constitutions'). There is a historical and political choice of perspective at stake: hysteria is a disorder which proves the law of sexual identity, the given order; hysteria is a protest against the oppression of that law of sexual identity, that given order, painfully envisaging in its disorder and economy, a quite different representation of men and women and the sexual. From the nineteenth century through psychoanalysis to the present day, sexuality is then the site of a veritable determination for law and order, of the continued sexual fix that is the concern of this essay.

The scene of the hysteric in psychoanalysis is done with discretion, nothing of the brilliance of Charcot's demonstrations, no audience even.* But it is the same scene nevertheless, the same arrangement: the master, the woman, the distance of the former's knowledge and position, eye and ear attuned to 'the problem'. The scene is never witnessed; it is read by you and me in the published works, the theoretical books, the case histories, the little incidents with which the analyst's path is strewn, even simply talking to a woman friend:

> I have a woman friend who lives abroad; we meet every two or three years, which enables us to discuss what we have been doing. Learning that I was working on female sexuality, she demanded: 'What do you know about that?' 'That's what we'll find out.' 'And why are you working on it? What is it you want to know?' My friend's intelligence is not in question, but not being an analyst, it did not occur to her that one does not write just the things one wants to know; why not also the things of which one would have preferred to remain ignorant. But anyway, as it is the elementary law of conversation to stay clear of hot waters, I ventured the answer that I was perhaps trying to find out whether a relation between the sexes was possible that would be a relation between equals. 'What's that you're saying? I want a being superior to me.' 'But Martha (that is my friend's name), there is no being superior to you.' It would be no exaggeration to describe the effect of this answer on my friend by saying that she was suffocated by it.

The concern is still 'female sexuality', the analyst still has the knowledge, polite but firm (there is no being superior to you, we are

---

*It should be noted, however, that the only subsequent equivalent in Paris life to Charcot's Salpêtrière lectures was provided in recent years by the public 'seminar' of the most famous of contemporary psychoanalysts, Jacques Lacan. In the late seventies, hundreds would flock to the Sorbonne to be fashionably seen and to watch the master tying knots (part of the theory), to be told that the sexual pleasure of women shows that 'God has not yet made his exit' or that 'Queen Victoria, there's a woman . . .' (the nineteenth century, the Woman, the One, Tennyson and Walter – 'when one encounters a toothed vagina of such exceptional size', continued Lacan).

all equals because all in the same phallic boat, all turning round the penis-phallus), the woman is amazed by it. Wait though . . . Martha is suffocated and suffocation, difficulty in breathing, is a classic symptom of hysteria. The friend is a hysteric, she's having problems of identity, with female sexuality – or else, perhaps, inconceivably, she's having problems with the identity, with the knowledge and its system held out to her, choking on that, entering a protest, but unheard.

V

'There were 117 psychoanalysts on the Pan Am flight to Vienna and I'd been treated by at least six of them. And married a seventh.'

Isadora Wing, heroine-narrator of
Erica Jong's *Fear of Flying* (1973)

'Sexuality became aware of itself in the person of Sigmund Freud, just as economy began to be aware of itself in the person of Karl Marx.' Thus Wilhelm Reich, disciple and critic of Freud, exponent of 'the sexual revolution' (the title of one of his books). 'They regard me rather as a monomaniac, while I have the distinct feeling that I have touched on one of the great secrets of nature.' Thus Freud himself, writing to his friend Fliess on 'the importance of sexuality'.

The detail matters little; what is of major consequence here is the fact of the establishment of 'sexuality', the fundamental importance accorded to and accepted for the sexual in those terms. The cultural reality of Freud today is that: sexuality, a few themes (the Oedipus complex), a notion of repression and so of a possible liberation, just a little more effort . . . Sexuality as imperative, the sexual fix.

Freud did not discover sexuality (nor even infantile sexuality, recognized by Darwin and a topic of research and debate for a number of Freud's contemporaries and colleagues); he developed a theory of sexuality that was lacking in the nineteenth-century medicalization which had been nevertheless a way of indicating its necessity, of envisaging 'the problem'. From Laws Milton to Freud to the latest instalment of *New Man & Woman*, there are, of course, shifts and changes. But the *concern* remains constant, all the busying around the sexual, the determination to get that right and the belief in its importance.

For hypochondria and hysteria we have substituted impotence and frigidity, pair for pair. In a way, it's different, a new perspective, new man, new woman; in another, it's not, simply the same system, the same old story. The pairs match, mirror each other in a perfect symmetry of the constant concern: the male and the female, the two sexual disorders, the man and the woman, the order of the sexual. In the nineteenth century: you're ill, you have a sexual life. In the twentieth: you're ill, something's wrong, you don't have a good sexual life. The shift is there and can mark in practice real improvement; what is in question here, however, is the general 'sexualization', the development of the concern and its terms, and the representation of ourselves given in that – is the propagation of 'sexuality'.

For the nineteenth-century physician, the sexual, 'sexual feeling', is problematic: socially, morally, it ought not to exist but, disturbingly, it does; for Freud, pessimistic: we are condemned to it, it leaves little individual peace and the instinctual renunciation on which society and human achievement are based cannot long be sustained, hysterics, neurotics, civilization and its discontents, gloom on all fronts; for the modern sexologist, optimistic: the gates of heaven are large and we can all pass through, be brought into the natural state of good sexual functioning, forward to the promised land. Yesterday, you would have been with the Victorian doctor, entered the world of hypochondria, hysteria, nervous diseases, organic causes, male needs, female disturbances: what you are suffering from can perhaps be regulated or, if a woman, we hope eliminated; we have a whole range of hygiene rules and rates, appliances, operations . . . Today, psychoanalysis and sexology share the work, not without occasional frictions, but on the whole in relative harmony; the former, though, has more class than the latter (a few Californian therapy institutes excepted), more intellectual respectability (mostly it comes out more expensive too). Go to the sexologist and you are in the world of the reassuring and the practical. You're impotent? Frigid? Not 'sexually effective'? No matter. You masturbate properly? You use pornography? Try this and that, vary your positions, get a full-length mirror ('every bedroom should have one!'), oil the bed, change partners or sign up with a trained surrogate, above all keep smiling, your problem is ours and everyone else's too. Go to the psychoanalyst and you are in the world of the intractable, insoluble predicament of sexuality. The cure will be long and there's not much hope. Moreover cure, you know . . . we're not sexologists, there is no cure, only 'something effectively incurable in the human being'. And even if there were a cure, we ethically couldn't risk it, 'we refuse to cure for as analysts we cannot be the love-object that would result'; our function is 'to produce the real symptom'. The best thing is to become an analyst yourself, practise the rite of the knowledge of the impossibility of cure. Let's be clear after all, you go into analysis, women especially, demanding ' "Make me come", or "Make me an analyst", the one or the other or both'.

The great find of the nineteenth century, the medicalization of the sexual and its treatment in nervous disorders, shifts and divides: sexuality as area for practical, medical-sexological therapeutic inter-vention, treatment and advice, produced in and supported by a general discourse of 'total loving'; sexuality as the secret of the nature of human being, a kind of metaphysics of the individual condition. The division is not a neat one inasmuch as there are continuities and exchanges between the two, above all from psychoanalysis to sexology, the latter being profoundly marked by the former, that cultural reality of Freud today (psychoanalysis itself, especially in Europe, often parades a strict sectarian separateness, protecting its special-knowledge position in the name of a Freudian 'purity'). Both have been – and are – instrumental in the sacralization of sexuality, our age's achievement from the inheritance of the nineteenth cen-tury: the modern belief, the contemporary religion, 'sexuality'.

The genuine originality of Freud should not hide the fact that his work is in many respects part of a whole context of investigation of the sexual and movement towards the conception of sexuality. The period of Freud's youth and medical training and first steps towards psychoanalysis sees a considerable development of research into the variety of the sexual in human experience. As the order of the sexual becomes a concern and a problem, so the question of its disorders arises specifically and can suggest, eventually, the need for a scien-tific study and understanding of what are then characterized as 'deviations' and 'perversions'. At the very time that Freud was attending Charcot's lectures, Richard von Krafft-Ebing, his col-league at the University of Vienna, published the first edition of *Psychopathia Sexualis* (1886), a treatise on sexual pathology to which we owe such terms as 'sadism' and 'masochism'. Another one-time

colleague in Vienna, Albert Moll, who had also been with Charcot in
Paris, undertook a comparative description of normal and patholog-
ical sexuality which he presented in 1897 in a book entitled *Libido
Sexualis*. While in London, Havelock Ellis was beginning his mas-
sive work *Studies in the Psychology of Sex*; in six volumes, from *Sexual
Inversion* (1897) to *Sex in Relation to Society* (1910).

Freud, that is, was far from alone, was within the overall concern.
The issues under debate were those exactly with which he was
struggling in the late 1880s and 1890s: the stages of sexual development, the incidence of infantile sexuality in adult perversions (is
infantile sexuality an indication of future sexual aberration or is it a
normal part of sexual development?), the causal factors in perversions (are perversions to be regarded as resulting from hereditary
degeneration or as acquired?), the explanation of homosexuality (an
acutely socially difficult topic, both in the German-speaking world
close to Freud and in England where the law was repressively
amended in 1885 and Oscar Wilde tried and condemned in 1895*).
Freud's thinking as set out in the *Three Essays on the Theory of
Sexuality* depends on those issues, stems from that contemporary
debate: 'a disposition to perversions is an original and universal
disposition of the human sexual instinct and . . . normal sexual
behaviour is developed out of it as a result of organic changes and
psychical inhibitions occurring in the course of maturation . . . [we]

---

* Mention should be made of another of Freud's sexology-initiating colleagues,
Magnus Hirschfeld, who was also a founder member of the Berlin Psychoanalytic
Society (founded 1908). Hirschfeld started journals and an institute devoted to
'sexual knowledge' and 'sexually intermediate stages' (he published material by
Freud and by Freud's followers at Freud's request). He was active in promoting the
legalization of homosexuality and achieved notoriety as a witness in a number of
legal actions (notably at the time of a public outcry with regard to a homosexual
group with influence on the German Kaiser and to a supposed 'homosexualization'
of the army). No doubt Hirschfeld was a curious person: there is something of the
Musée Spitzner about it all as one looks now at the documentation amassed by his
institute, photographs of genital deformations with Hirschfeld in whiskers and
frock-coat, boots and cuffs, pointing to this or that, holding open the genitalia of a
hermaphroditic boy and turning to face the camera with a Victorian solidity. He
seems to have been disliked by Freud and some of his key psychoanalytic colleagues
in a way bound up with his homosexuality. Writing to Freud of the Dutch
neurologist L. S. A. M. van Römer, Jung comments: 'He is big chief of homosexuals, the Dutch Hirschfeld, personally known to me from Amsterdam. He is, like all
homosexuals, no delicacy.' When Hirschfeld resigned from the Berlin Society,
Freud himself abandoned all restraint: 'Magnus Hirschfeld has left our ranks in
Berlin. No great loss, he is a flabby, unappetizing fellow, absolutely incapable of
learning anything . . . homosexual touchiness. Not worth a tear.'

regard any established aberration from normal sexuality as an instance of developmental inhibition and infantilism'.

The work on sexual pathology leads in return to the necessity for understanding sexual normality: deviations can only be properly grasped if there is a firm account of what constitutes a regular – straight – sexual development. Thus is opened up the general field of study: the psychology and practice of sex, 'sexuality'. Sexology, the would-be science of that sexuality, starts here, from the interest in the pathological and its necessary extension to include the non-pathological, operating with a norm and a variety: there is a normal development but an original disposition, manifest in infantile sexuality, made up of a multitude of component instincts; a number of these instincts may be brought together into a unity, giving a normal heterosexual genital-sex fulfilment, but may also, through inhibition or dissociation of some kind, be crystallized into fulfilment through deviant sexual activity. The task of sexology is description and understanding; the latter brings the order of the norm to the variety recognized in the former but that variety can also come back on the norm – since there is the variety, there cannot be any norm, or the norm is, simply, the variety. The history of sexology over the last hundred years could be traced in terms of the play of norm and variety, with 'sexuality' – its conception and representation – posed accordingly.

Havelock Ellis and Freud and the others put normal and deviant sexuality side by side; the normal is a model of development and a point of reference in the understanding of deviations. But what do we *really* know of the actual sexual lives of individuals? The second great moment of sexology sets out from this question to make good our ignorance. Mobilizing sociological inquiry and statistical investigation, medicine and psychology, its aim is to study the reality of sexual experience, the real practices and bodies of men and women, outside of the institute for sexual pathology or the analyst's consulting-room. This is field-work and laboratory research, based on 'scientific method' and 'objectivity'. The names of the key figures of this moment are American and familiar (their books, significantly, have become best-selling paperbacks): Alfred C. Kinsey, William H. Masters, Virginia E. Johnson.

Kinsey's work is essentially two large volumes: *Sexual Behaviour in the Human Male* (1948) and *Sexual Behaviour in the Human Female* (1953). Stories of Kinsey are those of a heroically indefatigable researcher who killed himself at his Herculean labour, always after the next record of a sexual life, ever on the move from town to town, up until dawn with a sailor just off ship and then on into the new day, noting, noting, noting. *Sexual Behaviour in the Human Male* was based on interview material from 5,300 white males, and that was only a sample of the material available, and that material was only a beginning . . . Masters and Johnson are above all *Human Sexual Response* (1966). Where Kinsey is statistical, Masters and Johnson are anatomical and physiological, concerned with 'observations of anatomic and physiologic response to effective sexual stimulation'. Their research was conducted in the Reproductive Biology Research Foundation of the University of St Louis, Missouri: 10,000 'complete cycles of sexual response' ('total orgasmic cycles') at least were studied for the book, with 'study subjects' observed, measured and recorded in laboratory conditions; 'Recorded and observed sexual activity of study subjects has included, at various times, manual and mechanical manipulation, natural coition with the female partner in supine, superior, or knee-chest position and, for many female study subjects, artificial coition [that is, using 'artificial coital equipment'] in supine and knee-chest positions.'

Kinsey and Masters and Johnson share the same ambition to expose sexual experience to detailed quantitative investigation. In both bodies of work, the idea of 'perversion' is no longer central or an initial context for the research. Both too have been culturally reassuring for individuals, you're not the only one and there's nothing wrong (for example, Kinsey's demonstration of the normal occurrence of male adolescent experiences with other males or of female masturbation or of a widespread practice of oral sex; Masters and Johnson with their measurements of penises, clitorises and so on or their discussion of female orgasm). Both are excellent sources of evidence.

Kinsey, however, despite the shift from the pathological to the normal as the defined focus of research, is near to the Krafft-Ebing beginning of sexology: variety brought into a picture of human sexual behaviour, 'the norm and its variety'. Indicatively, Kinsey founds an Institute of Sexual Research (in Bloomington, Indiana) for the collection of information and material on any and every aspect of sex (thus it includes, for instance, a large library of pornography with many extremely rare items – one of the only two known copies of Walter's *My Secret Life*). As Krafft-Ebing's descriptions and classifications of sexual activity could play something of an educative social role by showing and scientifically taking over, offering a framework of explanation for, the range of sexual practices (Krafft-Ebing himself urged greater leniency in the courts, deviants were to be treated not as criminal but as ill), so Kinsey's work, the data and statistics provided, is offered as a social document, exactly a picture for social understanding; 'this book', state the publishers correctly in a note to *Sexual Behaviour in the Human Male* designed to stress its seriousness, 'is intended primarily for workers in the fields of medicine, biology, psychology . . . and for teachers, social workers, personnel officers, law enforcement groups, and others concerned with the direction of human behaviour.'

Masters and Johnson, on the other hand, are resolutely medical (anatomical, physiological). Distant from it though they may be in so many respects, their sexological origin is in the world of Victorian medicine and the medicalization of the sexual; one can imagine Laws Milton in the St Louis laboratory, measuring and recording and testing the ingenious appliances; and it is not insignificant that their research should indeed be carried out in a foundation devoted to '*reproductive biology*'. At the centre of *Human Sexual Response* is a firm normalizing object of study, the '*complete* human sexual *cycle*', and an overall ethos of '*effective functioning*' (words such as 'effective', 'efficiency', 'function', 'functioning' are omnipresent). The next work *had* to be *Human Sexual Inadequacy*. Once human sexual response has been determined, failures can be identified, inadequacy recognized and eventually dealt with. The therapeutic pull, in fact, is already in evidence in *Human Sexual Response* in the example histories of individuals used in the research given in the final chapter ('Study-Subject Sexuality'). Many of the subjects were involved as 'family units' (that is, husband and wife both participated) and declare motivation in connection with partnership gain ('this man and woman have stated categorically that they have found program cooperation of significant importance in their marriage', 'subject C has vocalized a desire to return to the program accompanied by his wife as a contributing family unit'). Masters and Johnson did indeed go on to offer therapy, running special two-week courses of treatment, and *Human Sexual Response* has been a major point of influence and reference for the many clinics and therapeutic units established over the last few years, for the whole present reality of sexology.

There is a further strand of development which is important in that present reality, running alongside the work of Kinsey and Masters and Johnson and coming together with it into the current representation of sexuality: that of a sexology envisaging itself as directly politically radical, in which the terms of 'inadequacy' are translated into those of a socially-determined repression of energy and which is thus, as therapy, offered as political action, as a mode of liberation. It is the work of Wilhelm Reich and that, today, of the anti-psychiatrist David Cooper which is crucial in this context.

Both Reich and Cooper, though heavily indebted to Freud and psychoanalysis, are highly critical of psychoanalytic practice, of 'the talking cure' (Cooper is also critical of Reich). Reich: 'Psychoanalysis is bound down by its method. It has to stick to that method which is the handling of associations and word-images'; 'Freud . . . succeeded very well in penetrating to the borderline where language develops, about the beginning of the third year. And, then, he got stuck . . . Then, I went on to the bodily expression which is wordless. I went even further and reached the stage where the newborn infant is formed in the womb. Psychoanalysis knows nothing about this. It can't know.' Cooper: 'The "talking cure" cannot effect this deteriorization of love and sexuality' ('deteriorization' is said to be 'a matter of everyone *loving and proving the acceptability of the "unacceptable"*'). Psychoanalysis, that is, deals in 'verbal terms' not 'body terms'. 'New' forms of direct therapeutic bodily pressure and contact (full circle from hysteria and the ovaries) must be found, capable of liberating energy, orgasmic potential and so on. The radical sexology gives rise to and serves as inspiration for the various methods of body therapy, group experience, sexual attitude restructuring, the practice of institutes such as Esalen in

California, founded by a former pupil of Reich's, Frederick S. Perls ('we have to lose our minds and come to our senses'), or Sandstone, again in California, the creation of John Williamson ('Contact at Sandstone includes the basic level of literal, physical nakedness and open sexuality. In these terms, the experience goes far beyond any attempt to intellectualize it. This reality of action . . . is the essence of the Sandstone experience').

The range of the sexology of Masters and Johnson is individual, the individual in the couple, the 'family unit': particular individual problems, inadequacy affecting relationships, you and your partner; *not* social. Reich and Cooper and the various projects to which their work relates see themselves in differing ways and degrees as having immediate social implications, if not effects, and full credit should undoubtedly be given to Reich for pointing to the limitations of Freudian psychoanalysis and attempting to raise sexuality as a social and political question. Once again, however, what is important here is the general cultural context and reflection of all this in the current sexological scheme of things and representation of sexuality. Reich and Cooper fit easily and feed into this scheme and representation, show the very same rhetorical and thematic constructions, have the very same defined field as the bourgeois sexology/sexuality their work claims to oppose. The problem, in fact, is that sexology and sexuality are in no way adequate modes or concepts for political action and theory; their acceptance is the acceptance of the sexual as concern, of the historical terms and assumptions of the emergence of 'sexuality', its conception, that we have traced above. With that acceptance, Reich and Cooper run time after time into emphases – and into a style – that are profoundly coercive and reactionary: they repeat, precisely, the sexual fix.

It is then not surprising indeed that, in return, contemporary sexology overall presents itself so often with a certain 'radical' pose and with 'liberation' always on its lips. This is so much part of its persuasive power: a flavour of suggested radicalism, conformity and constraint got up as liberation, people firmly held and directed as individuals to this or that standard, under the orders of 'sexuality'. And there is no simple distinction in this respect between a good and a bad sexology, between the true radicals and the functionaries of the established system: the same assumptions, the same imperatives recur. Reich contends, for example, that Freud was 'very much dissatisfied genitally' and in fact that '*most psychoanalysts were genitally disturbed*'; Reich's therapy is designed to break through the 'carapace', the 'armour' enclosing the individual, and bring out – 'liberate' – the real, authentic 'genital character'. Fine, if one is willing to have the sexual and its relation to our individual social lives ordered in this way, to submit to a 'genital character' that we ought to have as the essential reality of our being. To say that someone is 'genitally disturbed' is meaningless unless a model is being provided to show up the disturbance, which model is norm, standard, requirement to conform. Whether the model be 'the complete human sexual cycle' of Masters and Johnson or the more or less mystical apostrophizing of the 'genital orgasm' and its constituents in Reich and Cooper, the result is the same (though we should certainly prefer the former which, in the research on which it depends, is useful and progressive): sexuality becomes a definable unified entity, the content of a narrative scenario, the model, an order to be followed with inadequacies to be repaired. Ironically, Reich has contributed a great deal to the definition and realization of the commodity 'sexuality', and to the imperatives of its use and exchange and circulation, which contemporary sexology represents and in which it confirms and supports the existing social organization: its ideology of the individual person as the ultimate point of reference, of 'reality', with his or her 'naturally-given' needs and desires and aspirations to fulfilment, the basic unit to be kept going freely – 'liberatedly' – in the circle of consumption.

VI

'The Erotic Path to the "Big O"'

'J', *Total Loving*, 1977

At the centre of sexology, the orgasm, and above all 'the female orgasm: 'the delicious erotic trip'. O for orgasm. Everybody's talking about it, endlessly, women especially. Evenings out, social occasions, are quite an ordeal for the sexologist who hears of nothing but *that*: 'I'm always very apprehensive about invitations to dinner for, sooner or later, the conversation turns to sex and the women round the table divide sharply into two categories: those who have the orgasm and those who don't.' Two categories, one topic: the 'Big O'.

Orgasm too has its history as a word and a concept. Derived from the Greek verb *orgān*, which has a variety of meanings connected with the idea of an excitation of the blood, 'orgasm' appears in English in the seventeenth century. The OED gives two meanings: first, 'immoderate or violent excitement of feeling; rage, fury; a paroxysm of excitement or rage', with a 1646 quotation from the physician and author Sir Thomas Browne: 'some fast retention or sudden compresssion in the orgasmus or fury of their lust'; second, a directly physiological sense of 'excitement or violent action in an organ or part, accompanied with turgescence [swelling with blood]', with a 1684 quotation from the translation of a French medical work: 'when there appears an orgasm of the humours, we rather fly to bleeding as more safe'. It is from this second meaning that the sexual usage particularly derives, probably in the course of the nineteenth century (once again). The OED has 1899 for the first instance of 'sexual orgasm', though an example of 'venereal orgasm' is recorded from 1802. The sexual usage eventually drives out more general or alternative ones, but these latter are still common during the period of the establishment of the former: thus a critic could write in 1847 of the poet Keats's 'vivid orgasm of the intellect', while a Dr Tilt is reported in *The Lancet* in 1862 as having commented with respect to menstruation on how 'for 30 years [the uterus and the ovaries] are thrown into a state of haemorrhagic and other orgasm every month'.

Many words, of course, exist to indicate sexual pleasure prior to the nineteenth century (and many forms of sexual pleasure too) but it is not surprising that the term 'orgasm' in this sense should emerge and begin to achieve status at that time and from within a medical-physiological context; and nor is it surprising that that term should still be ours today – in the mouths of dinner-party guests (so it seems) and the pages of just about every contemporary novel and magazine barring *Railway Modeller* (for sure). Sexual pleasure is ages older than the nineteenth century (though the obviousness of this should not blind us to the fact of a very long history in which there have been massive developments and changes, a whole evolution of human sexual life) but this does not mean that it is somehow simply a given, abstract from the particular historical, social, psychological complexity in which it is realized, that it is not always a historically-coded phenomenon. The word and the concept of orgasm are now part of our coding and of our representation (and realization) of sexuality. Physiology is determining? Yes, in the sense that we cannot merely transcend it, that it is a condition of our very experience. No, in the sense that it is not some unique essence of that experience, of our sexual being which is, always, a complex inclusion and definition of the physiological, a precise constituted materiality.

'Nature intends women to have orgasms.' The statement is, supposedly, encouraging; actually, it is meaningless, and in the end coercive (paradoxically, the same nature apparently also warns us that 'with orgasms so hard to come by, you shouldn't be so fussy!'). Nature did not, like some aimiable and primitive sexologist, intend women or men to have orgasms, for the very good reason that nature does not 'intend' or indeed even exist in the way that this projected image of an intending entity would have us admit. What can be said is that there is a natural history of men and women, the human species, in which the possibility of what we learn as sexual pleasure is developed. We can, if we really wish, declare that 'the naked ape is the sexiest primate alive' (though what we might do or seek to gain with such a declaration is another matter) and we doubtless should attempt to understand the terms of human sexual species being in that very long history, the whole evolution, referred to above. But none of this, other than by a trick of sleight of hand, can be allowed to become a 'Nature intends' justification of what is always this complex fact of the sexual, of sexual experience, in a specific and defining context.* The precise constituted materiality is that: the recognition that we are not some kind of hamburger in which bread and meat lie on top of but separate from one another in such a way that the natural has a simply autonomous and extractable existence, cooked up alongside and before the cultural into which it then fits, like meat into bread. That the sexual is universal to the human species, to all human being, does not place it outside of historical and social determinations, push it into some pure realm of its own. On the contrary, it suggests its permanent interaction with material conditions and definitions. Language after all is equally a human universal but that universality never exists but in a full particularity – this language, this speech in this society, this history, these modes, these uses, these possibilities. The sexual too.

Masters and Johnson have given clear and detailed anatomical–physiological accounts of the male and the female 'sexual response cycles', measuring and recording the body's reactions and changes

*For an example of such justification, consider the following remarks by Desmond Morris, well-known chronicler of 'the naked ape': 'By making the first copulation attempt difficult and even painful, the hymen ensures that it will not be indulged in lightly. . . . By putting a partial brake on this trend in the female [the trend to 'full copulation' before 'pair-formation', before a stable male–female bond of partnership], the hymen demands that she shall have already developed a deep emotional involvement before taking the final step, an involvement strong enough to take the initial physical discomfort in its stride.' Nature may intend women to have orgasms but it also intends that they shall not 'indulge' lightly, that they shall think carefully before 'the final step' and only go ahead when there is 'deep emotional involvement' – the hymen proves it, 'demands' it . . . Nature is not just sexologist but equally responsible young people's counsellor – we have to appreciate that when Nature started this whole business of men and women, it already had in mind marriage and going steady, virginity and what every mother should tell her daughter, the very language of the advice columns of our more conservative magazines.

during sex (heterosexual intercourse, male and female masturbation, female intercourse with artificial coital equipment). The 'orgasmic phase' in their accounts 'is limited to those few seconds during which the vasoconcentration [congestion of blood vessels; remember the origins of the word 'orgasm'] and myotonia [increased muscular tension] developed from sexual stimuli are released. This involuntary climax is reached at any level that represents maximum sexual tension increment for the particular occasion. Subjective (sensual) awareness of orgasm is pelvic in focus, specifically concentrated in the clitoral body, vagina, and uterus of the female and in the penis, prostate, and seminal vesicles of the male. Total-body involvement in the response to sexual tensions, although physiologically well-defined, is experienced subjectively on the basis of individual reaction patterns.' All of which seems at first sight so simple and well-rounded that one might wonder what all the agitation has been and is about: the orgasmic phase is specified as the moment of maximum tension discharge, bringing the idea of orgasm well into line with its common equation with climax, acme, coming, male ejaculation (used by Masters and Johnson as synonymous with male orgasm).

The problems, however, are there in the background, already casting their shadows. Thus, orgasm is never simply physiological: as Masters and Johnson go on to recognize, it is always also simultaneously and interrelatedly subjective, the fact of an individual's experience which includes the historical and social determinations of his or her individuality (it should be noted, moreover, that the emergence of the concern with orgasm goes along exactly with the development of extreme emphasis on subjectivity, on the reality and importance of individual experience). Thus, again, the stress on a – on the – moment of orgasm answers to an identifiable physiological reaction but is not at all equivalent to an identification and description of human sexual pleasure. The introduction of the question of the sexes, male and female, heightens this difficulty since, as Masters and Johnson decisively establish, the human female, quite different in this to the human male, is potentially multiple and prolongedly orgasmic, capable 'of rapid return to orgasm immediately following an orgasmic experience' and 'of maintaining an orgasmic experience for a relatively long period of time'. Outside of some reduction of the sexual to discrete physiological reactions, that is, 'moment' ('those few seconds') and 'cycle' ('sexual response cycle') are not very helpful, are part of a narrative that rapidly breaks down in the face of actual experience, individual sexual life; and for men just as much as for women once the imperative timing of ejaculation = orgasm = sexual experience is resisted and the real multiplicity of that experience recognized. Thus, again, following on from this, the conception of sexuality proceeding from the lives of men and women to the difference male/female anchored on the orgasm is a truly catastrophic limitation. The definition, maintenance and regulation of that difference, that identity of *the* difference, has been the concern with the sexual from the nineteenth century on, has been the very point of 'sexuality' and the impetus of sexology current today: Man, Woman, the Big O. For as long as orgasm holds the centre of the stage, we will never get out of a sexual norm, a reduction of the sexual, the realization of sex as exchange commodity with men and women placed and held essentially, as their 'nature', male and female, the difference, as the agents of that exchange. Orgasm, in short, is the key manœuvre in the sexual fix.*

Which is to say that investment in 'the orgasm' goes far beyond any physiological mechanism, that there is a veritable necessity of the orgasm, a historical and social entity of concern and discussion and debate, in relation to which we are to be defined and measured and identified. 'IT HAPPENS': something big, 'let go and float up, up and away', the stakes are high.

Consider here the matter of the 'quality' of the orgasm. In the beginnings of sexology, orgasm is relatively unproblematic in this respect because equated with a simple physiological release, a

---

* It is the manœuvre that is of *prime* importance, not any particular version of what orgasm might be, and the relation of women in that manœuvre. 'Other female primates do not appear to experience a climax to their sexual sequence', notes Desmond Morris (and we should note incidentally the omnipresent natural assumption of 'climax' and 'sequence'), therefore 'the female orgasm' is 'a "borrowed" male pattern'. Or let us envisage with Freud and many successors a genuine female maturity, 'the vaginal orgasm', authentically womanly as opposed to the 'blind beakishness' (as D. H. Lawrence could put it) of clitoral stimulation. Or let us stress women as 'multiply orgasmic', many 'climaxes', supermen. . . . What matters in the first instance is the stability of the concern, the orgasm, man, woman, same, different, same again, the question of the difference, everyone settled there, male and female, that as the great affair. And so it goes on. . . . *Playboy* just recently announced 'the uterine orgasm' – and under the title 'Female Orgasm, Where Are You?' Exactly. We need you.

basically male–model discharge of tension (continuing the Victorian 'spending'). Kinsey, in *The Sexual Behaviour of the Human Male*, works within this equation. Orgasm is 'sexual outlet', 'climax' obtained from any one of the six possible sources – masturbation, nocturnal emission, heterosexual petting, heterosexual intercourse, homosexual relations, animal contacts. No problems, and in a way no final need even for the term and the idea 'orgasm' which has these easy synonyms of 'outlet', 'climax', 'discharge', and so on. The 'sexual revolution', however, has produced and been caught up in a whole discourse of 'the orgasm', a whole elaboration and representation, a standard of sexual life.

'Radical sexology' has been in the vanguard of this. Orgasm is a qualitative phenomenon ('true orgasm'), refers to an authentic – as opposed to some inauthentic – level of experience and being. Reich: 'It's not just to fuck, you understand, not the embrace in itself, not the intercourse. It is the real emotional experience of the loss of your ego, of your whole spiritual self'; Cooper talks of '*the repression of orgasmic ecstasy* which differentiates making love from fucking'; you fuck, I have my orgasmic-potential-ecstasy-being experience. Kinsey happily recorded statistics of the kind 'average number of orgasms prior to marriage' totalled from all the possible sources (result: husbands, 1523; wives, 233). For Reich and Cooper this can only be a total misuse of the term, like lumping together in the single category of 'football' kicking a ball around in the park and first-division soccer: orgasm is authentic orgasm, not to be confused with 'partial releases of tension which are similar to orgasm'. This terror-ism of the true and authentic orgasm, that 'ultimate vegetatively involuntary surrender', then readily supports, as in Reich, such notions as that of the 'sexual maturity' of a 'vaginal orgasm' over a 'clitoral orgasm', Freud's pattern of the movement from male imitation to the properly female experience. Reich inveighs against the '*phallic-pornographic-clitoral* genitality of present-day man which has existed for some six to ten thousand years' (!); 'clitoral genitality is a neurotic *substitute* for a blocked vaginal excitation'. True orgasm is also mapped on to class-sexual characterizations in which the working classes are identified with a 'natural sexuality', a kind of primitive 'orgastic potency': for Reich, in a statement which is simultaneously unaccompanied by any evidence and unamenable to any provision of evidence since the terms of the argument are mystically assertive and beyond proof, 'there are human beings of a

certain kind, living and working here and there, unobtrusively, who
are equipped with *natural* sexuality; they are the *genital characters*.
They are found frequently among the industrial workers.' For
Cooper, who follows suit in all this, male orgasm is even rarer than
female orgasm, which is itself rare enough 'in the first-world
bourgeoisie and in the bourgeoisified elements of first-world working class and the third world'. Big deal for the non-bourgeoisified
'elements' of the third world – they may be starving but they sure as
hell can orgasm.★

Not surprisingly, pleasure comes through as of fairly minimal
importance. Orgasm, which is 'a form of work', is a deadly serious
affair, with strict standards of correct behaviour. Talking or laughing, for example, are definitely out: 'Orgastically potent individuals
never talk or laugh during the sexual act – with the exception of
words of tenderness. Both talking and laughing indicate a serious
lack of the capacity for surrender, which requires an undivided
absorption in the sensations of pleasure.'† The word 'pleasure'
occurs but imperatively, you must have it this way, work at it
undividedly, no laughter. There are protocols to follow, proper
attitudes. During and immediately after climax 'the healthy woman'

★ The objection, of course, is not at all to analysis and description of the relations
between class and sexual experience, of, for instance, the relations between
capitalist modes of production and specific orders and limitations and uses of the
sexual (which are exactly the context, indeed, of the emergence of 'sexuality' to the
construction and hold of which sexology, including in its 'radical' versions,
contributes). It is that there is no such analysis and description here but rather the
projection of a stock – and reactionary – idea of an essential 'natural sexuality', a
primitive sexual potency that the working class is mystifyingly supposed to
embody and express. Concomitant with which is then the revolution in themselves
accomplished by Reich and Cooper and their followers who have pierced the
armour of civilization and regained true orgasmic being, in the name of which the
experience of other people can be registered as inadequate, inauthentic. This brand
of self-believing sexual self-congratulation seems to have informed such fellow-
travelling fighters in the revolution as 'the beat'; Lawrence Lipton writes: 'In the
sexual act, the beat are filled with mana, the divine power. This is far from the
vulgar, leering sexuality of the middle-class square in heat.' The point, again, is not
that it is not possible and necessary to analyze and criticize and seek to transform
dominant middle-class orders of the sexual; it is merely that we should resist the
substitution of a new imperative ('new' only in its own eyes; in fact, another
complicit episode in the sexual fix).

† The steady gaze, eyes open, is also required: 'it is so essential to orgasm to look
the other in the eye'. Regrettably, Masters and Johnson forgot to note and measure
this, and Kinsey, hopelessly out, actually included it as a requirement for . . .
conducting sexological interviews! ('Looking an individual in the eye, and firing
questions at him with maximum speed, are two of the best guarantees against
exaggeration.')

wants 'to "receive completely"' (as the clitoral/vaginal reference above will have made clear, Reich's idea of orgasm is male-stereotyped). Things must be done according to the rules and the right outcome to 'the sexual act' achieved: 'orgasm is a matter of the right involuntary pelvic muscular contractions and, at the apex, a state of no-mind'. And don't think you can break the rules and get away with it: the orgasm police *know*, they *can tell*: 'One can always diagnose the non-orgasmic personality by minute ocular deflections and by sentences spoken to one that fail to connect because they are never properly ended.' 'Always', no escape; 'diagnose', illness, health and sickness, the medical back once more, the diagnosis from spermatorrhoea to impotence, hysteria to frigidity, to the non-orgasmic personality; 'minute ocular deflections', 'sentences that are never properly ended', so many signs and symptoms: no blinking or looking away, and speak fluently, in good grammatical sentences – orgasm demands it.

Run of the mill sexology stands away from this coercive shrillness and is nearer to a Masters-and-Johnson technical-type orgasm acceptance. At the same time, however, the central concern of the orgasm remains: just as David Cooper issues 'An Orgasm Manifesto', so 'J', author of *Total Loving*, gives 'Orgasm Messages' ('Orgasm Message 1 is: *Keep that erotic stimulation going or your sexual apparatus will close up shop*'). As orgasm is filled out with a content of definitions and norms, so the sexual fix is maintained, strengthened; a coerciveness returns, if more diffuse, bathed in a general atmosphere of common sense, straight talking, medical knowledge, permeating advice and description.

In a real sense it is precisely in the description and its *narrative* of orgasm that this can be most readily grasped. Masters and Johnson posit human male and female 'cycles' of sexual response which they divide up into: 1) the excitement phase; 2) the plateau phase; 3) the orgasmic phase; 4) the resolution phase. For them, this 'arbitrary four-part division' is simply an 'effective framework' for their descriptions of physiological reactions and changes. Yet already, arbitrary or not, we are into a delimited cycle, an order, a narrative, a little plot of sex: the Big O, a story in four episodes (not to be missed), from excitement to resolution. Reich has a similar but more elaborate version, a kind of orgasm model comprising: 1) forepleasure; 2) penetration; 3) triple movement from (I) voluntary control ('as yet harmless'?!) to (II) involuntary muscle contractions to (III) sudden and steep ascent to the acme; 4) orgasm, followed by a steep drop; 5) relaxation (time allotted for 'the sexual act': about five to twenty minutes). Masters and Johnson have two sexual cycles, male and female, but these two come together into the one overall cycle-narrative, 'the sexual response cycle'; Reich has one model with an emphasis on 'penetration' and a basic assumption that 'normally, that is, in the absence of inhibitions, the course of the sexual process in the woman is in no way different from that in the man'.

The narrative of the orgasm has become the staple fare of sexology (and, as we shall see, of other forms of writing, such as the novel, which share with sexology the role of maintaining 'sexuality' today). One must think, live and be orgasm, the good story. Just as one could be ill from nocturnal emissions or sexual feeling in the nineteenth century, so one can now be ill from poor orgasm, not doing it properly, 'orgastically ill' (Reich) or 'inadequate' (Masters and Johnson) or . . . and so on and on. A whole sexological literature, a constant representation, has developed that simultaneously assures you you are not ill or inadequate and not to worry (we are not the Victorians) while serving you up every time, again and again, the same story, the same model, the same sexual concern, the same orgasm (we are nearer the Victorians than we are told to think: we have kept the concern, its terms, its normalizations, that world). Orgasm is held out at you, complete with identikit description, and you and the sexual are held to that; but you can make it, you must, here are the stages, the techniques, the things to do and feel, this is what it is, the Big O:

> It starts with a tingle; then sensations of warmth and lightheadedness and quickening pulse; a catch of breath; a delicious swelling of the breasts and then OH! the sudden sweet ache in the mons area, and OH! that throb and first contraction in your moist vagina, and OH! the demanding pelvic gyrations that seem to have a mind of their own, and OH! the sudden arching of your back, pushing your breasts high, and OH! it's so nice to be able to let go and float up, up and away on waves of erotic feeling.
>
> Where do you float to? Orgasm, and then the gentle descent down into the solid warmth of your lover's embrace.

All the right phases: excitement ('It's a tingle . . . And this is just the *beginning!*'); plateau ('oblivious to everything but the intense pelvic drive for more and more and *more*'); orgasmic ('And then IT HAPPENS'); resolution ('You slide down slowly. . . . You smile and cuddle up close to him. . . . And there is no doubt in your mind that it's heavenly to be alive and a woman'). Match that.*

Sexology thus appears – and appeals – as a kind of orgasmic engineering (doubtless anticipated in the instrumental ingenuity of the Masters and Johnson project with its perfectly adjustable equipment, 'the equipment can be adjusted for physical variations in size, weight and vaginal development'). The body is a terribly complicated machine, like a computer; the sexologist is its technician, the engineer of 'the sexual equipment', organs, zones, the whole body (itself one big sex, the natural state of the child: 'his whole body is a sexual organ'). Machine, the body is also a work of art; technician, the sexologist is also human counsellor, a reassuring engineer, full of feeling and emotion. The symptomatic expression of this warm expertise (and there is a veritable rhetoric of sexology that we must begin to bring out) is the adjectival labelling of some physiologically conceived moment or some bit of the body: 'the fabulous love muscle', 'those fabulous orgasmic sensations', 'you are quivering with the exquisite feeling in your genitals', 'a delicious swelling of

---

* Naturally the orgasmic scenario is all-embracing (if that is not too risky a way of putting it):

'A pale light in the sky signals the nearness of dawn as the two bare bodies again stretch upon the bed. He nuzzles her skin, breathes her scent, and quickly rouses. He inhales deeply, presses urgently against her, and unwittingly pinches her nipple in the process. Flinching slightly, she rubs his nose and whispers softly, He fixes his eyes on her, and kneads one breast with his fingers as he relishes the other with his lips. As he forces his hips against hers, an ancient rhythm oscillates and ebbs. Gradually his grip relaxes and he drifts towards a deep, refreshing slumber. She tenderly disentangles her hair from beneath his body.'

No, not an entry in the world's tackiest erotic writing competition, but the opening of an 'assist your children' sex manual for parents; the next and final line reads: 'Then she covers him with the blanket and carries him to his cot.' Moral: the sooner the narrative the better, or, you're never too early with the fix.

the breasts', 'hands – accessible, sexy and sensitive', 'legs are excit-
ing', 'you have that delicious organ the clitoris'.*

Sexology is an order. It provides a target and a model, orgasm and
the narrative of its achievement, and commands assent. A basic
mode of its writing, a strategy in its rhetoric, is thus the imperative:
issuing 'messages' and 'manifestos', ordering your thoughts,
'ERASE . . . FEED IN . . . ERASE . . . FEED IN . . . ERASE . . . FEED
IN . . .'. Imperative injunction to women to orgasm:

> Rinse yourself down, dry yourself, perfume yourself. Rub yourself
> slowly with toilet water or skin softener. . . . Concentrate . . . incarnate
> the image you see in your mirror. Live your body instead of seeing it.
> Now lie down on your bed or on cushions. Wet your finger with
> saliva. . . . Caress your clitoris . . . If you are not still a virgin, you may
> put your left index finger in your vagina in order to simulate the
> to-and-fro of the penis . . . until the budding of orgasm.†

Yes, sir.

The sexological command can easily turn nasty, beyond the inane
offensiveness of the passage just cited (ten or more imperatives, do
this, do that, rub this bit, use this finger; part of the inanity is that the
next book one reads will prescribe 'a moistened middle finger' –
which finger matters not one jot, the point is that everything should
be *ordered*). On the crusading or 'radical' edge of sexology, 'inadequacy' becomes the basis for insult and a sexual tribunal sits in
judgement. Thus leading French sexologist Dr Gerald Zwang writes

---

*One begins to understand why Walter should have heroic status amongst
sexologists, accredited with good positive attitudes. No one has done better than
him in the fabulous-rapture line: 'Verily, cunt is queen, king, emperor, high-priest,
commander-in-chief, an army in itself, a necromancer, a wizard, a saint of
marvellous power – all these and more in one. Who can withstand it, who not yield
to it?' ('We cannot but commend Walter to his positive and appreciative attitude . . .').

† The giving of contradictory orders is also an aspect of the programme, adding
strength to its hold (you're really caught). The same sexologist who here commands concentration for orgasm equally stresses that one must stop oneself from
thinking about 'having' 'it' – 'it' comes unawares, Christ-like: 'On the subject of the
orgasm, I'd be tempted to borrow the words of Christ: "Behold, I come as a thief"!'

an *Open Letter to Poor Fuckers (Lettre ouverte aux mal-baisants)*. The title
says the self-belief and the contempt: this sexologist knows a good
fuck when he sees one, up to the rest of us to come up to his mark; or
else remain poor fuckers, the despised of this earth whom sexology
will offer to help, indeed, but also to confirm in their place by the
constant representation of 'sexuality' it produces and to which they
are held, the very concern. A typical example of the reflex recourse
to the sexual as judgement and dismissal is provided by David
Cooper when in the middle of a discussion of 'bed therapy' (his term
for analysts and doctors sleeping with their patients), he refers to a
survey carried out on the subject: 'In a recent questionnaire thirteen
per cent of doctors on the West Coast of the USA felt that sexual
relations with patients might sometimes be positive. As the incidence of impotence in the remaining eighty-seven per cent was
unknown, this figure might be significant.' No doubt such sexual
relations may sometimes be positive, no doubt they are often
disastrous, and certainly the factors of power and authority that
structure what is an easily exploitative situation would have to be
carefully analysed. But, and this is what is important here, Cooper's
logic is simple and crude: if you agree with me, you're sexually ok; if
you don't, you're impotent; you have objections to 'bed therapy'?
then you must have trouble in bed. . . . Opinion can be tied to and
dismissed in sexual terms (with the traditional male bravado, all
those 87 per cent West Coast doctors have no balls), and according,
of course, to a rigid version of what the sexual is supposed to be –
good sex versus bad, this right way, true, authentic orgasm. . . .

Let it be stressed that the mainstream of sexology is far from the
violence and crudeness of Cooper, but it does nevertheless work
constantly in a constrainingly imperative mode and on the basis of
the representation to us of the sexual as 'sexuality' as the key to our
being, as the grounds for the judgement of ourselves, our lives, our
worth.

A complement of this imperative mode is the unfailing appearance in
sexological discussion and writing of little 'Oh, horror!' stories,
shocking examples of wrong attitudes, what not to do or think:

A medical student and his young wife are able to speak about sex with his
mother, a newly liberated matron. The young couple tests the depth of

the mother's newfound philosophy by discussing many intimate details. The mother doesn't even blush. She replies with a shady joke and a sex manual quotation of her own. Finally, the young wife describes the intricate manipulations necessary for her vagina to lubricate. She suddenly turns and asks her mother-in-law, 'What does it take for *you* to get juiced up, Mother?' The mother blushes, stammers, and is unable to answer.

Oh, horror! Blushing and stammering! No marks for mother-in-law, that newly liberated matron caught hiding behind the shady joke and the sex manual quotation. No marks for you either if you're not regularly getting into your, her, his parents or grandparents or near relations and their juicing-up. Again:

One lady interrupted her mate in the middle of lovemaking to inform him that the toaster was broken.

Oh, horror! Nought out of twenty for inattention and lack of proper commitment. You have no right not to come straight out with the history of your juices when somebody asks you (so what are you resisting?); you have no right not to manage your love-making with deadly earnestness (so what's your inadequacy?). Maybe you have some vague notions of individual respect, maybe you try to define in your life modes of privately shared experience, maybe you don't much connect to 'juiced up' as the language of sexuality for you, let alone to the description of someone as 'a newly liberated matron', maybe you even think there are more important topics of conversation in most circumstances than 'sex'. Forget it. *Oh, horror!*

And inevitably the 'oh, horror!' stories are accompanied by 'well done!' ones in which, as though from some interminable American family TV series, model adults and model children do model things, like reading sexology books: 'Walter intimated that Michael was spending several hours each afternoon reading *Everything You Always Wanted to Know About Sex*. His mother, with a twinkle in her eye, confronted Michael, who readily admitted to his research. He giggled and said, "It's not going to be any of that three-minute stuff for me." Mother was convulsed with laughter. Michael was an unlikely candidate for sex therapy.' Well done, Mother! Well done, Michael! Twinkle, giggle, super lover.

One should note, too, in this context what might be called the *metaphorical command* of sexology, its series of images of you and your body and your sexual functioning, image after image for you to ponder and follow. *Treat Yourself to Sex?* Treat yourself to a good analogy, match that image, all of them, sex and food and cars and . . .

> Just imagine the time and careful preparation you are ready to lavish on cooking a really delicious meal for friends . . . and then compare it with the way you made love last night . . .

But,

> for most of the time we require the simple luxury of good plain cooking

Think of yourself as a Volvo, don't kid yourself you're a Rolls-Royce:

> If a man selling a Volvo car spent all his time explaining to this prospective buyer why it was not a Rolls-Royce, he would be doing the manufacturers, his customer and himself no good because he would not have conveyed the unique and special characteristics of the car he was offering.

Buying, selling . . . tough if you aren't up to a Volvo even, but never mind, don't be too shy if the car you're offering has a few faults:

> What if 'piston' were a taboo word like 'penis'? Were people to hesitate about telling a mechanic about a failing piston in their car the way they hesitate to talk to a lover or a professional adviser about a failing penis, the roads would be littered with broken cars . . .

And think of yourself as a radio, fiddle around a bit:

> it is like having a radio set which you never tune in to more than a few familiar wavelengths. Ask yourself why you have stopped experimenting with the reception. How often have you enjoyed an unexpected programme which you came upon by chance when playing with the knobs?

You may be able to get the Olympics, listen to the athletics, maybe try some yourself in a leisurely way:

It may be helpful to think of orgasm as being rather like the high jump where the bar can be made higher and lower, but the lower the bar the easier it is to go over the top.

At the end of all this is something like a constant of sexual identity, of identity as sex: *you are* your sexual nature or problem or whatever. A sexologist constructs a book out of a 'dialogue' with two young people, Hélène and François. Introduction, very first page: 'Hélène: "François is a precocious ejaculator and we differ on many points, notably concerning sexuality."' Who are you? François, precocious ejaculator (a few pages later he himself is happy to repeat this identity: 'I am a precocious ejaculator'). And you? Jane, pre-orgasmic female. And you? John, secondarily impotent male. And you? Sexology is the new identification, the roll-call of that 'sexuality' that defines our lives, us, you and me, who we are. Sex is the identity, you answer present to that.

This identity is also, at once, an obligation to act. If you are not doing or having sex and orgasm, you cannot really exist, are hope-lessly incomplete: 'while it is very satisfying to be today's multi-faceted female, able to explore and fulfill all of her intellectual and career drives, *nothing* beats the thrills and satisfactions of being totally responsive emotionally and sexually'. *Nothing* beats sex (which becomes, too, the standard of the emotions), so who are you, how are you doing, what's your rating on the 'Big O' scale? Inevitably, the extreme expression of all this is to be found in the 'sexual radicals'. What was wrong with the psychoanalysts? They 'put their fingers into the vaginas of their patients' instead of, like Reich, 'taking' or 'having' a woman: 'When the relationship with my first wife did not work out, I took another woman. . . . When I was through with my first wife, I had a second one.' What was wrong with Laura, one of Cooper's cases? She liked talking with other women: 'She wanted to live in a feministic universe rather than a male-orientated one. This involved spending much time with other women – "just talking", although the just talking, metaphori-cally, was mutual masturbation. . . .' And what's more, 'her or-gasms were centred on digital clitoral stimulation, not penile pene-tration' – how ill can you get?

Let us also mention here two watchwords of sexology, *hygiene* and *freedom*. Hygiene: 'Fellatio consists in receiving a so-called dirty organ, the penis, into a so-called clean cavity, the mouth. Yet a well-washed penis retains only a very few microbes, whereas a mouth, except after gargling or an antiseptic mouthwash, is full of them.' (So don't say you don't want to or don't like it . . . why are you resisting, what's wrong with you?) Freedom: anything you want, 'the advantage of a sex-shop is that you can browse through the books. If there is something that gives you an erection, no matter what the theme, don't hesitate, buy it. You've just found the right one.' (You get erections from snuff films, from photographs of the torture of men, women, children, animals, from dressing up in Nazi gear and shouting fascist slogans? Fine, carry on, you're doing well. . . . Of course, the 'freedom' held out is anyway heavily circumscribed by the central position of the idea of the orgasm and the relentless assumption of male-stereotype perspectives, of the stereotype of 'the man', is, in fact, the complete inability of sexology to think of sex – and hence recast its very conception – in social terms: sex is delimited as area and object, projected as a quality or property of the individual, cobbled up with a vague liberalism and proffered as a 'right', the freedom to . . . sexology.)

All of this comes with a thick spread of 'naturalness'; 'the natural state', remember, 'is good sexual functioning', 'Nature intends you to have orgasms'. Once again, there is a 'radical' as well as a mainstream version of the account then given.

For the former, 'the natural' is a lost and potentially regainable paradise, in contrast to which the present age reflects only sickness and violence. Reich is full of 'natural sexuality' and 'natural emotional life expression', of a 'natural (orgastic) sexual gratification' which has been blocked, 'damned up' by 'some four to six thousand years' of 'mechanical and authoritarian civilization' and which demands, for its liberation, 'surrender to the flow of biological energy without any inhibition', demands a therapy powerful enough to break through what is now in every individual an 'armouring against nature'. Cooper's guide to life, his 'grammar of living', is written with orgasm as 'a time-less moment in which an excess of vitality (body) generates death (no-mind as opposed to the sense of mind as a "head" hegemony that subjugates and would annihilate lower body centres)': 'For the sake of orgasm which is the secret centre of liberation we have to achieve a neat operation – we have to eliminate our poor poisoned brains by effecting a decapitation of ourselves that will at last lead us back to a lost life – and then forward.' 'Natural-ness' here can clearly be rather chilling, itself quickly and essentially violent: 'as a dream to explore the nature of sexuality', Cooper is able to 'recommend one of dissecting one's own head – and then kicking it away' (note too that even our dreams are to be *recommended*, subject to vigilance).

In the mainstream of sexology 'naturalness' is much more com-forting, calmer and generally untroubled, an individual's 'right to sex happiness', a pool into which one can and should dip at will (but with the necessary sexological help and guidance: the sexual may be natural but it also has to be worked at, properly developed; 'the natural state is good sexual functioning' and, *simultaneously*, 'good sex does not come naturally'). The stress is on a human natural, not the vegetative natural of Reich or the no-mind lost life of Cooper, on the 'expression' or 'realization' of 'oneself', not its breaking through or dissection. A sexologist writes a book entitled *I Love You: The Little Red Book of Humanist Sexology*. Exactly – a flavouring of the radical (the little red book, this *is* 'the sexual revolution'), the central weight of the human (*humanist* sexology), the aspiration of the universal, the all-embracing warmth of the sexological sunshine in which we are called upon to bask, quietly to take our place (I love you). Conclusion of the book: 'I have tried to show you the human being who is in me. I love you. *That* is humanist sexology.'

Opening ourselves up, finding the human being who is in us, is important, something we should dare to accept: 'sexuality is the privileged site of a fundamental questioning'. The sexual fix again, as always. Why 'the privileged site'? Why must we open ourselves up to some natural 'sexuality'? Why is that our 'human' identity? No doubt is permitted as regards this sexuality that sexology gives itself as its object and proclaims as the very basis of human being, of who we really are. It is our *duty* to open up and be a sexual story, to confess and overcome (the path of the 'fundamental questioning'), showing our true humanity and entering thereby the sexological kingdom of heaven, the happy family of sexually confirmed individuals.

There is no need for invention, the reality is sufficiently worse. Robert T. Francoeur, 'a man who left the Catholic priesthood to become a writer, a husband and a professor of embryology and sexuality', outlines a sex-education course called 'Human Values' and inspired by a similar course used in the Harrad College experiment imagined in the United States by Robert H. Rimmer, 'a long-time student of human relations'. The college was an equal-numbers co-ed establishment with shared boy/girl suites ('after some careful psychological tests to sort out compatible pairs'). 'Human Values' was the core course, a year-long series of weekly two-hour sessions designed to bring out the human natural of sex. Thus at one point, for example, students would be shown 'movies of sexual rites . . . among the Polynesians, Africans, and inhabitants of Borneo'. Francoeur comments:

> Rimmer suggests that this might be an appropriate place to compare and contrast the spontaneous, non-pornographic celebrated joy in one's sexuality so evident in these early images with two modern images. The natural exuberance and ease of some poems from college publications, excerpts from *Woodstock* or other underground movies that treat human sexuality, love-making and the human body in a joyful, playful way, could be contrasted with the joyless, posed, clinical sterility of *Playboy's* air-brushed bunnies and the less sophisticated images of today's pornography.

Hardly a stereotype is missing in this appeal to a supposed spontaneity: we have the appropriation of other cultures into the terms of the Western sexual concern ('Polynesians, Africans, and inhabitants of Borneo' can be lumped together as so many indistinguishable natives, natives are near to nature, nature is sex, therefore it is 'evident' that they will be celebrating 'joy in one's sexuality') and their accompanying definition from the perspective of that concern as the image of an original happy state, as contentedly primitive (note the symptomatic '*early* images'); the assumption of right and wrong, good and bad sex with no more in the way of specification than the self-endorsing display of words like 'exuberance' and 'playful' ('Polynesians, Africans, and inhabitants of Borneo' are like children, the same primitive 'joy' can be found in both★); the whole *lesson* of the natural (compare and contrast, top grades if you get 'joyful'/'joyless', learn it by heart; and have no fear, the course always works, cannot fail to produce some naturally exuberant poems). Everything is just as 'natural' and 'human' as it is programmed to be. Rimmer says as much himself, in a proud but unguarded moment in which 'nature' suddenly turns out to be a question of conditioning: 'we assume that the students who live together on this program will ultimately find a spouse among their fellow students, because they have become so conditioned by the program that they cannot relate easily with less mature young people who have not been exposed to this program'. Meanwhile, Francoeur is using the language of 'Human Values' to introduce us playfully to some of these same students: 'Sheila Anne Grove was a quiet plain Jane, prim at all times', 'Stanley Cole was every girl's dream of a hip guy – long wavy brown hair, sideburns, suave and poised'; or else exuberantly debating such natural issues as whether virgins or non-virgins makes better wives ('spouses', as Rimmer would say): statistics 'show that virgins are more intolerant, non-virgins more moody and changeable in their dispositions'; or else . . .

The Reich–Cooper sexology commands us to authentic orgasm in the name of a repressed or alienated nature to be recovered; the mainstream commands us to joyful orgasm in the name of the human being inside us to be grasped in total loving. The latter borrows from the former (the constant idea of liberation), which in turn is closer to it than it would care to suppose (orgasm providing an extensive common ground). From the one to the other, the overall representation is much the same, only its inflections vary: everywhere the sexual concern, the tie to that.

★ Sexology is thus keen to stress how playfulness can be encouraged in the early years with the right children's games. 'Ding dong' is a good one for the two to fives ('if a girl is present, she may play also, but she has an unfair advantage'). Girls enjoy 'tie the boat': 'although obviously they can't play without at least one boy. Unless the player who provides the mooring happens to have an erection, the game becomes frustrating. Fortunately neither side can tie an effective knot. . . .' From seven on 'nudist party' offers 'frolics and fantasy': 'In one such party, girls decorated every available penis with streamers, balloons, and a painted face. In "nudist party" boys receive the lion's share of attention and a prodigious increase in penis pride.'

The nineteenth century contains and Freud grasps sexuality in the woman as hysteric: female sexual experience, the great problem, the drift of all this sexual concern and pressure, the point of its ties. From hysteria to frigidity to anorgasmia, the woman stays in place as the question to which the newly defined 'sexuality' answers. In current sexology, within the mainstream itself, two adjoining but differently orientated positions can be seen in connection with the question of 'sexual liberation' and the terms of man/woman relations.

The first is more traditional, in the sense that it accepts and maintains an idea of 'feminity', of 'being a woman', to which women should correspond (not to do so is to deny this essential femaleness). Women now have this and that, are right in their wish for and action towards obtaining independence, *but* there are ways of going about it, *feminine* ways: be neither 'doormat' nor 'superior woman'. Take, precisely, 'the militant feminist'. Sure, why not? 'You don't have to bind your feet, fill your brain with sawdust, always walk three paces behind . . . but you should present a female image to him and the world.' Don't be mistaken 'for a badly groomed boy or a second-string halfback for the Los Angeles Rams': 'One glance should tell him that you are female, very female.' Feminism should mean femininity: 'Realize that the more feminine a militant feminist you are, the more likely you will be able to accomplish your aims – in bed and out.' Nature intends women to have orgasms so that is what every woman needs and wants, but don't be 'fussy', and, above all, keep the image up for men, fit in, that's what they need and want and must have: '*Tell* him that your body is quivering in anticipation of receiving his magnificent penis deep in your hot, hungry vagina.'

Crucial to this position is the notion of *completion*. Men and women are complementary: the former are completed by the latter, who find their fulfilment in that completing role, are themselves completed in the orgasm men give them and the love they can then express (love is 'your wanting him to have the bigger filet'). Secretly, truly, real happiness is always there, in that completion: 'The modern woman may spend her days happily running countries and corporations and citizens' committees, church socials and Camp Fire Girls' Cookouts. She may win Pillsbury Bake Offs and Nobel prizes, but when she totters into bed at night, she still needs to be held close, to hear – and to say – the three little words that are the *essence* of her life: "I love you."'

The second position is manifestly modern, in the swim of things. We've understood women's liberation, it means sexual liberation, our sexuality. That's what they're on about and we'll give it to them, of course: a well-oiled genital sexuality, orgasm-tuned and functioning to perfection for man/woman exchange, the maximum circulation of women to men. Naturally, everything is fine, anything goes. Relations between women? You mean lesbianism? Yes, of course. Whatever you want. Ah, but watch out for your resistances, don't fool yourself. What's blocking you? What are you defending yourself against? What's the *trouble*? Don't you *really* want the orgasm – the genuine one – that I can help you towards? Frigid? Anorgasmic? Pre-orgasmic? Just follow me.

The prize in this modern double bind – anything but only 'sexuality' – must go to the French Freudian orthodoxy of sexological psychoanalysis which, entirely given over to devotion to the penis-phallus ('the glorified body' of the psychoanalytic cult and 'the alpha and omega of the alphabet of desire'), has understood to its satisfaction that women who stand away from this sexual economy are simply frigid, extinguished, whatever they might think of their own experience and say to the contrary: 'An extinction of which the women in question are not even aware, and which seems quite normal to them, indeed in the order of things; in short, which for them has no value as symptom but rather adds to their "value".' The 'reasoning' is that there are two possibilities: either the equation "vagina = phallus" or the equation "clitoris = little penis". The latter leaves the way clear for 'some hope', apparently because if you think your clitoris is a little penis, you know you lack the big one and you'll set out on the path to it and orgasm. The former is without hope, since if you think you've got the phallus, you're not going to start looking for it and will stay blocked in 'a frigidity half unknown, half well-accepted'. (One might suppose that you might not have any equations for your vagina at all or that you might think about it as anything, a teddy bear, say: just as, while we're at it, someone else might think about his penis as a red herring. But no, the phallus it is, and psychoanalysis in tow, deadly serious. Do I hear 'teddy bear'? Ted, daddy, bare: bare of daddy's penis, precisely. And 'red herring'? Red, her, ring: her red ring, her castration grasped in the image of his penis. Phallus, lack, you see it works, no more shying away, the problem you must have is ours, 'sexuality').

Agitation round the orgasm: the male analyst-sexologist-therapist/the female symptom–case–object (and let us not be deceived by the appearance of men and women on both sides, this is the basic scenario, the history in which that appearance is written). Identities. Establishing positions, law and order. 'These young women, authentically orgasmic through masturbation . . .': there they are, signed, sealed and delivered, certificate of authenticity guaranteed, sexologist-approved merchandise, ready for consumption.

Establishing positions, confirming places. 'After having hesitated, for form's sake, out of coquetry, perhaps because she didn't particularly want to, I don't know, she at last accepts making love. Ah! She starts me a fellatio, I reply with a cunnilingus, we meet in a 69 of the best style, something my wife still refused me at the time, then I penetrate her and we conclude with a synchronic orgasm. She came, I came, ah, what an admirable experience!' Game, set and match to the Doctor in this sexological exchange of balls: for form's sake, out of coquetry (you know what women are like), even perhaps because she didn't particularly want to (impossible that she didn't want to at all), no matter, her behaviour was hesitation, a kind of teasing reluctance to come to the inevitable decision, and at last she accepts, the best style, synchronous orgasm, admirable experience – one up on the wife who was desperately behind, making very slow progress.

Establishing positions, identities. What do women want? Orgasm. Mine. Pray heaven for the security of the phallus, anything for that, as long as everything can be kept in those terms. Total phallic abjection. Women are not to worry, they are better than men, *more* phallic still: 'the woman's whole body may become experienced as a phallus'; *'women have much bigger "penises" than men'.*★ All of which

---

★This phallic nature of women equips them for radical therapy, the 'Big Fuck' or '*mutual* penetration of the being of each other by the being of the other'. Penetration indeed is the order of the day for authentic orgasmic sex being: 'today we recognize the woman's clitoris and periclitoral zone as penetrating', 'the feeling quality of a woman's body . . . may be more emotionally penetrating than the man's', etc. 'We' would no doubt be hopelessly wrong to see in all this the transference of an old male stereotype on to women in order to keep things in phallic terms, to keep up the genuine, certified orgasm. But the question nevertheless remains: what do we want with the 'Big Fuck', why should we let ourselves be made to take that as the imperative of sexual experience?

leaves us – or sexologist David Cooper – with 'the beautiful, frenetic, uncontrolled movements of her body in full, free sexuality'. Now where have I read that before?

VII

'while Millicent bucked and writhed and chortled breathlessly'

J. J. Scott, 'The end-away justifies
the means', a 'fiction' in the magazine *Mayfair*, 1980

A characteristic of the kind of society in which we live is the mass production of fictions: stories, romances, novels, photo-novels, radio serials, films, television plays and series – fictions everywhere, all-pervasive, with consumption obligatory by virtue of this omnipresence, a veritable requirement of our social existence. We cannot live today without contact with this fictioning continuum.

This mass production of fictions is the culture of what might be called the 'novelistic', the constant narration of the social relations of individuals, the ordering of meanings for the individual in society. With the development of industrialism and urbanization, what are then seen as traditional forms of community definition and cohesion give way to a social organization, that of capitalism, in which, precisely, society and the individual become the terms of reference, in which the social relations of the individual – 'the individual and society' – become exactly a problem as such. 'Man', says Marx, 'is an animal that can be individualised only within society.' The point now is a social organization which, dependent in its economic instance on the relations of people as individual agents, producers and consumers assuring a circulation of commodities and money, institutes human being as individual being; Marx again: 'the various forms of the social texture confront the individual as merely means towards his private ends, as external necessity'. There is then a powerful work of *social* representation of 'the individual', the socially cohesive realization of the latter, people given that sense: stories of life, of lives, patterns of recognition, the ceaseless account of the social as meaning for the individual, experience always in these individual terms. In the nineteenth century this work was the province of the novel and written fiction generally; in the twentieth it has been that also of cinema and television: transmitters of the novelistic, social-for-individual representativity – my, your, our stories, our definitions.

In this 'individual and society' organization, the family has occupied a decisive position, proposed as a kind of mediation between the two: assuming the production of the new individuals needed for the reproduction of the social work-force, it is the first arena of socialization, preceding and then running alongside the systems of formal education, and, equally, it is the given arena of sexual relations, of the social ordering of the sexual. The great subject of the novelistic was thus crucially the family, the family as the bridge between individual and society, private and public, site of their meeting and conflict and resolution in the separate world apart it supposedly offers, the individual's fulfilment as individual in love and affection and the sexual within that love and affection. That so many nineteenth-century novels end in marriage, the union with the perfect mate, is not, of course, by chance or simply some formal convention: the marriage-union ending represents the resolution of 'the individual and society', a firm social unit offered as the privileged mode of the individual, the haven of his or her personal happiness, personal life.

Much of this family feeling and representation is still strong today (switch on your television set or look through the magazines at your newsagent's) but clearly many of the nineteenth-century terms have shifted, and this especially in connection with 'sexual liberation', 'the sexual revolution', leading to various adjustments and rearrangements in the overall representation. For the novelistic is never simply fixed, some static content. On the contrary, its institution in the mass production of fictions is the assurance of a continual *process* of representation, capable of taking up and working over actual social change, responding and redefining, maintaining the social-for-individual intelligibility. When in 1857 divorce laws are passed, there is at once a spate of 'divorce novels' (including the bestselling *East Lynne* by Mrs Henry Wood): the new must be brought into stories, focused in meanings, placed. Today with, for example, the pressure of the women's movement, there is an immediate response in novel after film after television programme, catching up from that pressure, drafting it into an available representation – and then in a way, which is the point, we cannot but deal in that representation, its terms, have difficulty in thinking beyond and grasping the challenge to them that the pressure always was and is and must be.

What has been described in previous chapters forms a central part of the current articulation of the novelistic, sexology contributing to a general representation from which, in turn, it draws many of the strategies of its writing. I want now to examine something of the sexological terms – the development of the sexual fix – in today's novelistic, referring particularly to written material – novels, stories, 'fictions'.

The strength of the sexological grasp of the novelistic can be seen straightaway in the appearance of a new and widespread literary genre: the sexual-life testimony. The influence of the Freudian psychoanalytic case-history in which hidden sexual impulses are revealed and laid out as the basis of an individual's character and behaviour is heavy here, as too, subsidiarily, is that of the work of Kinsey involving as it did the collection of the narratives of thousands of individual lives. People are summoned to bear witness, to report their private worlds, to narrate themselves as sexual experience. Nancy Friday, doing 'research in sexual identity', records, sifts, publishes fantasies: *My Secret Garden: Women's Sexual Fantasies, Forbidden Flowers: More Women's Sexual Fantasies, Men in Love: Men's Sexual Fantasies: The Triumph of Love over Rage.* Bestsellers. Gay Talese researches, field-works, interviews, practically experiments (becomes, for instance, client and manager of a massage parlour), publishes *Thy Neighbour's Wife: Sex in the World Today,* an account of his findings in the form of the 'intimate stories' of a number of Americans, a hymn to the dramatic personal awakenings of 'the sexual revolution' with every story a real life, fully authentic ('private papers further authenticated the sexual scenes and attitudes, feelings and fantasies, that appear in the book'). Bestseller.

The idea of the authentic document, of the publication of *research*, is constant and important. Typically, *Mayfair* runs a feature entitled 'Quest: the laboratory of human response', interviews in which the interviewees are asked to testify on some aspect of their 'sex life' ('Receptionist, 30 years old, redhead, town of origin Truro . . . it felt marvellous as he edged into me. I begged him to let it go in all the way, to fill me, but he took it very calmly. . . .'). The point is not that the presentation as research serves as justification or alibi, though no doubt it does for many writers and readers, but that the sexological is fundamental to 'sexuality'. In the same way that Victorian pornography and sexual representation generally are permeated by medical definitions and conceptions, so too, and following on in a basic continuity, our current idea of sexuality is everywhere informed by the terms of that sexology which has indeed been crucial for its very development: 'sexuality' comes quickly and easily as a sexological picture – the clinical picture of the sex life, the laboratory of human response, documentation of that.

Witness, confession, testimony. 'The first time I saw an adult penis, I was very young, perhaps around three', begins a *Playboy* feature article by Lynda Schor ('Some Perspectives on the Penis'). How to produce a book today? Get a number of personalities, from Dr Spock to Erica Jong, to recount their sexual 'initiation' and publish the results as *For the First Time*. When television and Sunday newspaper performer Clive James offers us his *Unreliable Memoirs* we can reliably expect – and we will not be disappointed – that much of them will be given over to details of his anguishedly exuberant, youthful tonk-pulling. And this is not just a question of public figures. We should all narrate, recount, tell ourselves, fill the testimony columns of *Penthouse* or *Mayfair*, *Playboy* or *Playgirl* ('I had sex with my stylist – it was a sizzling experience'). In the democracy of universal identity, we are all equal, all *the same*. Simply, there are also the experts, those with the knowledge and the experience, those who can report, give us the fruits of research, the lives and fantasies we must buy, consume, match.

Women by John Philip Lundin Ph.D., 'pseudonym of a world-traveler and scholar'; 'explicit sexual memoirs', with a preface by a specialist in 'forbidden sexual behaviour', strong praise for Lundin, for the example he sets ('one might wish that all sexual relationships were conducted on an equally high plane'); epilogue essay 'On Women' by the Ph.D. author, summarizing his conclusions ('women are possessed of very little logic as compared to men' but 'they fortunately have sexual cravings as strong as those of men'). Sequel to *Women*, *Mistresses*. Bestsellers. Available on any bookstall.

The imaginative prefacer of Lundin's *Women* ends with a glowing tribute to his literary achievement: 'Better than most novelists, and better than most authors of psychological case studies, he has presented a slice of the sexual life of our times.' Case study, slice of sexual life, novel: this complex of terms is important and is the definition of the terms of the contemporary representation, its writing. Their separation out there, of course, is only a strategy the better to praise Lundin whose books are directly dependent on case study and novel for their composition, as too is Talese's *Thy Neighbour's Wife*, as too are the innumerable other memoirs and reports, slices of sexual life. The latter is now the very stuff of the novelistic which gives it forms, structures, its representation: sexual life as sex lives, a whole narration of oneself, the story of who and how we are.

As well as the novel, written fictions, there are films and television programmes, not to mention posters, photo magazines, and so many other different modes. Yet the novel occupies what is still in some sense a privileged position, fulfils the crucial role of the work of *saying* sex and sexuality, of giving a solid mesh of meanings, of making available sense. Alongside and informing photo and film, our most powerfully invested modes of sexual imaging, is a constant production of novels, a stream of written fictions: every month, every week, the absolutely 'contemporary' bestseller; every month, every week, 'an entirely new accuracy of fact and of valuation in speaking of sexual experience' (from a blurb–quoted review of a novel by James Jones and by any other bestselling author).

The Victorian novel deals in family romance, in sexual situations (adultery, divorce), in certain of the period's sexual images (the fallen woman), in a certain grotesque comedy of the period's problem and economy and panic of the sexuality newly defined and felt (look at Dickens's *Bleak House* with its young woman narrator simultaneously child and mother to her father-figure guardian who wishes to marry her, surrounded by a host of male characters swelling up out of their skins or else phallically weak, and in even their very names: Rouncewell, Boythorn, Smallweed, Skimpole; no existence for a woman, only a child or a mother; and no stability of the identity of the man, troubled by the possibility nevertheless of the existence of a woman, castrating and only resolvable by marrying her as child-and-mother). A firm presence of women writers gives one form of the novel – the first-person woman narrator, perhaps in some governess-type situation – that allows a different expression of sexual affectivity and identity but within confines that can quickly return a conventionally given position of the women (subordination, marriage as resolution, female emotionalism – this being the possibility and the limit of any sexual expression).

What is generally constant in the Victorian novel is a fascination with the image, the figure of 'the woman' – depicted, defined, displayed, diagnosed in a kind of ceaseless concern (the concern for identity, for who I, male, am if she, female, is elsewhere to *my* difference, 'the man'/'the woman', the one *from* the other, like Eve from Adam, *the* difference secured); and this simultaneously with her emergence as a medical problem for society and with her increasing reality as disturbance, engaged even in struggle against her position as 'the woman' and hence against his as 'the man'.

One might take as an epitome-example here of this novelistic fascination and concern Thomas Hardy's *A Laodicean*, published in 1881. The title, a biblical reference (the Christians of Laodicea were 'lukewarm' in their faith), is aimed at the novel's heroine and her lack of determination, her waverings, her unsettled place. She has independence and force, her name is Paula *Power*, but no particular course of action or decided commitment, her name after all reflects only the strength of her engineer father ('the heiress of a name so dear to engineering science as Power'). Inevitably (the inevitability of the terms of the novelistic, the general representation), she falls into error, is deceived, has the truth revealed to her and ends the book in the right marriage; inevitably too (for this is at the basis of those terms, that representation), she is accompanied throughout, and even against the emphases put on her independent character, by a running commentary derived from and confirming the available cultural psychology of woman: 'the illimitable caprice of a woman's mind', 'this was not the sort of reasoning likely to occupy the mind of a young woman; the personal aspect of the situation was in such circumstances of far more import', and so on. Perhaps the key articulation, however, is the male vision of 'the modern woman', with 'modern' involving the sexual problem of independence of body. In a crucial scene, one of the male characters – Captain de Stancy – looks through a peephole into a gymnasium in which Paula is doing exercises:

> What was the captain seeing? A sort of optical poem.
> Paula, in a pink flannel costume, was bending, wheeling and undulating in the air like a gold-fish in its globe, sometimes ascending by her arms nearly to the lantern, then lowering herself till she swung level with the floor. Her aunt Mrs Goodman, and Charlotte de Stancy, were sitting on camp-stools at one end, watching her gyrations. Paula occasionally

addressing them with such an expression as – 'Now, Aunt, look at me – and you, Charlotte – is not that shocking to your weak nerves,' when some adroit feat would be repeated, which, however, seemed to give much more pleasure to Paula herself in performing it than to Mrs Goodman in looking on, the latter sometimes saying, 'O, it is terrific – do not run such a risk again!'

It would have demanded the poetic passion of some joyous Elizabethan lyrist like Lodge, Nashe, or Greene, to fitly phrase Paula's presentation of herself at this moment of absolute abandonment to every muscular whim that could take possession of such a supple form. The white manilla ropes clung about the performer like snakes as she took her exercise, and the colour in her face deepened as she went on. Captain de Stancy felt that, much as he had seen in early life of beauty in woman, he had never seen beauty of such a real and living sort as this.

The scene is a seduction (Captain de Stancy had vowed himself to celibacy; from this moment on, he will want to marry Paula): Paula is unaware of her spectator but this is nevertheless her 'presentation of herself'; wheeling and bending and risking, she performs to the audience, the others and him and us watching with him (he who has the pleasure which Mrs Goodman cannot have, he for whom the scene must *really* be set). His fascination structures the scene, his gaze surprising and penetrating an intimacy of women (that 'intimacy' existing only from the term of its intrusion, that gaze, only as a male image), running into a pointed voyeurism (that Hardy recognizes, commenting a little later that to gaze on the festival of Paula's goddess-like beauty was 'though so innocent and pretty a sight, hardly fair or gentlemanly' – hardly goodmanly! – and 'would have compelled him to withdraw his eyes, had not the sportive fascination of her appearance glued them there in spite of all'). The writing holds us to this voyeurism, this fascination, saying its incapacity to deal with the 'optical poem' we are watching ('It would have demanded the poetic passion of some joyous Elizabethan lyrist') at the same time that it lifts Paula away from the reality of a woman (she 'like a goldfish in its globe' or somewhat eclipsed in her 'pink flannel costume'; earlier it has been stressed that in the gymnasium she wears 'such a pretty boy's costume, and is so charming in her movements, that you think she is a lovely young youth and not a girl at all') and simultaneously underscores a sexual content, suggesting erotic spectacle and threat ('like snakes') as her colour deepens in 'this moment of absolute abandonment to every muscular whim that could take possession of such a supple form'.

Sexology, psychoanalysis are contemporary with that,* a whole pressure in and on this vision, the whole sexual concern. The novel is part of their history and they of its. The problem is general, one of representation; the holding to and reconstruction of this 'sexuality', with its terms and positions and identities, is a task for the times, from the late nineteenth century on. D. H. Lawrence is a novelist, yes, but also, and with no break, sexologist–cum–sex–educationalist, analyst–cum–sexual–anthropologist (look simply at the titles of his writings from novel to essay to theoretical tract: *Women in Love*, 'Do women change?', 'Matriarchy', *Psychoanalysis and the Unconscious*, and so on). James Joyce wanders Europe with his daughter Lucia from psychiatrist to psychoanalyst to psychiatrist, the playing out of an impossible drama of sexual identity, the very material and functioning of his major works, ends them both (*Ulysses* and *Finnegans Wake*) with a 'female monologue', the woman figure (Molly Bloom and Anna Livia Plurabelle) slipping away, the problem again, the disturbance of position, has himself praised by the psychoanalyst Jung for his unparalleled insight into women's psyche while his wife, Nora Barnacle, says flatly 'Jim knows nothing about women . . .'. And that exactly is what it is all about: that fringe of ignorance which 'the woman' poses even as 'she' is set up to establish identity – 'the woman' confirms 'the man', giving a clarity of position, but then also projects an absolute otherness, different, in contradiction, potentially threatening – and which has thus, continually, to be made up, securely fictioned.

The work of fictional security today – of the novelistic – can be seen in the development and consolidation of terms of representation as strong as those of the nineteenth century with its hypochondria and hysteria which in many ways are continued in this new statement of the sexual concern, in this new picture of 'sexuality'. As would be expected, it is in response to the struggles and movements against established identity and position that that work is most acutely engaged, that statement and picture are most easily grasped in their making up.

* Interestingly enough, *A Laodicean* itself was discussed in 1883 in the *Westminister Review* by future sexologist Havelock Ellis, who gave particular consideration to 'the love history of Paula': 'Independent, self-repressed, "deep as the North Star", that enigmatic lady is supposed to be representative of the modern spirit.'

Take *Kinflicks* by Lisa Alther ('wildly, ribaldly funny, the dazzling American best-seller'), which at one point describes a commune women's movement meeting ('the Free Farm Women's Weekend'). The heroine wanders from seminar group to seminar group: 'Women and Politics' ('locked in a match of revolutionary oneupmanship'); 'Women and Their Bodies' ('Laverne was demonstrating to the intrigued gathering how it was possible, if one possessed the flexibility of an Olympic gymnast, to view the inside of one's vagina and the mouth of one's cervix. I stood transfixed, gazing at the moist red hole. But for the life of me, I couldn't grasp why anyone would *want* to view the mouth of her cervix as reflected in a mirror. I felt I couldn't ask Laverne at the risk of sounding bougie [= bourgeois]'); 'Women and Rage' ('where the woman was in the process of hacking her ex-lover to bits'); 'Women and Work' ('I knew that housework and childbearing were being roundly dumped on, and that I would feel agonizingly bougie once I felt compelled to mention what a trip I found cleaning the shower to be'). In its details, the description mixes moments of sympathy with a continuing irony; overall, it gives an incident in the life of the individual heroine, an aspect of present-day reality that needs to be included and placed as a stage she must go through – and that place is quickly tied and limited to the terms of the contemporary sexual concern. Thus, for example, Laverne, organizer of the 'Women and Their Bodies' group, is earlier portrayed as provoking and revelling in gang rape: ' "Faster! Faster! Don't stop *now*, you mother fucker! Oh mother of Christ! Don't *stop*!" Her body was arcing up off the ground and twitching spasmodically, like a frog's leg hooked into an electric current. Three men lay in panting heaps next to her, like bees after stinging' (note the return of the image of the hysteric: the spasmodic twitching, the *arc-en-cercle*). Naturally, like all women, the heroine *really* wants that too: 'My nipples began tingling with excitement. I realized I wanted to join the fray.' And then for the rest of her time in the novel, Laverne is shown as perpetually involved with an electric vibrator with which she finally blows herself out: 'The doctor held the phallus-shaped vibrator, turned it over, sniffed it, scratched his head. It had a big crack all the way up it. Laverne had apparently achieved her goal of the Ultimate Orgasm.'*

---

*The back cover of the English Penguin edition gives prominence to the following quotation from a *Cosmopolitan* review: 'Reinforces our new-found knowledge that woman *can* and *do* write just as powerfully . . . and unsqueamishly about sex as men.' Exactly.

Orgasm is everywhere, the very material of the picture, the life. Heroine's name, Virginia Babcock: virgin, baby, cock; married, after the free farm episode, to Ira Bliss IV: I are – or higher? – bliss; preoccupation, orgasm; girlfriend of high-school football star Joe Bob Sparkes, 'this was my first experience with the concept that I have now, after extensive experimentation, formulated into a postulate: It is possible to generate an orgasm at any spot on the human body'; student of Worthley College, A-grade paper on 'Venous Congestion and Edema as a Determining Factor in the Intensity of Human Orgasm';* lover of Eddie, a female co-student with whom she experiences 'a breathtaking series of multiple orgasms, triggered by the insertion of greased little fingers into each other's anus'; wife of Ira in a marriage that involves an emotional retreat from orgasm until, deciding she would like to have a baby, she manages 'one that outdid even those with Eddie'; encounter with Hawk, Vietnam deserter, into meditation and mysticism, who, critical of her 'bougie' attitudes ('If you have sex, you want an instant orgasm'), leads her through the ritual preparations for an authentic cosmological sexual experience which fails to come off . . .

This is difficult. *Kinflicks* contains more than this, contains, for instance, a complex presentation of the relationship between the heroine and her dying mother in which terms of experience and understanding are worked out which go far beyond those in which she is constantly cast in the narrative of her life. But then, precisely, that narrative does everywhere run into orgasm and sexual concern as suggested in the brief account given above. But then again, why not? After all, the sexual *is* a fundamental part of a life, of life itself. The assumption of 'life', however, has to be handled with care. A novel is not 'life' but a form of representation and 'life itself' anyway is never simply given outside of forms of representation, of which in our society the novel is one, importantly so (the production of the novelistic). There is a crucial *responsibility* of forms, of representations. Suppose we say that *Kinflicks* reflects aspects of contemporary life; for example, women's groups *do* have sessions devoted to women and their bodies, teaching and developing methods for

---

*Having your heroine write a Masters and Johnson term paper on orgasm is probably only capped by giving her an orgasmic name. Thus Praxis Duveen, heroine of Fay Weldon's novel *Praxis* ('her new bestseller'): 'Praxis, meaning [in Greek] turning-point, culmination, action; orgasm; some said the Goddess herself.'

self-examination and knowledge – *Kinflicks* merely reflects this, shows something that we can easily find in real life. Admitting this reflection idea for the moment, *Kinflicks* is nevertheless a novel, is involved in certain modes of organization and depiction. The linking of the women's group with a character who enjoys gang-bangs and spends all her time with a vibrator is a *certain* way of representing with a *certain* stance, a *certain* position; as too is the narration of the seminars from the heroine's nonparticipatory and ironic point-of-view, the use of such phrases as 'a match of revolutionary oneup-manship' or 'the flexibility of an Olympic gymnast'.

But more than this, there can be no simple idea of reflection: life is permeated by and – as 'life' – made up of representations, grasping and rendering and ordering all experience. 'Women and Their Bodies' sessions are not pristine phenomena out there in some untouched world waiting to be described. Like everything else, they exist always within a complex of meanings, of representations in relation to the terms of which they are posed, understood, *ap-prehended*. No referent – nothing in the world – can be allowed to guarantee a discourse (the suggestion of such a guarantee is itself a discursive strategy, an attempt to naturalize the meaning given, the position constructed); on the contrary, a discourse must be ques-tioned in its own particularity, its specific forms, its characteristic engagement with the complex of meanings, representations, that is the present existence – the cultural-historical reality – of this or that phenomenon, this or that referent. *Kinflicks* does not reflect life like some mirror, it repeats and reworks representations, structures of organization and understanding, falls in with the sexological picture, the sexual concern. It must take responsibility for that repetition, for the meanings and positions it adopts, and that responsibility cannot be avoided by appeals to the rights of comedy, satire, or whatever. There is no reason why, say, the women's movement should be exempt from comedy and satire (and no evidence that internally it is) but comedy and satire are again made up at any time of particular forms which involve choices of meaning and position, of representa-tion. *Kinflicks* refuses, simply, to consider the implications of the forms it adopts; like so many other contemporary novels, it tries to avoid the responsibility of its commitment with the alibi of an engagement in 'the comedy of life itself': so doing, it can only repeat and confirm at so many points the dominant order, make the dominant – and the dominant sexual – sense.

Kinflicks's representation hinges on a basic narrative of the contemporary novelistic, involving orgasm as central and the problem of the woman raised round the themes of her independence and her eventual completion by the discovery of a true femininity. A major emphasis here has become the tracing of the progression from 'feminist' to 'feminine' (remember sexology's advice to women not to be mistaken for 'a badly groomed boy' or 'a second-string halfback').

Take the emphasis and its narrative articulation at their simplest and crudest, as, for instance, in Ian Fleming's *Goldfinger*. Hero James Bond – whose concentration of stereotypes of 'the man' needs no description – confronts two women. First, Tilly Masterson: 'She was beautiful – physically desirable. But there was a cold, hard centre to her that Bond couldn't understand or define.' The woman-enigma, the woman–problem. But, of course, Bond *can* understand and define the cold, hard centre: she is 'one of those girls whose hormones had got mixed up' (the result of 'fifty years of emancipation'), one of 'a herd of unhappy sexual misfits – barren and full of frustrations'. Men are men, women are women (or should be); Tilly is a hysteric, neither one nor the other or both, aggressive and masculine (acts like a *son*, not a daughter); a misfit, she is unhappy and frustrated in her failed femininity (what she really wants and needs is a *master* – Masterson should be master's daughter*). Since she cannot place herself correctly to Bond, as woman to man, she gets killed: ' "Poor little bitch. She didn't think much of men . . . I could have got her away if she'd only followed me." ' Second, Pussy Galore, leader of a lesbian criminal gang, a natural challenge: Bond 'felt the challenge all beautiful lesbians have for men'. Tilly falls for Pussy, Pussy falls for Bond, ' "I never met a man before" '. QED. It then only remains to *explain* her lesbianism: she is anti-men (lesbianism is being anti-men) because of a traumatic childhood rape by an uncle (shades exactly of Freud's seduction theory of hysteria); and to prescribe treatment from practising sexologist Bond: ' "All you need

---

*This is suggested and acted out in a host of little details and incidents throughout the book. Thus, when Bond tells Tilly what to do after a motoring mishap: ' "While I fix up about the garage, here's some money. Please buy us lunch – anything you like for yourself. For me, six inches of Lyon sausage, a loaf of bread, butter, and half a litre of Mâcon with the cork pulled." Their eyes met and exchanged a flurry of masculine/feminine master/slave signals. The girl took the money.'

is a course of TLC . . . Tender Loving Care Treatment . . . "When's it going to start?" Bond's right hand came slowly up the firm, muscled thighs, over the flat soft plain of the stomach to the right breast. Its point was hard with desire. He said softly, "Now." His mouth came ruthlessly down on hers.' So she fits in the end, finally cured, identity established, his and hers, in her place, name confirmed – pussy galore.

Emphasis and narrative articulation are common; they can be played in different ways, varied in their realization, decked out with new stylistic frills, but their basic grounds stay constant, the basic position the same. In *Eyes of Laura Mars*, a suspense-story involving a series of murders of women written by H. B. Gilmour as the novel of the film of the same title, the heroine Laura, a successful New York photographer, tough, independent, and with a peculiar ability to hallucinate the murders as they happen, falls in love and goes to bed with the inspector assigned to the case ('"it took me all my life to find you"'). On waking:

> She studied herself in the dressing-room mirror. Another face was emerging, brighter and more beautiful . . . more feminine . . . Laura Mars, she chided herself, you are becoming a reactionary. Where is that revolutionary fervor the reviewers spoke of? That 'masculine sensibility' and 'defiant independence' so raptly associated with your work? Do you know who you look like now? Do you know *what* you look like? A sleepy little girl just waking from a dream. A little girl curled warm in a canopied four-poster bed.

There are two set poles, masculine and feminine; a woman confusing them (thus nearing hysteria, subject to visions, hallucinations); a treatment, sex, under which the masculine overlay comes away and the underlying reality emerges, brighter and more beautiful, more feminine (twisting on this theme of identity, the novel then provides a plot in which the inspector turns out to be the murderer, avenging himself for the trauma of a prostitute mother, for *her fault*, a kind of original sin of the woman).

And the same recurs, again and again, and just as well in what is regarded as 'serious' literature. For instance, *Hers* by A. Alvarez distinguished critic and lecturer, a novel clearly far removed in the ambition of its writing from *Goldfinger* or *Eyes of Laura Mars*. The paperback cover promises 'a story of sexual jealousy and one woman's icy pursuit of self-knowledge', already edging us nevertheless into the recognition of a perfectly common ground (note the 'icy', this is Bond's chocolate-box theory: a woman should be warm and soft but Tilly Masterson has 'a cold, hard centre'). First page: 'Yet she looked like a child: blonde, fragile, with cool blue eyes and the smooth face of a fourteen-year-old girl. High cheekbones, delicate mouth, untouchable.' The narrative is there already: the woman 'cool' (part of her iciness; 'deft body and cool stare', Alvarez himself, not Ian Fleming or the cover) and 'fragile' ('a child', as Laura Mars is really 'a sleepy little girl') and above all *'untouchable'*, a challenge (again) for the other characters, the men who surround her, and for the novel, resolved through her story ('*Hers*'!) – her story through her lovers right back into the German past she carries deep inside her and which she finally exorcises in the arms of the son of a former Nazi:

> Why had nobody ever told her that sex was for use, that through pleasure she extended her boundaries? She moved Kurt's hand against her wetness. He half woke and began to stroke her lazily, lazily. She lay still to attend to the far off tremblings in the pit of her body, while the rain shushed down outside. There had been too much sweetness and light. It was time to find out about the darkness. Her hand moved with Kurt's, probing, touching herself.

Untouchable, touching herself, the book's movement, find out about the darkness, the truth through sex, the revelation of yourself and life: 'And as she reached her climax, her head cleared of all its confusions. . . .'

'Brought face to face with her own sexuality', says the cover. A curious notion but one that is the very assumption, the very vision of all this. Hers, his, two poles, to be correctly aligned; she must be brought, imperatively, face to face with her own sexuality, finish in the place assigned, pull through by orgasm – the climax of the book, the untouchable touched, return to normal: 'My husband, she thought. Responsible, domestic, laborious, immovable, flat. He'll do.' End of novel. A world away from Bond and Laura Mars? Of course. Serious writing comes down from the orgasmic heights to a 'mature' perception of the everyday, the icy pursuit of self-knowledge brings you back to a more balanced, authentic acceptance of yourself for that ordinary life. But then self-knowledge is sex, sex is how you know who you are, your real identity. Pussy Galore on Bond: 'I never met a man before'; a lover on Alvarez's heroine: 'I've never seen a real woman before'. The same world, the usual fix: 'the man', 'the woman', 'sexuality'.

At one point in his novel *The American*, Henry James is involved in the depiction of a moment of awareness and admission and expression of love between his hero, Newman, and a lady named Madame de Cintré. The novel was first published in 1877, but was subsequently revised for the 1907 New York edition of James's works; in the course of which revision, the particular passage in question was initially altered and expanded in a way which in fact leaves us with three versions as follows:

> But this time, in the midst of his golden sunrise, Newman felt the impulse to grasp at a rosy cloud. 'Your only reason is that you love me!' he murmured, with an eloquent gesture, and for want of a better reason Madame de Cintré reconciled herself to this one.   (1877)

> But this time, in the midst of his golden sunrise, he felt the impulse to grasp at a rosy cloud. 'Your only reason is that you love me!' he almost groaned for deep insistence, and he laid his two hands on her with a persuasion that she rose to meet. He let her feel as he drew her close and bent his face to her the fullest force of his imposition; which she took from him with a silent surrender that he felt long enough to be complete.   (revision for 1907 edition)   *222469*

> But this time, before his golden sunrise, he felt the impulse to grasp at a rosy cloud. 'Your only reason is that you love me!' he almost groaned for deep insistence, and he laid his two hands on her with a persuasion that she rose to meet. He let her feel as he drew her close, bending his face to her, the fullest force of his imposition; and she took it from him with a silent, fragrant, flexible surrender which – since she seemed to keep back nothing – affected him as sufficiently prolonged to pledge her to everything.   (final text as printed in 1907 edition)

The first version is the shortest. Newman's passion is present only as eloquence – the eloquence of the writing with its vague 'golden sunrise' and 'rosy cloud' and his own 'eloquent gesture' (almost a comment on the writing itself, eloquently gesturing) – and Madame de Cintré reconciles herself 'for want of a better reason' to his murmured assertion of her love. The second version erases the eloquent gesture and adds a strength of passion to Newman's little speech, he almost groaning 'for deep insistence'; it adds, too, physical contact; the persuasive power of his two hands that she rises to meet, his drawing her close, face bent to her in 'the fullest force of his imposition' which she takes 'with a silent surrender that he felt long enough to be complete' – a whole rehearsal of their wooing which comes near to an explicitly sexual account that nevertheless cannot be given, envisaged as such (hence perhaps the hint of embarrassment in the syntactical hiatus of 'bent his face to her the fullest force of his imposition'). The third version retains these elements (attempting somewhat to improve the troubled syntax) and adds in turn a luxuriance to the surrender, a memory of romance fiction, 'silent, fragrant, flexible'; the surrender now essentially the woman's body, the adjectives marking the desire for its yielding pliancy, she to pledge herself 'to everything'.

Thus it is that characters make love in Henry James. One recognizes the clichés, the stereotypes, the given positions – male force/female surrender – but also a certain play, as though everything is *not quite* sewn up. The first version is understated and complex in that; the second and third versions, some twenty years later, lay on the stereotypes but without perhaps fully losing the complexity, the resistance of the conception of these characters and their interaction to a simple sexual positioning, to the explicit terms of 'sexuality'. James is writing, and the versions can make us aware of this, in the turn from the nineteenth century to the twentieth; he, his writing, knows the pressure of the sexual as fundamental area of concern – knows it more gently than Lawrence, less radically than Joyce – but without as yet the establishment of the terms of the nineteenth-century problem as the twentieth-century vision, with instead a psychology of infinite subtlety, endlessly ramifying analyses of consciousness and behaviour in men and women and their interactions, the complexity of the confusion of identity.

From version to version of the passage from *The American* the physical is entered more explicitly, the stereotypes of making love are hardened, a typical position re-engaged. Today this explicitation, hardening and positioning has become the stuff of the novelistic, its structure and goal, the ground of its elaboration and truth. Orgasm is the question of the day, what everything bears on: ' "Do you ever have an orgasm?"', Matt Hooper to Ellen Brodie in Peter Benchley's *Jaws*;★ '"Simon, have you never come? Had an orgasm?"', Ronnie to Simon (short for Simona) in Kingsley Amis's *I Want It Now*; and so on, novel after novel. As marriage is the end and resolution of the nineteenth-century novel, so orgasm – good, proper, authentic, real, successful, total, mind-blowing, truth-revealing, the moment when IT HAPPENS – is that of twentieth-century fictions, the point of representation: 'And then they both began to move again, interlocking, cock and cunt, and nothing else in the world mattering. She came with a shudder that shook her whole body and released another scream from her that scarcely seemed human . . . They lay not moving in the absolute peace after the earthquake . . .', final moment of Erica Jong's *How To Save Your Own Life*; 'Then suddenly it happened – like a great, glorious, whooshing washing machine – it's the only way I can describe it – leaving me shuddering and shuddering with pleasure at the end, like the last gasps of the spin-dryer. And afterwards I cried some more because I was so happy, and he held me in his arms, telling me how much he loved me until I fell asleep . . .', last pages of Jilly Cooper's *Octavia*.

In the nineteenth-century novel the concluding marriage was above all the resolution for women; men could cross from the world of feeling to the world of society in which they were accredited active agents, move from private to public and back again for the emotional strength and fulfilment the private is instituted to stand for and provide. The orgasm of the twentieth century binds women and men, the social agency of the latter giving way more and more to an inward-turning engagement on the sole – offered as *the crucial* – terrain of 'personal relations', 'intimate life': 'nothing else in the world mattering'. The use of and investment in love-making is in these terms; the representation is that of a general, 'sexuality'-determined psychology which is the very essence of 'life', the basic and deepest reality – I may do this and that in society but I am only really me in bed, confronting my own sexuality, stripped down to a purity of self and experience. John Updike expresses it perfectly in his *Marry Me*: 'Jerry and Sally made love lucidly, like Adam and Eve

★ Hooper follows up this lunch-date question by suggesting a session in a motel: '"we should have a name, just in case we run into an old-fashioned innkeeper. How about Mr and Mrs Al Kinsey. We could say we were on an extended field trip for research."'

when the human world was of two halves purely'; Adam and Eve,
two halves purely, matched in flawless complementarity, 'the original man and woman'. That is where we should be, where we should
find ourselves; the novels, their stories, tell of the problems of the
achievement of such truth, filled with the sexual concern, written
out of the all-pervasive sexological imagination. The contemporary
plot is exactly that of the erotic path to the 'Big O', the realization of
elemental, original, real being, man and woman, the two halves,
cock and cunt; woman brought to reality through man: 'and she
thought, feeling that cock slide in and out of her as if it owned her
soul, that if she died then, if she died that very minute, it would be all
right, she would have known most of it, have lived, have felt it'; man
through woman: 'through the strait gate between your legs I had
entered this firmament'.

If we had to point to one key figure in the literary history of this
representation, this engagement of the novelistic, that figure could
be none other than Lawrence. It is Lawrence supremely who catches
up the new pressures of the sexual concern, who is aware of current
thinking in sexology and sexual psychology and psychoanalysis,[*]
who follows and reacts to feminist struggles and early 'free sex'
theorists, whose novels focus shifts in experience across the genera-
tions from the nineteenth through to the twentieth century and
define a mode of understanding in which love-making becomes the
site of the demonstration of authentic or inauthentic being, of the
problems and relations of man and woman, male and female. *Lady
Chatterley's Lover* is simply the best known of these novels in which
the equation of personal with sexual development is increasingly
strongly produced, with social questions run into and lost in the
latter, left peripheral: Mellors the gamekeeper and Connie Chatterley, John Thomas and Lady Jane (an earlier title for the book and

---

[*]Frieda Lawrence (his German wife who as a young woman had been close to
some of Freud's disciples): 'Lawrence knew about Freud before he wrote the final
draft of *Sons and Lovers* [in 1912]. . . . I was a great Freud admirer; we had long
arguments and Lawrence's conclusion was more or less that Freud looked on sex
too much from the doctor's point of view, that Freud's "sex" and "libido" were too
limited and mechanical and that the root was deeper.'

expressions used by Lawrence to refer to the male and female genital
organs), cock and cunt, the man and the woman meeting, with
Connie learning to find herself through 'the phallic hunting out',
brought 'to the very heart of the jungle of herself', 'to the real
bedrock of her nature' – 'the phallus alone could explore it'. Everywhere in Lawrence, and given powerfully influential definition, the
establishment of the one area of crucial concern, of the importance of
the sexual; with explorations of that principle from novel to novel,
of the blocks and disturbances of the order of male and female, the
original and vital force of man and woman – blocks and disturbances
caused above all by the commotion, the challenge of the woman,
petulantly admonished for her refusals to fit: 'She was withstanding
him, and his male super-power, and his thunderbolt desire. She was,
in some indescribable way, throwing cold water over his
phoenix . . .'*

What we have today is a powerful sexual economy of the novel (and
of the novelistic, in the production of which the novel plays its –
important – part). 'Sexuality' is the stake and the purpose, the
constant wager of the representation, over a scale of variations that
runs from the elemental Lawrentian, ever present and appealing, to

---

*The decisive significance of Lawrence as a figure in this history can be measured
too by the contemporary function of his work as an extreme point of debate and
controversy. Feminist Kate Millett's critical account of Lawrence's sexist writing of
women in her *Sexual Politics* provoked heated replies, such as Norman Mailer's *The
Prisoner of Sex*; and, more interestingly, gave rise to attempts to provide a positive
evaluation of the novels for women, most recently Carol Dix's *D. H. Lawrence and
Women*, concerned to argue that 'far from treating them as inferior objects, as
Lawrence is accused of by Kate Millett, he saw more in women, and the feminine
principle, than did most of his contemporaries'. No one could deny that Lawrence
was massively concerned with women, that his writings are full of references to and
statements about 'the feminine principle' and that those references and statements
very often reflect the impetus behind and the determining conception of the
characters and actions in the novels. But precisely what is in critical question is this
investment in women as woman ('the woman pure woman'), these terms of
concern (the whole fact of the sexual fix). 'Recalling his fascination with duality,
The Lost Girl and *The Plumed Serpent* draw upon the triumph of the bowels over the
breast, the loins over the face. This is the expression of the feminine mode of being.'
Dix simply repeats Lawrence, the concern, assents to a 'feminine mode of being'
(and in counterpart to a masculine one), sexually grounded and bodily defined –
bowels and loins, the essence of women's being lying there.

its banalization, its ordinary 'aroundness', the simple and immediate acceptance that *it* is the fundamental topic of interest and preoccupation. A novel by Kingsley Amis can serve as a brief example of this banalization, its very title catching the standard conception – *I Want It Now*.

The novel is flavoured with Amis's brand of social satire: the ironically self-deprecating humour that glibly shatters glibness and pretension, the hero who is a 'shit' in a world of shits, right and left, and who can be allowed to come through with a certain sympathy, emerging as a kind of centre of genuine human shittiness. The narrative lives up to the expectations of the title. Television personality Ronnie, the hero, meets Simon-Simona at a smart party; Simon proceeds to announce that she 'wants it now'; home to Ronnie's bed where it becomes clear that, whatever she may say about wanting it, Simon doesn't like it; Ronnie prepares to kick Simon out of his life as fast as she entered it but discovers her to be the daughter of excessive wealth and aristocracy and rapidly changes his mind; from then on, the novel mixes its satire with the basic story of Ronnie falling in love with Simon and his painstaking attempts to overcome her sexual resistance and bring her to orgasm. Simon is nervous, tense and frigid (the traces of hysteria recur as usual: she speaks in a 'hypnotized tone', she comes on with a refusal of her femininity, confusedly boyish in appearance, behaviour and name). Ronnie's treatment of her condition is an uphill battle (not like Bond dishing out TLC to Pussy with instant success), involving psychoanalysis: 'Handicapped by almost total ignorance of what made women frigid, he tried some amateur psychoanalysis, asking her for instance to recall her first man and just what it was that was horrible about him'; sexological inquiry: 'Simon, have you never come? Had an orgasm?'; practical exercise sessions, with failures: 'her body went into overdrive. With nobody at the wheel, the Porsche left the M1 in an accelerating ascending spiral' (Simon's surname is *Quick*); and advances: 'We're making a bit of progress. It's bound to be slow'; up until the unmistakable signs of approaching triumph: 'Then he took hold of Simon. Her response was that of a girl who simply wants what is coming, a different being from the stiff, shuddering, gasping personage he had encountered that first evening. It had come to seem impossible that anything could prevent him from satisfying her . . .' From here to orgasm, sexology wins again, sexuality is where we're at, our position, you and me, man and woman, this is our life.

If the novelistic is now generally referred to the sexual in this way, locked into 'sexuality', what of pornography as a distinct and classified area of sexual representation?

Pornography in Britain is usually seen as dating from the seventeenth century, above all from the period of the Restoration in 1660, Charles II's court bringing with it a new licence and a large output of manuscript poems and farces together with translations from French and Italian works. An important date then cited in its development is that of the publication in 1748 of John Cleland's *Memoirs of a Woman of Pleasure (Fanny Hill)*, the first original English pornographic work in prose – the first novel. Yet the term 'pornography' is again essentially a nineteenth-century one. OED gives 'pornographer' 1850 and 'pornography' 1864 ('pornographic' following in 1880): 'Description of the life, manners, etc. of prostitutes and their patrons; hence the expression or suggestion of obscene or unchaste subjects in literature or art.' The etymology of the term is Greek: *pornê* – prostitute, *graphein* – write; hence OED's reference to the description of prostitutes: much early pornography is exactly that, lists or directories of prostitutes with details of prices and accounts of anatomy and speciality (the appearance of *pornographe*, pornographer, in France in the later eighteenth century is exactly in this 'technical' sense: the pornographer is the author of a treatise on prostitution; and that sense is the basis of the rare uses of the pornography words in both French and English until the middle decades of the nineteenth century).

The nineteenth-century crystallization of a named phenomenon *pornography* is indicative. Pornography is the necessity of the age of the beginnings of the sexual concern, of the problem of sexuality. Earlier, we pointed to something of a medicalization of Victorian pornography, its assumption and repetition of the massively developed hygiene-and-physiology conception of the sexual: the world of Walter's *Secret Life* is the world of Acton and Laws Milton and their medical treatises; there is a common ground of intelligibility. We might now say indeed that pornography does not exist outside of – and thus comes into being with – the production of the sexual as a general social/individual problem and concern. The 'bawdy' or 'lewdness' of previous centuries is dispersed, relatively literary, relatively private, the province of small and wealthy groups; pornography, from the nineteenth century on, is a systematic vision, unliterary, mass-produced and given wider and wider social distribution and circulation.

This is difficult; after all, Walter's autobiographical work has no circulation, is privately printed in a few copies, and Davenport's books likewise were by no means widely available. What has to be grasped is that in many ways the pornography of the Victorian age – and this is a condition of its development as such – is elsewhere, is in the medical treatises, the hygiene manuals, the advice pamphlets, the advertisements and prospectuses for this or that remedy, and so on. The medical is the foundation of the pornography because it is the basis of a sexual *system*, of the definition and understanding of what will eventually be adapted and theorized as 'sexuality'; and because, too, it is thereby the possibility of a social availability of sexual representation. Slow at first in its extension, that social availability is exactly initiated in the kind of medical and quasi-medical literature mentioned above. Walter and Davenport have the terms of the system – the content – which are all-pervasive but lack a social form (the social-pornography modes of novel and magazine, photograph and film, once sexology has clarified 'sexuality' as the truth and reality of individual life, an authentic area of public exchange and depiction and propagation); they remain minor figures in the movement of an overall system that they privately confirm, the new order of phallic concern and economy.

The last phrase is again difficult. *New*? When Walter records his opinion that showing a woman his penis is an unfailingly effective method of seduction (no woman can resist) we can go back at least to the seventeenth century, to, for example, an anonymous poem entitled 'The Dreame' and the clinching argument made by the gallant narrator to 'a bucksome girle': 'An Argument noe Sister can withstand / I put my Prick into her hand.' So much for the newness of the phallic order. And anyway, how can we reasonably say that pornography is a nineteenth-century phenomenon? On 9 February 1668 Samuel Pepys notes in his *Diary*: 'I to my chamber, where I did read through *L'escholle des filles*, a lewd book, but what doth me no wrong to read for information sake (but it did hazer my prick para stand all the while, and una vez to decharger).' Clearly Pepys is here involved with what we now call pornography: the lewd book ('dirty book' is our equivalent) used for purposes of sexual stimulation (Pepys even has the modern 'for information sake' alibi). But the emphasis is not (of course not) that there is no sexual writing nor any relation of that writing to a strictly phallic scenario prior to the

nineteenth century; it is, quite simply, a stress on the establishment
in the nineteenth century of the *system* of phallic identity in the terms
of an emerging social concern with the sexual – and in connection
with which something called pornography is importantly developed
and assigned as such, part of the pressure of the sexual representation
and maintenance.

Everything turns on the penis-phallus and the potential disturbance of its identity by the woman (as women must be seen from its
perspective, the opposite and mirroring pole to that of the man to
which men are held). Hence the major commonplaces of the Victorian sexual imaginary: the central and socially-circulating medical
account, defining the order and its disorders, the containing system,
flanked by the two main displacements-recognitions of that order,
whipping and the cult of the little girl (neither of which is limited to
clandestine minority sexual depiction and practice; both spread into
areas of public acceptance and activity: the former in homes and
schools and prisons, and a topic of much debate and celebration; the
latter in the popular petting and imaging, little girls an adorably
innocent allowed focus of attention). The point of whipping in this
sexual imaginary is its avoidance of genital sex, investment inflected
on to the buttocks in a confirming production of the same: no
difference between man and woman (let alone differences in and
between individuals outside of that fixed polarization), fulfilment in
carefully ritualized situations that reproduce an unproblematic
domination, receiving punishment as from schoolmaster or mis-
tress. The point of the little girl is her existence before womanhood,
supposedly before sexual life, before the critical moment 'when the
stream and river meet' as C. L. Dodgson (Lewis Carroll) could put
it: investment in an untroubling image of female beauty, avoiding
any reality of women and men, the ever-possible disorder of relations (art critic and moralist John Ruskin, admirer of the little girl, is
divorced for non-consummation of the marriage by his wife Effie
Gray: 'he had imagined women were quite different to what he saw I
was, and . . . the reason he did not make me his Wife was because he
was disgusted with my person the first evening').

The medical account recognizes and allows sexual feeling on the
side of men, a matter of physiological regulation, the economy of the
male body; women have no sexual feeling or else, since they do, are
sick; order and disorder. Whipping and the little girl say that order
and disorder again: women have no sexual feeling but at the same

time here are modes against the threat that they do, escapes into realms of a sexual safety in which the order of the man is not disturbed by any presence of women, she banished altogether or erected into the role of a punishing mother-figure for the erotic transport of the man as little boy or, the reverse, held as the image of the little girl, deliciously intimating a femininity from which the man remains nevertheless secure. Pornography is developed at the centre of that system with two crucial – systematically interdependent and effectively equivalent – functions: repeat the penis–phallus as order, answer the question of women and sexual feeling, the enigma of female sexuality (as Freud and psychoanalysis will later phrase it).

Which is why an author such as Lawrence, who constantly declares himself to be writing against pornography, is in fact very much bound up with it, directly pornographic; as too is sexology, as too is psychoanalysis (and to mention these last is to underline again the importance of the medical and paramedical in the system which defines the place and terms of pornography). Lawrence: women in love, the phallus, its universal order, as learnt for example by Connie Chatterley: 'I *know* it is the penis which connects us with the stars and the sea and everything. It is the penis which touches the planets, and makes us feel their special light.' Psychoanalysis: the hysteric, 'what does a woman want?', the phallus as universal signifier, 'alpha and omega of the alphabet of desire', everything dependent on that, Oedipus complex and so on: 'The concept phallus is that from which is supported the desire of *both* the man *and* the woman . . . The fact that "attention", whether that of the man or that of the woman, is directed on the penis and not on the testicles is clearly linked to its possible erection, that is to say, to a visible manifestation of desire.' It has to be admitted that psychoanalysis spends a certain amount of time insisting that the phallus is not the same as the penis (which nevertheless, as in the passage just cited, seems always to be popping up and giving the lie to such oily double talk), that it is the universal signifier to which men just as much as women have to submit. But then so also did Lawrence, Lacanian before Lacan, and more poetic even: 'the penis is a mere member of the physiological body. But the phallus, in the old sense, has roots, the deepest roots of all, in the soul and the greater consciousness of man. . . .' Quite why the phallus should be the universal signifier and star-reaching consciousness raiser, as it was in the beginning, now and ever shall be, is never revealed (except for psychoanalytic lapses into admiration for the 'visible' nature of the penis and its 'possible erection'). To do so would be to have to recognize and analyze the fact of a *historical* construction of 'sexuality', of a *specific* order of the sexual – in the terms of which pornography and psychoanalysis, not to mention Lawrence and sexology, write supportively together, repeating the order and construction they help to confirm in a universal mask.

In the nineteenth century the need is to speak – to say – sex and sexuality, to provide ways of articulating the new concern. Pornography is established as part of that production of speech, of that making the needed sense, and goes along in this with the developing medical discourse of sex; the novel meanwhile occupying a middle ground of the generally available social defining of the individual. The difficulty for representation of this separation of discourses as between the medical and the pornographic on the one hand (with their direct treatment of sexual material for restricted groups) and those given in the novel on the other (the novel which works with the concern and the terms of its understanding but which is precluded by its central social position from directly identifying that concern in such terms) increases throughout the century, round exactly the depiction of *individual* experience and notably the experience of women. What is felt more and more urgently is the need for a supple holding of the sexual concern, against the rigidity of the discursive separation, within the central definition of the novel, for showing the sexual now as the very basis of the individual, as the very reality of – of a – life. Sex (medical, sexological) enters the novel which in turn constantly informs the given (medical, sexological) account. Freud writes sexual novels, the case histories of individuals, the reader plunged into the world of family relations and romance; Lawrence fills his characters with the new ideas of sex, debates psychoanalysis and sexology, pushes the phallus to the forefront of the novel; Freud and Lawrence, novel and psychoanalysis go together. In the midst of which redistribution, pornography as writing, written material, loses its importance as a separate enclosed area: the representation of the sexual as 'sexuality' enters the novel and the novelistic generally, until we reach the situation today in which pornography, the repetition of the penis-phallus, is no longer marginal – and thus no longer really specifically exists as such – but is *the* mode, the general and endlessly available vision: she wants it now ('deep inside of me, where I need it'), he must have and give it ('she went into raptures when she saw how monstrously excited she had made me') – or as Lawrence had Connie Chatterley put it, 'I know the penis is the most godly part of a man'.

This generalization and overall diffusion of the pornographic in writing, moreover, has been accompanied by its respecialization as 'pornography' in images, photographic images. To think of pornography today is to think at once of photographs and films; significantly, the Williams Committee, set up in 1977 to review 'the laws concerning obscenity and violence in publications, displays and entertainments', recommended that there should be no restrictions or prohibitions on the printed word and concerned itself almost wholly with the question of visual material. Photography is quickly linked with pornography in the nineteenth century and a full-scale commerce of images rapidly developed (*The Times* of 20 April 1874 reports a police raid on a London shop in which 130,248 obscene photographs were seized, plus 5,000 stereoscopic slides) and then extended into one of films with the coming of cinema, moving photographic images. So that there is a double functioning. On the one hand, the pornography of the visual image as phallic proof: 'showing everything', *the* scene, *the* act, and hence 'more and more', which is the determinant of a constant repetition, again and again the male difference, the triumph of the phallus, woman's 'genital place' (as psychoanalysis puts it from within the system of this difference, 'the visual is the perception of the genital place of the mother or daughter and the perceptual consciousness of the penis'), what she wants and gets (thus the necessity in the films for 'cum-shots' in which the man pulls out to be seen ejaculating and 'orgasm-shots' in which the woman is seen frenziedly writhing and twitching and heard panting and moaning – the proof that it all works, no problems, the Big O, this is it). On the other, the written word, the novel, the scenarios of narrative film and television play and so on, saying the sexual as 'sexuality', taking up the difficulties (the problems that nevertheless arise for men and women in fitting the order, matching the images) earlier left to medicine and which are now held, worked through and resolved on a general terrain of medical-sexological-psychological-novelistic representation, worrying over the phallus and its order of men and women, responding to challenges to its identities of man and woman, fixing things up.

VIII

Pornography, Victorian sexual medicine, sexology, psychoanalysis, the whole contemporary novelistic, all turn on that question formulated by Freud as 'What does a woman want?', the question of 'sexuality', constantly and variously answered but always the same, the same story of the phallus and her orgasm, the Big O, preferably vaginal, the real thing; her sexual feeling denied, asserted, feared, patterned – 'give her a pattern' (the title of one of Lawrence's essays). Woman = sex = orgasm. QED of the male position, the man whom men are supposed to be for their identity. What does a woman want? 'What Marsha craved was a man, a real live, lascivious male. . . .'

It is evident though, as has been stressed, that the question 'What does a woman want?' is a certain trouble, the point of a breach in the edifice that needs constantly to be repaired. Hence what appears as the possibility of taking the question *radically*, of using it to widen the breach and bring down the edifice, showing up and ruining its assumptions. The French writer Hélène Cixous does just this:

For me the question 'What does she want?' that is asked of the woman, a question that the woman indeed asks herself because she is asked it, because exactly there is so little place for her desire in society that she ends up, through not knowing what to do with it, by not knowing where to put it, or even whether she has a desire, overlays the most immediate and urgent question: 'How do I have pleasure? What is female *pleasure*, where does it happen, how is it inscribed on her body, in her unconscious? And then how do we write it?'

Cixous takes up the question, runs it into the specificity of female pleasure and at once grasps the latter as a question of meaning, representation – how is it written, how do we write it?

Traditionally, the relation of women to language has been one of exclusion and silence; as Saint Paul decreed, in a text regularly referred to throughout history as justification: 'Let the woman learn in silence with all subjection. But I suffer not a woman to teach, nor to usurp authority over the man, but to be in silence.' The Victorian regime was simple: little girls should be seen and not heard, the first virtue to treasure – and demand – in a wife is obedience; the man, head of the household, possesses the power of language and word. Areas of authority of language were then, as before, institutionally closed to women, from the priesthood through to the professions and beyond; and remain of course, a site of struggle (consider the women to men ratios of members of parliament, television 'experts', and so on). Supplementing the biblical reference, various systems of thought offered and offer theoretical justifications of the exclusion: for the new true-to-Freud psychoanalysis of Lacan and his followers, for example, women, since they lack the penis-phallus which is the universal signifier determining the very existence and functioning of language, are 'excluded by the nature of things which is the nature of words'.

Simultaneously with the exclusion, and as its exact complement, women have also been traditionally represented as out of control in and in relation to language, the agents and dupes of gossip, tittle-tattle, gibble-gabble, prattle, idle chatter, the trivial surface of blandishment and flattery. Adam ignored but Eve listened to the serpent's cajolings, fell for language: 'And Adam was not deceived, but the woman being deceived was in the transgression.' Men make dictionaries, the law, can speak the truth; woman are in the transgression, seduced and seducers, a dangerous temptation of language – hence the complementarity: the association of temptation and seduction with women's speech requires their exclusion from all authority of language.

Cixous's reappropriation of the 'What does a woman want?' question is thus the project of a movement against the oppression of exclusion and limitation to triviality, for a new – or newly recovered – existence of women in language, another and authentic possibility, a specific writing of female pleasure, a true women's language.

There is a passage towards the end of *A Room of One's Own* in which Virginia Woolf sums up something of her thinking as regards the introduction of determinations of sex into writing:

> Even so, the very first sentence that I would write here, I said, crossing
> over to the writing-table and taking up the page headed Women and
> Fiction, is that it is fatal for anyone who writes to think of their sex. It is
> fatal to be a man or woman pure and simple; one must be woman-
> manly or man-womanly. It is fatal for a woman to lay the least stress on
> any grievance; to plead even with justice any cause; in any way to speak
> consciously as a woman. And fatal is no figure of speech; for anything
> written with that conscious bias is doomed to death. It ceases to be
> fertilized. Brilliant and effective, powerful and masterly, as it may
> appear for a day or two, it must wither at nightfall; it cannot grow in
> the minds of others. Some collaboration has to take place in the mind
> between the woman and the man before the art of creation can be
> accomplished. Some marriage of opposites has to be consummated.
> The whole of the mind must lie wide open if we are to get the sense that
> the writer is communicating his experience with perfect fullness. There
> must be freedom and there must be peace. Not a wheel must grate, not
> a light glimmer. The curtains must be close drawn. The writer, I
> thought, once his experience is over, must lie back and let his mind
> celebrate its nuptials in darkness. He must not look or question what is
> being done. Rather, he must pluck the petals from a rose or watch the
> swans float calmly down the river.

'It is fatal for anyone who writes to think of their sex.' That
proposition reverses Cixous's emphasis on the need specifically to
pose sex, woman, her wants, female pleasure, writing that. Suppose
in turn we re-reverse it: it is fatal for anyone who writes – reads,
speaks, takes up language – not to think of their sex, not to bring into
reflection their sexual positioning and its effects in language, speech,
discourse, writing.

Reading the Woolf passage, we can grasp something of the
difficulties, the meshes of sex in language. The thesis is clear – it is
fatal for anyone who writes to think of their sex, one must be
woman-manly or man-womanly – but it is not clear that we are not
given a quite different position in the writing itself. 'Some marriage
of opposites has to be consummated', for example. 'Consummated'
is already a whole sexual history: 'consummate', 'to complete
marriage by sexual intercourse', as the OED defines it, giving 1540
as the date for its first appearance; a legality, the law of marriage, a
male scenario. How is consummation defined? The legal procedures
for the invalidation of marriages from the seventeenth century on are
explicit: by penetration and emission (in France there existed an
extraordinary and extreme procedure known as '*congrès*' under

which judges could order trial consummations before witnesses, the husband or wife against whom the demand for annulment was made having to defend themselves by demonstrating that they could actually manage intercourse). Woolf is writing discursively here in a male-defined position; the 'marriage of opposites' is one-sided in its representation – creation as consummation, a finality, an end, penetration and climax, male climax. After which, 'when his experience is over', the writer 'must lie back and let his mind celebrate its nuptials in darkness'. Perhaps it might be said that here exactly Woolf does bring in the balance, shifts to different terms, elements of a potentially female position, lying back, as earlier, more evidently, she had stressed that 'the mind must lie wide open'. But this 'female position' is equally male, part of the same scenario: the penetrating active man, the receptive passive woman. The marriage in the writing is one single order with its two given sides, its two specified positions. The very notion of 'opposites' is from within that order: man and woman, male and female, complement one another, with the latter derived as the difference from the former, so many essential female qualities in counterpart to his essential and defining maleness. Working with marriage, consummation, opposites, man and woman added together, Woolf is returned, even against the possibilities of her thesis, to what is a representation that assigns women to a certain place as woman, in relation to a certain domination and evaluation from men, the place of man.

The concluding images underline this return. The writer 'must pluck the petals from a rose or watch the swans float calmly down the river'. Has the image of the rose ever been used from woman to man? The weight of the language and literature that are Woolf's inheritance is on the equivalence of rose and woman, on the rose as a male image for the woman. 'Goe, lovely Rose', says the conventional seventeenth-century poet – in this instance Edmund Waller – and the rose is both messenger and visualization:

> When I resemble her to thee
> How sweet and fair she seems to be.
> ('Song')

Plucking the rose is quickly an image for the climax of male desire, as in the Victorian poet Robert Browning:

> I kiss your cheek
> Catch your soul's warmth,—I pluck the rose
> And love it more than tongue can speak
> Then the good minute goes.
>   ('Two in the Campagna')

Watching the swans floating is less definitely marked perhaps, but again has the swan ever been a woman-to-man image? Traditionally the whiteness of the swan has been that of her body, breasts especially: 'Between thy breasts (than down of swans more white)', writes Robert Herrick in one of his several poems 'To Julia'. Nearer to Woolf's own time (Herrick was writing in the seventeenth century) the Anglo-Irish poet W. B. Yeats can assume swans as mystery, beauty, a delight for men's eyes:

> But now they drift on the still water,
> Mysterious, beautiful;
> Among what rushes will they build,
> By what lake's edge or pool
> Delight men's eyes when I awake some day
> To find they have flown away?
>   ('The Wild Swans at Coole')

or else, through the myth of Leda raped by the god Zeus in the form of a swan, can produce the swan as fascinated image of male power over the woman:

> A sudden blow: the great wings beating still
> Above the staggering girl, her thighs caressed
> By the dark webs, her nape caught in his bill,
> He holds her helpless breast upon his breast.
> How can those terrified vague fingers push
> The feathered glory from her loosening thighs?
>   ('Leda and the Swan')

Lawrence takes the swan directly as the sexual being that man gives woman, image of her in the climax and liberation he gives: 'He had performed a little miracle, and felt himself a little wonder-worker, to whom reverence was due. And as in a dream the woman sat, feeling what a joy it was to float and move like a swan in the high air, flying upon the wings of her own spirit. She was as a swan which never before could get its wings quite open. . . .' Not surprisingly then, the German philosopher Nietzsche, in the late nineteenth century, finds the swan exactly as the supreme image of English womanhood:

'watch the most beautiful Englishwomen *walk* – in no land on earth are there more beautiful doves and swans'.

It is fatal for anyone who writes to think of their sex but, even as she sets out that thesis, Woolf is caught up in a web of words and images and ways of writing that bring with them a position, a sexual stance, a certain representation. Cixous's question, how is female pleasure to be written? Or, how is the fatality – the historical fatality, the fix – of this position of 'sexuality', male and female, the man and the woman, the one and the other, the difference, to be broken, written away from?

This is an important area of theoretical discussion and literary practice today, most notably from the perspective of feminism and in terms of the possibility of the development of a specifically woman's language. 'Woman's desire would not speak the same language as man's' (this and following quotations are from French feminist writers, Cixous herself, Michèle Montrelay and, as here, Luce Irigaray); the point now is to achieve an authentic language of that desire – and thus to write thinking of one's sex.

In this context, a number of theses and arguments are advanced and made as regards the relation of woman and language:

– The woman is more naturally a writer, since close to the mother tongue, close to creation: 'it is the woman who is more the writer, by the very fact that she creates an idiom; and the poet well knows that it is the mother tongue he speaks and no other'; woman's pleasure being in excess and at the expense of the phallus, the phallic order of the signifier, it is like a process of writing (understanding the latter as a play in language, the disturbance of fixed meanings): 'female pleasure can be seen as *writing* . . . this pleasure and the literary text (which is also written like an orgasm produced from within discourse) are the effect of the same murder of the signifier'.

– The woman is close to the body, the source of writing: 'it is obvious that a woman does not write like a man, because she speaks with the body, writing is from the body'. Writing resembles the body and the sexual division of male and female is expressed in the difference of women's writing: 'a feminine textual body can be recognized by the fact that it is always without end, has no finish, which moreover is what makes the feminine text very often difficult to read'. Against 'the "I" of phallocratic language' (this formulation in fact taken from an American feminist, Mary Daly), erect and single, the 'two lips' of the female sex in a female language, constantly moving and plural.

– A woman's writing is anti-theory, has no metalanguage ('cannot describe itself from outside or in formal terms'); it has no place for 'the concept as such', is 'fluid' in style, breaking syntax and developing towards a new syntax of 'auto-affection' (the 'two lips' of the female sex are perpetually joining in embrace), with 'neither subject nor object'.

Clearly what these theses and arguments do is to assert a very powerful sexual determination in language and language use, and in particular to valorize sexual difference as male/female, female versus male, by an appeal to signs and correspondences of a femininity, a femaleness – flow, liquid, lips, holes – as well as to specifically women's experiences – menstruation, pregnancy, and so on. All of which, of course, bears first on literary production, women writing, but equally on literary reception, women reading and their literary criticism. Thus an English critic, Gillian Beer, follows the idea of the feminine textual body as being without end exactly when she talks in connection with Virginia Woolf of how 'the eschewing of plot is an aspect of her feminism. The avoidance of narrative climax is a way of getting outside the fixing properties of event'; and Woolf herself, despite her fatal-to-think-of-one's-sex stress, could praise her contemporary fellow-novelist Dorothy Richardson for her invention of 'a woman's sentence', 'the psychological sentence of the feminine gender' – 'of a more elastic fibre than the old, capable of stretching to the extreme, of suspending the frailest particles, of enveloping the vaguest shapes'.

Problems quickly emerge however. To lay the emphasis on difference and the specificity of women (as of men) in the paradigm male/female is a gesture within the terms of the existing system, for which, precisely, women are different *from* men. Patriarchy, men in its order, has never said anything but that women are – the woman, the female, is – different: they are not men. Lawrence's novels, for instance, are full of 'pure man'/'pure woman', 'male soul'/'female soul', the antithesis derived from and justifying the reign of the phallus. Different as female to male, women are readily pinned to and identified with their sex, their bodies, a biology (the poet Ezra Pound: 'the female/Is an element, the female/Is a chaos/An

octopus/A biological process'): woman as the female animal, as
sexuality, in every sense a sex object. The signs and correspondences
claimed are none other than those of the system itself: women as
fluid, flowing (Lawrence, regretting the rise of 'the modern
woman': 'But women used to know better . . . Women used to see
themselves as a softly flowing stream of attraction and desire and
beauty, soft quiet rivers of energy and peace'); women as maternity
(Lawrence again can argue *for* matriarchy, meaning by the latter 'full
self-responsibility as mothers and heads of the family', leaving men
alone to get on with 'the life of society').

And so the litany of difference has gone on and continues,
attributing ('recognizing', as it would say) 'qualities' (often defects as
far as its view of women–woman is concerned). 'If the male orgasm
is in some sort "consonantic", is not the female orgasm "vocalic"?'
At school, as we were guided through Palgrave's *Golden Treasury of
English Poetry*, we were much taken with liquid vowels and hard
consonants but were not quite together enough to make the obvious
connections which only a French psychoanalyst today could so
felicitously spell out for us (and doubtless tomorrow we will be
reminded that men are active and women passive verbs – or is it
transitive and intransitive?). 'Feminine in its lack of restraint, its
wordiness, and the utter absence of feeling for form', wrote Arnold
Bennett of George Eliot's style; 'feminine forgetfulness of one's self',
added his contemporary Walter Pater writing generally; while
David Holbrook sums up the tradition within which such remarks
are automatically made with his recent unsparing praise for 'the
female elements of intuition, creativity, and sympathy'. A pat on
the back from the solid men and women can be sent happily clucking
back to the farmyard, to what Lawrence calls 'the lovely henny
surety, the hensureness which is the real bliss of every female'.

Difference, that is, is difficult, speedily comes round to an essence
of woman and man, male and female, a kind of anthropologico-
biological nature. But men and women are not simply given biologically; they are given in history and culture, in a social practice and
representation that includes biological determinations, shaping and
defining them in its process. The appeal to an 'undeniable' biological
reality as essential definition is always itself a form of social representation, within a particular structure of assumption and argument. It
is this appeal indeed that is made by the existing system and its
'sexuality', which holds to the clear identity – determined and fixed,

rooted in nature – of the man and the woman, with the latter the difference, and runs over from there into an elaborate account of 'masculine' and 'feminine' modes of behaviour, characteristics, styles – the whole gamut of 'qualities' that the theses and arguments on the relations of woman and language uncannily reproduce (compare the idea of a breakdown of syntax, a writing with 'neither subject nor object', never-ending, an 'elastic' sentence 'enveloping the vaguest shapes', with Bennett's 'feminine in its lack of restraint, its wordiness, and the utter absence of feeling for form'; the whole idea of resemblance to the body is that of the system: women are like – *are* – their bodies which then specify their nature, define them essentially, their condition for ever).

This is difficult again, however, in that in a given situation the appeal to difference can be a powerful and necessary mode of struggle and action, can take the force of an alternative representation, turning difference against the order of the same that it is used to support (the single identity of man and woman from him); thus, for example, the reappropriation of the question of 'what does a woman want?', at once a question in the system *and* a moment of trouble that can be brought round against it, as its contradiction. The attempt to distinguish specifically feminine elements of writing, to develop a specifically female language, can clearly become important as a basis for movement and challenge and transformation. Virginia Woolf can perfectly well lay down that it is fatal to think of one's sex (as though there were one sex that one was, an absolute identity of sex) and at the same time praise Richardson's 'woman's sentence', this having a precise radical value, 'only in the sense that it is used to describe a woman's mind by a writer who is neither proud nor afraid of anything that she may discover in the psychology of her sex'. A critic such as Gillian Beer can perfectly well reverse Arnold Bennett's commonplace about the feminine inability to manage form into a feminist valuation of Woolf's eschewing of plot and narrative climax, inasmuch as in the context in which Woolf writes the latter are exactly strategies of the system, part of its novelistic resolution.

There are two sets of – interlocking – problems here, round this question of a specific female, or male, language: those concerning the reference to 'female' and 'male'; those concerning the reference to 'language'. Leaving the former in suspense for a moment, let us

briefly consider the question of language and determinations on the
basis of sex.

What is at stake here cannot be language as faculty or as system,
the system studied by linguistics in its attempts to show how any
particular language works: the faculty of language is neither male
nor female but human; the system of a language may well specify
sex-difference constraints (in Thai, for example, men and women
have a different first-person singular pronoun, equivalent to the
undifferentiated English 'I': man *phom*, woman *dichan*) but there is
no way in which a particular feature of language functioning such as
syntax, understood linguistically, can be identified as somehow
inherently and essentially male. The effective concern of any discussion of sexual determinations must be language in use, its reality as
practice, mode of representation, discourse.

A discourse is a social organization of the elements – the signifiers
– of language into the relation of an order of meanings and a subject
posed as such in that order, a positioning, a certain representation for
the individual of the place of his or her sense, his or her desire. What
can be critically analysed in respect of sexual determinations are the
terms each time of this certain representation. Analysis thus focused
avoids any naturalism, the confusion of the sexual positioning
inscribed in a discourse – its representation – with the sex of the
author or producer of the discourse, its speaker or writer: in any
given instance, men do not *necessarily* speak or write male positioning discourse nor women *necessarily* female positioning discourse;
the link between sex (in the sense of gender) and the sexual is not
direct – there is no natural expression of one's sex – but is always
mediated, realized in language in use in society, in discourses, is
always a matter of representations (of 'the man' and 'the woman',
'masculine' and 'feminine', 'male style' and 'female style', and so
on). If the sexual were not this cultural fact, there would be no hope
of any transformation: men would be men and 'women are women'
(as D. H. Lawrence put it in an essay with the suggestively answer-
able title 'Do Women Change?'), the man and the woman given and
eternal, the natural fact of their sexes, Adam and Eve – beginning
and end of story, and the end of history.

There is no essential male or female language, immediate and
inevitable, determined by the sex. But there are, for example, very

definitely, uses of language, discourses, inscribing male positions
(spoken or written in and from the representation of the man in the
particular – phallocentric – system of 'sexuality' we have been
describing here); as also there are uses of language attempting to
break the dominance of the inscription of those male positions
(against and alternative to that phallocentric system), uses that have
indeed been developed especially by women from the force of their
experience . . .

Let us take some passages of writing in illustration of discursive
sexual positioning and of the general remarks just made concerning
language and sex:

a   She looked very lovely under her black hair hung loose over her
     neck and bosom, sparkling with drops to imitate dew, and it
     seemed a pity that only ladies were to look at her.

     Gustave was made to kneel down on the ground in front of the
     sofa, and support a round mirror, before which the wilful little
     lady had elected to try on the silken hose and dainty boots.

> Margaret Anson, *The Merry Order of St
> Bridget: Personal Recollections of
> the Use of the Rod* (1868).

These passages are from a work of nineteenth-century pornography
(an example of the common whipping literature of the period), the
author and narrator of which is given as being a woman. This
assertion of female author/narratorship is, in fact, a convention: the
desire of the book, which depicts an enclosed and exclusive little
world of women whippers ('the merry order'), is for the *intimacy* of
the woman, which intimacy is preserved by the idea of a woman
author-narrator (and the book is furthermore set out as Margaret's
letter-report to a woman friend). But then, of course, this 'intimacy'
exists only as a spectacle *for men*, exists only from the projected male
gaze that defines it as such (remember the intimacy created by the
Captain's gaze in the extract from *A Laodicean*). The passages, given
as by a woman, thus offer a particular representation of desire which
is entirely within that of the current sexuality – a whole panoply of
the male, voyeurism and fetishism, the gaze and the boots, the
young Gustave as man allowed into the fiction only as child,
preserving the intimacy while simultaneously exploiting the
fetishistic moment at the woman's feet. The writing invites the

reader's male vision, 'it seemed a pity that only ladies were to look at her'; the text itself shows off like a little lady wilfully trying on for him. What we have is the fixed perspective of 'the man' and 'the woman', the latter from the former and the writing in position there. And were the author of *The Merry Order of St Bridget* to have been a woman (and no gender essence prevented this), she would have been in that same position, repeating its terms, doing the male thing, the standard version of sex.

b   Not a human being was out of doors at the dairy. The denizens were all enjoying the usual afternoon nap of an hour or so which the exceedingly early hours kept in summer-time rendered a necessity. At the door the wood-hooped pails, sodden and bleached by infinite scrubbings, hung like hats on a stand upon the forked and peeled limb of an oak fixed there for that purpose; all of them ready and dry for the evening milking. Angel entered, and went through the silent passages of the house to the back quarters, where he listened for a moment. Sustained snores came from the cart-house, where some of the men were lying down; the grunt and squeal of sweltering pigs arose from the still further distance. The large-leaved rhubarb and cabbage plants slept too, their broad limp surfaces hanging in the sun like half-closed umbrellas.

He unbridled and fed his horse, and as he re-entered the house the clock struck three. Three was the afternoon skimming-hour; and, with the stroke, Clare heard the creaking of the floor-boards above, and then the touch of a descending foot on the stairs. It was Tess's, who in another moment came down before his eyes.

She had not heard him enter, and hardly realized his presence there. She was yawning, and he saw the red interior of her mouth as if it had been a snake's. She had stretched one arm so high above her coiled-up cable of hair that he could see its satin delicacy above the sunburn; her face was flushed with sleep, and her eyelids hung heavy over their pupils. The brim-fulness of her nature breathed from her. It was a moment when a woman's soul is more incarnate than at any other time; when the most spiritual beauty bespeaks itself flesh; and sex takes the outside place in the presentation.

Then those eyes flashed brightly through their filmy heaviness, before the remainder of her face was well awake. With an oddly compounded look of gladness, shyness, and surprise, she exclaimed–

'O Mr Clare! How you frightened me – I –'

There had not at first been time for her to think of the changed relations which his declaration had introduced; but the full sense of the matter rose up in her face when she encountered Clare's tender look as he stepped forward to the bottom stair.

'Dear, darling Tessy!' he whispered, putting his arm round her,

and his face to her flushed cheek. 'Don't, for Heaven's sake, Mister
me any more. I have hastened back so soon because of you!'

Tess's excitable heart beat against his by way of reply; and there
they stood upon the red-brick floor of the entry, the sun slanting in
by the window upon his back, as he held her tightly to his breast;
upon her inclining face, upon the blue veins of her temple, upon
her naked arm, and her neck, and into the depths of her hair.
Having been lying down in her clothes she was warm as a sunned
cat. At first she would not look straight up at him, but her eyes
soon lifted, and his plumbed the deepness of the ever-varying
pupils, with their radiating fibrils of blue, and black, and gray, and
violet, while she regarded him as Eve at her second waking might
have regarded Adam.

Thomas Hardy, Tess of the d'Urbervilles (1891)

Angel Clare, a parson's son, has declared his love to the socially
inferior Tess, a milkmaid, and Hardy is here describing their next
meeting (she has not had time to think of 'the changed relations',
Angel whispers 'Don't, for Heaven's sake, Mister me any more. I
have hastened back so soon because of you!'). The 'brim-fulness' of
Tess's nature (she 'warm as a sunned cat') continues the sweltering
sensuality of the scene and the moment ('broad limp surfaces hanging in the sun'). Clare confronts Tess in a quite definite social
relationship which maps the unequal status of women on to a
difference in class but the passage confronts man in the face of
woman, of sex ('sex takes the outside place in the presentation'). The
writing then drops into the language of romance fiction ('plumbed
the deepness of the ever-varying pupils') and counterpoints the fact
of the meeting with the signs of 'the woman' and their male
perspective. From 'the red interior of her mouth as if it had been a
snake's' and the echo of that image in 'her coiled-up cable of hair' to
the final reference to 'Eve at her second waking', a little subplot is
developed of the primal, tempting, sexually guilty and corrupting
woman (the second waking is after Eve, beguiled by the snake, has
persuaded Adam to eat with her of the forbidden fruit). In the book's
narrative, Tess is the victim of Angel, who is unable to forgive her
after their marriage when she confesses she is not a virgin (she was
seduced by a supposed kinsman, the upper-class Alec d'Urberville);
in the book's assumption of 'sexuality', as here, she is at fault as
woman, the writing moves into the position of her guilt (she luring
the now significantly named Angel, the cause of his fall).

C   After three verses she faltered to an end, bitterly chagrined.

'No,' she said. 'It's no good. I can't sing.' And she dropped in her chair.

'A lovely little tune,' said Aaron. 'Haven't you got the music?'

She rose, not answering, and found him a little book.

'What do the words mean?' he asked her.

She told him. And then he took his flute.

'You don't mind if I play it, do you?' he said.

So he played the tune. It was so simple. And he seemed to catch the lilt and the timbre of her voice.

'Come and sing it while I play,' he said.

'I can't sing,' she said, shaking her head rather bitterly.

'But let us try,' said he, disappointed.

'I know I can't,' she said. But she rose.

He remained sitting at the little table, the book propped up under the reading lamp. She stood at a little distance, unhappy.

'I've always been like that,' she said. 'I could never sing music, unless I had a thing drilled into me, and then it wasn't singing any more.'

But Aaron wasn't heeding. His flute was at his mouth, he was watching her. He sounded the note, but she did not begin. She was twisting her handkerchief. So he played the melody alone. At the end of the verse, he looked up at her again, and a half mocking smile played in his eyes. Again he sounded the note, a challenge. And this time, as at his bidding, she began to sing. The flute instantly swung with a lovely soft firmness into the song, and she wavered only for a minute or two. Then her soul and her voice got free, and she sang – she sang as she wanted to sing, as she had always wanted to sing, without that awful scotch, that impediment inside her own soul, which prevented her.

She sang free, with the flute gliding along with her. And oh, how beautiful it was for her! How beautiful it was to sing the little song in the sweetness of her own spirit. How sweet it was to move pure and unhampered at last in the music! The lovely ease and lilt of her own soul in its motion through the music! She wasn't aware of the flute. She didn't know there was anything except her own pure lovely song-drift. Her soul seemed to breathe as a butterfly breathes, as it rests on a leaf and slowly breathes its wings. For the first time! For the first time her soul drew its own deep breath. All her life, the breath had caught half-way. And now she breathed full, deep, to the deepest extent of her being.

And oh, it was so wonderful, she was dazed. The song ended, she stood with a dazed, happy face, like one just coming awake. And the fard on her face seemed like old night crust, the bad sleep. New and luminous she looked out. And she looked at Aaron with a proud smile.

'Bravo, Nan! That was what you wanted,' said her husband.

'It was, wasn't it?' she said, turning a wondering, glowing face
to him.

His face looked strange and withered and gnome-like, at the
moment.

She went and sat in her chair, quite silent, as if in a trance. The
two men also sat quite still. And in the silence a little drama played
itself between the three, of which they knew definitely nothing.

D. H. Lawrence, *Aaron's Rod* (1922)

The passage describes the woman getting free, her own soul moving
pure and unhampered at last; the impediment is overcome, 'now she
breathed full, deep, to the deepest extent of her being'. But this
getting free and coming to a climax that leaves her dazed and
glowing is brought about by Aaron and his magic rod, the flute with
its 'lovely soft firmness'. Bitter and obstructed, twisting her handkerchief and dropping in her chair, Nan is seduced by the challenge
of the flute and Aaron's half-mocking smile: giving into him, the
flute's gliding music and rhythm, is finding herself, 'her own pure
lovely song-drift'; he is her initiation, leaving the husband 'strange
and withered and gnome-like'. Of the little drama that plays itself
out, the writing knows definitely everything, its phallic sexual-fixed
position is clear; and if Aaron is said to know nothing when he so
evidently directs the passage and Nan's liberation, this is a feint the
better to confirm the impersonal force of 'male super-power', 'the
magic feeling of phallic immortality' with which the writing leaves
Aaron and seeks to leave us. For the phallus is 'the third creature',
between man and woman, prior to personality; for, as Lawrence
puts it in *John Thomas and Lady Jane*, 'the personality must yield
before the priority and the mysterious root-knowledge of the penis,
or the phallus'.

That the phallus is the fundamental belief and the main protagonist
of Lawrence's writing is well known but Lawrence must be seen in
the context of the whole development and propagation of 'sexuality'. His work is a major contribution to the 'gaining ground' of the
latter (we have already mentioned the number of sex-related terms
he introduces or gives currency to), a decisive moment in the shift

from the Victorian medicalization to the more general representation of sex as the basic fact of experience and identity – and to which an intense value is now assigned (sex as authentic being, the imperative of good sex). Sex and sexuality become the direct and determining concern of the novel, making love is the crucial big scene – what in the end it's all about. From *The Rainbow* on, Lawrence plays his influential part in this; and *Lady Chatterley's Lover*, of course, has its own particular and important delayed effect when finally published in unexpurgated form in 1960 as an instantly best-selling paperback.

How many contemporary novels have you read that do not run into and depend on love-making scenes? But then art reflects life, it may be said, and people do after all make love . . . Fine. Except that art does not simply reflect life which in turn is not some pristine guarantee or alibi but itself a constant process of construction and understanding: art organizes and condenses and weighs and proposes, gives a representation that here replies to and helps to make up the myth of 'sexuality' which is central to the current ordering of life and lives. Writing love-making is again a problem of complicity with and support for the sexual fix, going over and over the standard pattern. Here if anywhere, one might think, differences would be fundamental, a plurality of positions and inscriptions would be possible. Yet here precisely the same is made and remade, the very fact of these scenes determined by the myth and its repetition; with the difficulty of writing otherwise, outside that repetition, immense. Consider the following, beginning with a passage from *Lady Chatterley's Lover* as reminder and point of comparison:

d   He took her in his arms again and drew her to him, and suddenly she became small in his arms, small and nestling. It was gone, the resistance was gone, and she began to melt in a marvellous peace. And as she melted small and wonderful in his arms, she became infinitely desirable to him, all his blood-vessels seemed to scald with intense yet tender desire, for her, for her softness, for the penetrating beauty of her in his arms, passing into his blood. And softly, with that marvellous swoon-like caress of his hand in pure soft desire, softly he stroked the silky slope of her loins, down, down between her soft warm buttocks, coming nearer and nearer to the very quick of her. And she felt him like a flame of desire, yet tender, and she felt herself melting in the flame. She let herself go. She felt his penis risen against her with silent amazing force and assertion and she let herself go to him. She yielded with a quiver that was like death, she went all open to him. And oh, if he were not tender to her now, how cruel, for she was all open to him and helpless!

She quivered again at the potent inexorable entry inside her, so strange and terrible. It might come with the thrust of a sword in her softly-opened body, and that would be death. She clung in a sudden anguish of terror. But it came with a strange slow thrust of peace, the dark thrust of peace and a ponderous, primordial tenderness, such as made the world in the beginning. And her terror subsided in her breast, her breast dared to be gone in peace, she held nothing. She dared to let go everything, all herself, and be gone in the flood.

And it seemed she was like the sea, nothing but dark waves rising and heaving, heaving with a great swell, so that slowly her whole darkness was in motion, and she was ocean rolling its dark, dumb mass. Oh, and far down inside her the deeps parted and rolled asunder, in long, far-travelling billows, and ever, at the quick of her, the depths parted and rolled asunder, from the centre of soft plunging, as the plunger went deeper and deeper, touching lower, and she was deeper and deeper and deeper disclosed, the heavier the billows of her rolled away to some shore, uncovering her, and closer and closer plunged the palpable unknown, and further and further rolled the waves of herself away from herself, leaving her, till suddenly, in a soft, shuddering convulsion, the quick of all her plasm was touched, she knew herself touched, the consummation was upon her, and she was gone. She was gone, she was not, and she was born: a woman.

Ah, too lovely, too lovely! In the ebbing she realized all the loveliness. Now all her body clung with tender love to the unknown man, and blindly to the wilting penis, as it so tenderly, frailly, unknowingly withdrew, after the fierce thrust of its potency. As it drew out and left her body, the secret, sensitive thing, she gave an unconscious cry of pure loss, and she tried to put it back. It had been so perfect! And she loved it so!

D. H. Lawrence, Lady Chatterley's Lover (1928)

This is close to the previous passage from *Aaron's Rod* (c). The woman follows the man into herself, yielding, the resistance gone, daring for once 'to let go everything', brought to a climax in which she is born again: 'a woman'. The insistent incantation of the word 'soft' serves to suggest a melting tenderness of the moment which is nevertheless always also directed and framed by the penis–phallus and admiration before its 'silent amazing force' – its 'potent inexorable entry', the 'ponderous primordial tenderness' of its 'dark thrust of peace' that floods her being, the 'plunger' that touches 'the quick of all her plasma' until the 'pure loss' of its withdrawal. Lawrence's

writing knows only *consummation*, the perpetual demonstration –
'the consummation was upon her' – of that position.

e   In the bedroom he switched on a sidelight, illuminating the vast
double bed, and drew back the fur counterpane. As he undressed
me with undeniable deftness, I thought of all the women he must
have laid on that bed before me . . . I felt like a novice horse
entering the Horse of the Year Show for the first time, with the
jumps up to six feet and all the previous competitors having had
clear rounds.

Once we were in bed he just held me very gently until the
horrors of the day began to recede. Then he said:

'I'm not going to lay a finger on you tonight. You're too tired.'
I felt a stab of disappointment.

'At least I don't think I am,' he went on, putting a warm hand on
my tits, spanning both nipples with finger and thumb.

'Look,' he whispered, 'I can stretch an Octavia.'
I giggled.

'That's better. Come on lovely, remember, from now on I've
got custody, care *and* control of you – and I'm not going to leave
you, like your bloody mother did, ever again.'

And with infinite tenderness he kissed me, until I felt the waves
of lust begin to ripple through me.

'It's Friday,' he said, as his hand edged downwards. 'We've got
the whole weekend ahead. We needn't get up at all.'

Then later he said, 'Relax sweetheart, don't try so hard, there's
no hurry. I actually *like* doing these things for you.'

Then later, more harshly, 'Stop fighting me; we're on the same
side.'

Then suddenly it happened – like a great, glorious, whooshing
washing machine – it's the only way I can describe it – leaving me
shuddering and shuddering with pleasure at the end, like the last
gasps of the spin-dryer. And afterwards I cried some more because
I was so happy, and he held me in his arms, telling me how much
he loved me until I fell asleep.

A few hours later the dawn woke me. We'd forgotten to draw
the curtains. All I could see were huge windows framing the plane
trees of Holland Park. I blinked, turned and found Gareth looking
at me. I must be dreaming.

I put my hand out to touch his cheek.

'Are you real?' I said incredulously.

He smiled. 'I am if you are.'

His eye had turned black, his chest was covered in bruises.

'I think I'm in bed with Henry Cooper,' I said. 'I never dreamt
he'd make such a sensational lover. Do you think we could
possibly do it again?'

And we did, and it was even better than the last time, and I
screamed with delight and joy because I'd been so clever.

Jilly Cooper, *Octavia* (1977)

By comparison with the *Lady Chatterley's Lover* passage (d), this
piece is banal, clearly much less exalted, but it stands none the less as
something of an assimilated version of it, a kind of currency of the
contemporary fiction and assumption of sex. Orgasm is the point
and the end of the novel. Romance – the genre within which Cooper
is writing ('her super jet-set Romance') – now incorporates this into
its representation, ending not simply or even necessarily with marriage. Octavia, the heroine, finds her man, the one who can play on
her, stretch an octavia, turn her on to a washing-machine spin. The
element of tongue-in-cheek humour is indicative of the currency.
There is nothing of the crusading, preaching, imposing feel of
Lawrence's writing; everything can be taken for granted, this is
naturally and inevitably what it's about, no questions are left and
playfulness can therefore be indulged, indulged within the limits of
that natural inevitability: washing-machine and spin-dryer may add
a little comedy for some readers and for the author herself but that
comedy is on the basis of the strength of the position, the structure –
the narrative of 'sexuality' holds firm and firmer.

f   It was no good. All her feminism, all her independence, all her
fame had come to this, this helplessness, this need. She needed
him. She needed this man.

When he entered her, when his hot cock slid into her, she was
moaning something about that, about surrender, and how
ashamed she was of needing him so, of loving him so desperately.
'But I need you just as badly,' he said. 'I can't do this without you, I
need you too.'

At first she was on top of him, sliding up and down rhythmically
on his cock, while he held her clitoris between two slippery
fingers, and pushed another finger up her ass. The whole world
went out except for the throbbing in her cunt, which seemed to her
like a universe, a galaxy, a deep black hole in space. She came the
first time with a shuddering that made her scream and bite his
shoulder. It was almost as if the orgasm was not only in her cunt,
but in her throat, her voice, her whole body, and the scream was
part of it, part of the release. He turned her over roughly but
tenderly and began fucking her from above. And she thought,
feeling that cock slide in and out of her as if it owned her soul, that
if she died then, if she died that very minute, it would be all right,

she would have known most of it, have lived, have felt it. There
was more: she wanted his baby, their baby, she wanted to feel that
pain, that pleasure, but still, if she died at this very moment, life
would not have cheated her.

She was coming again. She told him. Could he wait? she asked.
Could she stop moving for a minute? he asked. She slowed, she
squeezed his cock with the muscles of her cunt, he moaned. His
mouth was very tender and soft on hers, his eyes were wide
enough to let all the darkness in. He rolled her over again, putting
her on top, holding his cock very still, his hips very still. She was
squeezing his cock with her muscles but trying not to slide up and
down on it until he quieted down somewhat.

And then they both began to move again, interlocking, cock and
cunt, and nothing else in the world mattering. She came with a
shudder that shook her whole body and released another scream
from her that scarcely seemed human. Everything released as she
screamed and came; she also peed, and was embarrassed and
apologized. 'I love your pee, your farts, your shit, your tight
snatch,' he said, digging his nails into her ass, and then he pulled
her cunt down on his upraised cock like a glove over a finger. 'Do
you want my sperm,' he asked, rhetorically – because of course she
wanted it, wanted to feel it spurt straight up to her womb, her
heart, her fingertips, and he moaned and began to come, sobbing,
shaking, crying, and she felt the base of his penis throbbing as all
the filaments flew flew flew into her womb and hopefully caught.

They lay not moving in the absolute peace after the earthquake.
She felt a small sun glowing in her solar plexus, and her legs and
arms too heavy to move, mercury-filled moon suits, leaden limbs.
He held her to him even as his cock grew soft and curled away from
her. 'I'll never leave you,' he said, 'never.'

'Do you suppose', she said, her voice hoarse from screaming,
weak with love, 'that many lovers felt this and then died anyway?'

'It doesn't matter,' he said, 'it doesn't matter at all,'

'That means *yes*, doesn't it?'

He hugged her very tight.

Erica Jong, *How to Save Your Own Life* (1977)

The passage offers to express perfect complementarity, 'interlocking, cock and cunt, and nothing else in the world mattering': the
perfect match, 'like a glove over a finger', he and she, she needing
him but equally he her in a stressed interdependence, she and he 'too'
– 'But I need you just as badly,' he said. 'I can't do this without you, I
need you too.' Traces of the primordial and cosmic investment in
'sexuality' from Lawrence to the radical sexologists are heavily
present at moments, from the 'deep black hole in space' to the 'small

sun glowing in her solar plexus' (this latter very close indeed to Lawrence's own writing). The frame for the expression of the complementarity, moreover, is male; *he* marks the progress of the passage, its movement: 'he entered her . . .', 'he turned her over roughly but tenderly and began . . .', 'he rolled her over again . . .', until *he* closes passage and novel, 'He hugged her very tight.' And once again *this* is *the* experience, the culmination of a life and a novel, the final truth, Eve before Adam: 'All her feminism, all her independence, all her fame had come to this, this helplessness, this need. She needed him. She needed this man.'

g   But Nancy appealed to his body, and roused it, with a couple of caresses. She had small, swift, soft, brown, cool hands. She also had her – as it was in relation to him – gift of tactlessness. She talked to him. Marcus had always imagined that when he did at last make love to a woman it would be in terrible silence, interrupted only by such noises as their bodies might involuntarily make, which he had already conceived might be embarrassing. But Nancy talked to him about what he was to do, about what he was doing, in a low, rather deep, swift voice which provoked in his skin almost the same sensation as her hands. When he entered her body, he felt he was following her voice.

Where she led him was a strange world that was not new to him, since he had always known it existed, subterraneanly: a grotto, with whose confines and geographical dispositions he at once made himself quite familiar, as with the world of inside his own mouth: but a magic grotto, limitless, infinitely receding and enticing, because every sensation he experienced there carried on its back an endless multiplication of overtones, with the result that the sensation, though more than complete, was never finished, and every experience conducted him to the next; a world where he pleasurably lost himself in a confusion of the senses not in the least malapropos but as appropriate and precise as poetry – a world where one really did see sounds and hear scents, where doves might well have roared and given suck, where perfectly defined, delightful local tactile sensations dissolved into apperceptions of light or darkness, or colour, of thickness, of temperature. . . .

Sensuousness and passion, which his imagination had apprehended to be antithetical, were in Nancy's world plaited into such a perfect interpenetration of opposites that the one could grow as a climax out of the other. Her face would lie for a slow moment above his, her eyes piercing his, until gradually her lips would descend on his full lips, slowly enclosing and enfolding them into a tender intensity of such sensuousness that it comprehended the sensations not only of taste and of texture, but of gentle, exhausting exploration. And yet, even as he felt drained, a climax would gather out of his pebbly dryness like a wave reforming in its moment of being sucked back, and he would heave himself up, curling above her like a wave, and would snatch, rape, her into an embrace of bitter, muscular, desperate, violence, that could only, he felt, be resolved by a death agony. . . . Yet in reality even this crisis opened, as if on the clash of a pair of cymbals, into a sunlit, flowering landscape, in which one of the flowers proved, subtly, surprisingly, to be his left ear, into which Nancy's finger was inserted – making an effect of wit, to which his response of a sharply indrawn breath made an effect of repartee.

Brigid Brophy, *Flesh* (1962)

The interest of this passage here is its reversal of the standard scenario of initiation: she initiates him. Brophy can then achieve effects that transpose and rewrite the male statements of the Jong extract (f). 'When he entered her body, he felt he was following her voice' softens and leads away from a single position, a single frame: he enters and follows all at once in a kind of mix of movements and directions and sensations that gives something new, no longer quite held in the stasis of 'the man'/'the woman'. This mix carries over into the account of the love-making which is to some extent thereby pulled off from the narrative point of the orgasm into a 'multiplication of overtones' that is never finished, an endless rippling of sensations, with a different version of male pleasure and sexual being now proposed, beyond the terms of the usual phallic appropriation (elements of which remain, however: snatching and raping her 'into an embrace of bitter, muscular, desperate, violence'). Humour can escape from the confirming playfulness of the Cooper passage (e) and become the wit of a sense of surprise and pleasure in the mobility and irruptions of experience (the flower becoming 'subtly, surprisingly' the ear into which her finger is inserted). Yet it is still the case that the writing is set into the pattern of an initiation and this is not without problems. It is as though, indeed, there is very great difficulty in breaking the idea of sex as sexuality as voyage, initiation. Brophy's writing leads close to and hesitates with the male representation and imagination of women as woman as sexuality as depth of discovery and revelation, 'a magic grotto, limitless, infinitely receding and enticing'. The passage strives for a different reality, for a different language, but the appropriateness and precision of poetry to which it appeals can give way to a heavy literariness and the difference it suggests comes tangled with previous images, something still of the current fiction.

h   Study sensation, the sea food light the senses in the moisture of the flesh. Body's mouth open in the friction even of a stray hair feel it pulled or rubbed upon the clitoris. Its pain is pleasure better understood. I lie as her hand plays upon me, the words repeating themselves inside my skull, study the senses these days live in your eyes in your skin give yourself to experience the present. Give yourself as you learn, become her teacher so she will never leave you, the joy of the flesh so great it can never be forsworn nor I who taught it. Give yourself like a Persian forgetting goals, coming is the end not an end sought for. It finishes therefore postpone the convulsion divert the mind, try other tricks insert tongue into the cleft waiting each nerve listening and alive as the nub of tongue licks and points itself upon the other nub hard stabbing softly and rhythm mounting. While my fingers sly finding another hole in her shy to enter pecking at the entrance for admission granted. Softly and with infinite gentleness turn over on your stomach rejoicing to look down and see them round waiting me while she lies below me the cheeks of her ass such lust I feel and firm, tenderness in my finger moving slowly gently in its rhythm in her, back and forth steady until she rolls away and cannot bear it. And did I hurt you struck with sorrow trying again my mouth watering her first tongue licking the place fill you with water with rain like watering a plant, I will bring all liquids to our rescue that there is no pain or friction bringing wet of her cunt too then enter easy slipping she is opening it for me for our pleasure. Only the sight of her below me, such kindness I feel for these cheeks such greed feeding upon her given and open defenceless vulnerable, but I shall never cause her harm careful to relish our abandon to savour each thrust as she does and my hand ever so slowly deliberate moving her closing on my finger's steady in and out, feeling her feeling in my own anus contracting as hers does the secret joy of it found at last.

For we can do anything. Everything. Nothing is forbidden us, always are open. Watching her suck me, the round of her cheek next to the round of my breast, the very sight watched excites me. As it does her too when I feed upon her, sucking hard till she erects in my mouth grows stiff as a lilac bud while I pull in the pride of it knowing she sees. Complicity so close we are each other's cunts. Feeling the hot cold rush when I touch her clitoris imagining I have her finger on my own, dizzy with the very sensation which I give her so real it is to me, our two bodies one I can no longer separate them. Her cunt from mine, feeling her fingers filling me while mine fill her and thrust against the wall inside her, feeling the pull in my own gasp while I probe the cervix like a flower hanging

upside down, my fingers searching around its turrets. While I give
I am given. The same storm, the same upheaval. One never has
this with a man, his experience hidden as mine is. But two women
have the same nerves. The merest flick of my finger on her clitoris
hidden like a pearl in its folds alerts its head and my own throbs
touched as surely as by a hand and my legs grab hers between them
in a vice, roll then opening to the strength of her leg so satisfactory
I can bring myself to a fever upon it while she shoves it hard against
me, pleased with herself the pleasure she brings me gasping now as
we come together one shaking cry. But I am still greedy to touch
her, ringing changes upon the clitoris, this most sensitive moment
after you've come. And touching it so insidiously the warmth
slowly spreading upwards from her toes till it becomes a chill she
can no longer bear it but bear further until you are faint with it you
can always go on beyond to the next wave and further. So much
further than you thought, such exquisite torture nearly you grow
dizzy in stoicism further still further. And break off. Rest, she says.
But I will not rest, my tongue shall bring her further until she cries
out surprised and comes again, the long difficult ecstasy of nerves
shuddering as after a shipwreck she lies within my arms, passion
and innocence.

Kate Millett, Flying (1974)

The passage is difficult, difficult to discuss here (what relation is one
to have to this representation as a man or indeed as a woman still
caught and fixed in the terms of phallic identity, of 'sexuality'?).
Millett is not – cannot be – entirely outside the accepted representation, little moments and expressions bring with them the memory of
the contemporary novelistic, the standard version – 'my legs grab
hers between them in a vice' is part of the usual rhetoric. There is
something of the commonplace even in the very position of this
description towards the end of her novel-autobiography. Yet the
passage *is* strongly different, turning initiation into complicity into
reciprocity – 'Give yourself as you learn, become her teacher',
'Complicity so close we are each other's cunts', 'While I give I am
given' – in a movement that simultaneously fuses and identifies
experiences: 'dizzy with the very sensation which I give her so real it
is to me, our two bodies one I can no longer separate them', the two
bodies become one *and* the sensation of that is so real to the *I*, given
an intensity there, me slipping and sliding into new identities, new
places, a syntax in shifts and flows from 'I' to 'you' to 'we' to 'I' again
– 'forgetting goals, coming is an end, not an end sought for'.

'One never has this with a man . . .' Let us put Millett's phrase to the writing. What we have seen looking at these passages is a lack of any simple correspondence between sex and language and writing: the fact of being male or female does not involve any essential male or female language nor any essential male or female way of writing; being a woman does not guarantee that your writing will inscribe positions or possibilities different to those of the dominant male-centred order (look again at the passages by Cooper and Jong); being a man does not mean that you will always, automatically and inescapably, produce the fixed discourse of oppression (men are not all some essential same unchangingly expressing itself until the end of time with no hope of transformation). Millett's writing itself is, of course, rooted in her experience and specific to that but this is not equivalent to saying that it is female in any sex–gender sense. The syntax it uses, the displacement of positions, the slip of any one identity into a mobility of intensities are implicated in an important tradition of modern writing that includes work by both women and men authors, Virginia Woolf *and* James Joyce. What is interesting is that modern writing has been precisely bound up with the question of female language, feminine discourse (remember the 'female monologues' with which Joyce ends *Ulysses* and *Finnegans Wake*), where that question emerges – as it does at the same time to psychoanalysis unable finally to hear it as such – as a challenge to the fixity of identity, as a challenge to the 'male' and 'female' which are the very terms – the places – of that identity, as a challenge to the very principle of sexual identity, the whole fix of 'sexuality'.

The American poet and writer and feminist Adrienne Rich has a poem entitled 'The Stranger' with the following lines:

> If they ask me my identity
> what can I say but
> I am the androgyne
> I am the living mind you fail to describe
> in your dead language
> the lost noun, the verb surviving
> only in the infinitive.

They are lines we should almost repeat to ourselves every time we read, asking not for the old identities, 'male' and 'female', 'the man' and 'the woman', but noting and knowing the deadness they bring as they appear repeated and confirmed again and again, and then looking towards other relations of language in writing (Millett shows us a possible example), towards desire and pleasure beyond the orders, the commandments, of identity – which was the Cixous question we started from here, writing that experience.

IX

'sexual in the sense that one's manhood, balls, were involved'

James Jones, *Go to the Widow-Maker* (1968)

What remains in abeyance from the last chapter is the set of problems concerning the reference to 'male' and 'female'. How are we critically to understand and evaluate the use of these terms such as 'male' and 'female', 'masculine' and 'feminine', 'man' and 'woman'? How are we to approach the whole notion of sexual difference and, in fact, *sexuality*?

'The concepts of "masculine" and "feminine" are of no use in psychology', stressed Freud to a meeting of the Vienna Psychoanalytic Society in 1910. Yet Freud and psychoanalysis continued to use them. Revising the *Three Essays on the Theory of Sexuality* in 1915, Freud added a long footnote on these same concepts of 'masculine' and 'feminine' ('among the most confused that occur in science'), distinguishing three meanings at least:

'Masculine' and 'feminine' are used sometimes in the sense of *activity* and *passivity*, sometimes in a *biological*, and sometimes, again, in a *sociological* sense. The first of these three meanings is the essential one and the most serviceable in psychoanalysis. When, for instance, libido was described . . . as being 'masculine', the word was being used in this sense, for an instinct is always active even when it has a passive aim in view. The second, or biological, meaning of 'masculine' and 'feminine' is the one whose applicability can be determined most easily. Here 'masculine' and 'feminine' are characterized by the presence of spermatozoa or ova respectively and by the functions proceeding from them. Activity and its concomitant phenomena (more powerful muscular development, aggressiveness, greater intensity of libido) are as a rule linked with biological masculinity; but they are not necessarily so, for there are animal species in which these qualities are on the contrary assigned to the female. The third, or sociological, meaning receives its connotation from the observation of actually existing masculine and feminine individuals. Such observation shows that in human beings pure masculinity or feminity is not to be found either in a psychological or a biological sense. Every individual on the contrary displays a mixture of the character-traits belonging to his own and to the opposite sex; and he shows a combination of activity and passivity whether or not these last character-traits tally with his biological ones.

Thus for Freud there is an easy biological meaning (for which 'male' and 'female', rather than 'masculine' and 'feminine', might be thought to be the more appropriate terms), a sociological meaning derived from the observation of actual men and women, and then, in addition, between the biological and the sociological, a psychological meaning, the essential one, the most serviceable in psychoanalysis: 'masculine' and 'feminine' as active and passive. But what reason is there for this last meaning? 'Active' and 'passive' are, after all, perfectly good and clear terms. Why, on what grounds, translate them into 'masculine' and 'feminine'? Why is this so 'serviceable'? One answer to these questions could be given sociologically and historically with reference to dominant representations and containments of men and women: in the nineteenth century into which Freud is born, women were matched and constrained to an overall idea of woman as passive (feeble, weak, liable to all sorts of female disorders), necessarily subject to and dependent on active man, the decisions and actions of men. This kind of answer, however, is no concern of Freud's. 'Masculine' and 'feminine' are given an absolute psychological status as 'active' and 'passive' and his answer can then only be on the basis of some universal psychology of sexual difference, precisely that universal psychology which psychoanalysis provides, with its whole paraphernalia of Oedipus complex, penis-phallus, castration, the woman's lack, and so on, its whole definition of masculine and feminine positions, developments, norms. Without any such basis, calling 'active' and 'passive' 'masculine' and 'feminine' would be totally arbitrary; one might just as well talk of the 'biscuits' and 'cheese' aspects of behaviour. That this latter would seem ludicrous while the 'masculine'/'feminine' pair appears as obvious and perfectly natural is exactly the point. The social division and representation of men and women as active and passive has a long history, in relation to which Freud's footnote is written and the terms of which it repeats. Using 'masculine' and 'feminine' for 'active' and 'passive' is thus not arbitrary but eminently reasonable – inevitable indeed – given the strength of this history. But then, equally, without a grasp of the historical construction and convention involved, 'masculine' and 'feminine' are, to echo Freud's own words to the Vienna Psychoanalytic Society, of no use in psychology – any psychology, that is, that is not simply designed to support, to naturalize, a social-historical status quo, set up to provide a description of men and women, man and woman, as essentially this or that by virtue of some innate maleness or femaleness, as essentially active and passive or whatever.

The final sentences of Freud's footnote touch on a fundamental theme of his work, the *bisexuality* of human beings. 'Pure masculinity or femininity is not to be found either in a psychological or a biological sense.' Every individual has both masculine and feminine dispositions and there is conflict and repression in the process of coming to assume the identity of one's own sex as man or woman (failures in this assumption of identity can then be understood as such in these terms – hysteria, for example, is a confusion of sexual identity, a breakdown in the movement to womanhood). That process, moreover, structures rather than eliminates and the resulting individual is left displaying 'a mixture of the character-traits belonging to his own and to the opposite sex' (once again, the grounds for assigning character-traits to one or the other sex, for the whole 'masculine'/'feminine' designation, are left unexplained and can only depend on particular cultural definitions and conceptions of what is 'male' and 'female' behaviour). Thus one has the absolute fact of sexual difference, the opposite sexes, and the simultaneous absence of that difference absolutely in any individual, who is always bisexual, involved in a physical and psychical 'hermaphroditism'.

Here is Freud summarizing his thinking in this difficult area in one of his last pieces of writing:

> We are faced . . . by the great enigma of the biological fact of the duality of the sexes: it is an ultimate fact for our knowledge, it defies every attempt to trace it back to something else. Psychoanalysis has contributed nothing to clearing up this problem, which clearly falls wholly within the province of biology. In mental life, we find only reflections of this great antithesis; and their interpretation is made more difficult by

the fact, long suspected, that no individual is limited to the modes of
reaction of a single sex. . . . For distinguishing between male and female
in mental life we make use of what is obviously an inadequate empirical
and conventional equation: we call everything that is strong and active
male, and everything that is weak and passive female.

Biological fact and the mental reflections of that fact are complicated
in their relations in the individual, the psychical having a kind of
simultaneous independence from the physical: the biological development is accompanied by a psychological development that
effectively determines an individual's sexuality. Both developments
are important in the bisexual nature of every individual, with a
physical and a psychical hermaphroditism running alongside one
another on separate tracks (again, 'in both sexes the degree of
physical hermaphroditism is to a great extent independent of psychical hermaphroditism'); psychically, 'the reactions of human individuals are of course made up of masculine and feminine traits'. All
of which adds up to the emphasis, frequent in Freud's writings, that
'pure masculinity and femininity remain theoretical constructs of
uncertain content'.

That uncertainty can be seen in the passage quoted. What Freud
half recognizes is that the content of 'pure masculinity and femininity' is not just uncertain but impossible: they can have no scientific
content. In order to maintain these concepts, he is thus condemned
either to run them back into an asserted necessity for the biological to
find expression in the psychological: 'the morphological distinction
[i.e. the physical fact of two sexes, male and female] is bound to find
expression in difference in psychical development'; or to give in, for
better or worse, to 'an inadequate empirical and conventional equation' that simply accepts a dominant representation of men and
women as active and passive, that takes that as a reality (the equation
is described as being not just conventional but also *empirical*: men
and women, that is, are *observably* active and passive so we might as
well use 'male' and 'female', 'masculine' and 'feminine', as
synonyms for these characteristics – which is to leave aside, yet
again, history, culture, the social terms of the realization of men and
women, is to imagine a kind of natural being of man and woman,
immediate and eternal).

But let us come back to bisexuality. The idea of bisexuality is not
peculiar to Freud, to be found in the development of psychoanalysis
alone. It was an important part of Darwin's work and of evolution-

ary theory generally (postulating a remote bisexual human ancestor, this phylogenetic or history-of-the-human-race bisexuality being repeated ontogenetically, in the history of each individual, as the presence in the early embryonic stages of the foetus of sexual organs of both sexes), as also of sexology (for Krafft-Ebing and others bisexuality could offer a progressive understanding of homosexuality), to name two major intellectual contexts of Freud's psychoanalytic thought. It was too, increasingly, a central reference for a modern literary understanding and practice, writing away from the assumptions of a fixed identity, calling into question the static terms and images of the Victorian 'life' (those innumerable solid biographies, people set into an acceptable public definition): witness Woolf with her 'woman-manly', 'man-womanly', cast as a theory of 'androgyny'; or Joyce with *Finnegans Wake*, a long adventure of transmutations and displacements, male and female running together in an endless 'bisexycle' ride; or Proust, described by Woolf as 'wholly androgynous'.

The difficulty – the contradictory struggle – comes exactly in respect of the question of identity, of the maintenance of sexual identity. Freud here is rather like D. H. Lawrence, who himself refers to the idea of bisexuality. For Lawrence, 'every man comprises male and female in his being . . . a woman likewise consists in male and female'; at the same time as which, however, 'the man is pure man, the woman pure woman, they are perfectly polarised': the bisexual mixture, male and female elements, rests on an underlying identity, precisely the possibility of saying 'male' and 'female', of assuming and using those terms in such statements as 'every man comprises male and female in his being'. So too Freud. Bisexuality at once recognizes the incredible problem of male and female, masculine and feminine, and maintains those identities nevertheless, the one difference, the two sexes, 'sexual polarity' – and for Freud as for Lawrence the basis of that polarity, the key to the identity of men and women is the man, the phallus, the phallic organization of the sexual. Bisexuality, that is, becomes a theoretical and ideological trap: a plurality is posed, the individual as made up of masculine and feminine traits, that is reduced in the very beginning, in its very terms of 'masculine' and 'feminine', to the system of the one – phallic – identity (thus bisexuality will serve in Freud to universalize 'penis-envy', the girl's and woman's wish to be a man in accordance with the masculine elements of their bisexual nature).

Bisexuality remains two-edged today in theoretical arguments. It can function to some extent as the beginning of an alternative representation, as an insistence against the one position, the fixed sexual order, man and woman; and it can return constantly as a confirmation of that fixity, a strategy in which differences, varieties of existence and experience, are neutralized into the given systems of identity, the two halves – masculine and feminine – adding up to the same old *one* (and according to the usual phallic fantasy of unity, of the perfect complementarity and harmony of 'the sexes'*). What has to be resisted is the whole psychology of bisexuality, the movement – and so often via the confusion of 'male' and 'female' in 'masculine' and 'feminine' – from a biological level (where 'male' and 'female' can be given a certain content and aspects of a 'bisexuality' effectively recognized and demonstrated) to a psychical level (described and explained as reflecting the biological one which is thus its essential determination). Freud was right: 'masculine' and 'feminine' are useless; or rather, they serve only and oppressively to naturalize cultural realizations and representations of human activity that should and must be analyzed as such, understood as part of the sexual fix. 'Masculine' and 'feminine' – and 'male' and 'female', too, in as much as they appear in the same way – are 'concepts' we need to learn to refuse.†

In the early stages of embryonic development, the human foetus is biologically male and female, having both mullerian ducts (the structures that will develop in the female into the uterus, fallopian tubes and upper segment of the vagina) and wolffian ducts (the structures that will develop into the internal reproductive anatomy in the male). Differentiation is of the male from the female (*not* vice

---

*Consider the current conversational usage of bisexuality. 'Is he/she homosexual?' 'No, he's/she's bisexual.' You have to be identified, fit 'sexuality', be one or the other or both, the same one in the end. Somehow the sum has got to be made to come out right, the problem preserved, the required answer produced. The regiment marches on, one–two, one–two, one . . . What you cannot be allowed to be is *sexual*, multiple, various, a kaleidoscope of moments and possibilities, infinitely desiring . . .

†It should go without saying that 'feminine' has no equivalence with 'feminist': feminism, feminist practice and theory, is based on the analysis of the real experience and situation of women, part of which analysis has involved exactly the demonstration and refusal of the fixing of the 'feminine', 'femininity'.

versa): if the gonads or sex glands, which differentiate according to directives carried in the genetic coding of the chromosomes, are removed prior to the beginning of hormonal differentiation (about the sixth week of embryonic life), 'then the embryo will proceed to differentiate as a morphologic female, regardless of genetic sex'. We start with male and female possibilities and the latter will be realized should nothing interrupt and change the course of foetal development. Development as male, in other words, depends on additional factors ('to masculinize, something must be added'): a mullerian inhibiting substance which suppresses the development of the mullerian ducts and testosterone, the male sex hormone, which promotes the development of the wolffian ducts and dictates the developmental programme of the external sexual organs (so that, for example, the initial genital tubercle of the undifferentiated embryo becomes a penis instead of a clitoris). Thus one has a 'bisexuality' or 'bipotentiality' in which male and female coexist from conception in an undifferentiated embryo, with sex differentiation beginning about six weeks after conception, and in which the female has a certain priority over the male.

Sex differentiation, moreover, is not a matter of any once-and-for-all one moment in the history of an individual. On the contrary, it is a long series of stages and something of the original sex bipotential ambivalence continues throughout the whole life (for example, the male and female sex hormones, androgens – of which testosterone is one form – and estrogens, are both present in men and women): 'Biological bisexuality comprises a series of relays, spaced out in time, each of which plays its role in the determination of the sex (chromosomal sex, gonadal sex, hormonal sex, internal genital sex, external genital sex, secondary sexual characteristics) . . . One can thus speak of a biological development of sexuality, from conception to puberty, which is carried through according to a discontinuous and differentiated process . . . but which is superimposed with other relays – an autonomous psychical development different from the biological one and responsible for psychosexuality; the human relay being the fundamental determinant of the individual's sexuality.' With the latter emphasis, we come back to the physical *and* the psychical, the biological *and* the psychological, to something of the more interesting perceptions of Freud and psychoanalysis: the individual's sexual being is a long history and that history includes, fundamentally, the human social terms of realization and definition, is a question not just of chromosomes and hormones and so on but equally of gender assignments and identifications, of meanings and representations.

There is a good deal of debate over the relation between the physical and the psychical, the genetic and the environmental or however the two sides are conceived. It is very uncertain that the idea of an autonomy of the psychical would find much favour among contemporary scientific authorities for whom psychosexual differentiation is much more a continuation of the biological development; for whom, indeed, the very idea of some juxtaposition of two levels is hopelessly outmoded ('modern genetic theory avoids these antiquated dichotomies and postulates a genetic norm of reaction which, for its proper expression, requires phyletically prescribed environmental boundaries'!). What is important here is simply: 1) that sexual difference is not an immediately given fact of 'male' and 'female' identity but a whole process of differentiation; 2) that differentiation is a *history* of the individual, takes place over time in the world (is not just something to do with the embryo in the womb, itself anyway not outside the world), involves always an interaction of the biological with the cultural and social (there is never some pure biological essence but always the individual as precise constituted materiality); 3) that biological, genetic or other similar scientific accounts define and describe men and women in respect of a specific differentiation as man and woman, not as 'masculine' and 'feminine' but as 'male' and 'female' where these terms have a precisely limited content based on the fact of sexual reproduction, define and describe men and women in respect of sex or gender not sexuality (unless the latter is simply taken in what was its earliest sense of relating to sexual reproduction, 'the quality of being sexed or having sex').

The human animal is involved in the reproduction of the species like other animals but is equally distinguished from them by a number of crucial factors. Thus, for instance, sexual activity is not tied to the finality of reproduction, is carried on just as well during periods when there is no possibility of conception: people make love all the time and not only at specific times of biologically determined receptivity (compare monkeys or apes where the period of sexual receptivity of the female is usually limited to a week or so of the monthly cycle, or lower mammals where it is limited to the actual time of ovulation). Further, moving on to central conditions of humanness, human beings develop outside the womb to a quite exceptional degree: we are not born finished or anywhere near finished but in a state of total dependency, gradually developing, growing and learning to become individuals in a process that lasts from birth to puberty and beyond. This process of becoming in the world – our unfinishedness and so our openness – gives the possibility of the extensive transmission of information and knowledge from which we are able to benefit: we are able to acquire, and we develop in relation to the acquisition of, a whole range of complex skills, procedures, ways of thinking and so on. The human being has the biggest brain of all the primates and almost 80 per cent of the growth of that brain takes place after birth; our capacity to learn, to define, structure and control experience, our world, is enormous – human being is first and foremost cultural, social, historical. And in this learning, the specifically human fact of language is of fundamental importance: we find ourselves always in language, in meanings and representations, in the most extraordinarily complex systems of sense, in the terms of which we grow, exist, are what we are. The sexual, to come back to that, is reproduction but it is also (and reproduction with it) always human activity and realization, defined, structured, given in meanings and representations: a cultural phenomenon.

What we need above all to grasp and retain is this: there is no natural sex or sexuality (the only thing that might conceivably be called 'natural' is the reproduction of the species but that too is to run the risk of abstracting from culture and ending up by essentializing – exactly naturalizing – some particular social organization and representation of reproduction: reproduction might be natural, mothers and fathers never are). There is no natural sex or sexuality; sexuality is not some absolute and eternal entity at the beginning of an underlying human being – it simply does not exist. Or rather, its only existence is as specific construction, specific definition of the sexual.

'Sex,' wrote the poet Pound, 'in so far as it is not a purely physiological reproductive mechanism, lies in the domain of aesthetics.' He was right in his way, in agreement with Isadora, heroine of Jong's *Fear of Flying*: 'Because sex is all in the head. Pulse rates and secretions have nothing to do with it.' We make love with our heads (so many more positions), bring into the play the facts of our human life (with language replacing the stork). Where does sexuality come from? Assuredly not from within like the kernel of a nut or the stone of a peach but from our being in the world, from our movement in the whole mesh of meanings and representations in which we find and come together as ourselves, in which the terms of our desiring are posed, in which we – mind and body – have our history. For this is the point: a conception – the feeling – of sexuality arises in connection with the slippage over and above the goal of reproduction. Imagine a game in which there is some compulsion on you to score but most of which as far as you are concerned is taken up with quite other motions and motivations, a kind of elaborate ballet choreographed for you in respect of a variety of additional steps and moments – that's the possibility of sexuality, that exorbitance. Individuals participate in the reproduction of the species in relation to which they are transient, held to the price of individual death, but are at the same time, as individuals, in excess of that simple species function, caught up in all the sense of the individual history that is theirs, all the desire that gives. It was this excess of which the nineteenth century was so strongly aware and which it sought so strongly to tie, to bring back into acceptable definitions, controlled limits; it is this excess that we in turn, and in continuation of the nineteenth century which gave us the problem and the word, conceive for ourselves as 'sexuality', today's marching order, the thing we believe in as hard as we can – after all this is where we imagine ourselves to be, where we are really at; our identity, male and female, masculine and feminine, man and woman, depends on it. Trust David Cooper for the contemporary slogan: 'bread *and* orgasm' . . . Give us this day . . .

X

'But say you have two motor cars. One has the front half bashed-in, the other has the back half bashed-in. From the two disasters you can make a good car. That's probably what sex is doing.'

John Maynard Smith, Professor of
Biology at the University of Sussex,
quoted in the *Sunday Times* (1978)

The idea of the importance of sexuality today is out of any proportion, the place it occupies is that of the new religion. Sexuality is your imperative, the thing you cannot and must not escape, the deepest reality with which it is your duty to come to terms. *This* is sacred and binding. The sanctification of the sexual as 'sexuality' indeed is one of the major characteristics of our culture.

Any good religion involves some kind of salvation or new life, some process of revelation and awakening with subsequent elevation to a higher state. The new religion of 'sexuality' will not disappoint: you start in darkness, then you discover your fallen and failing condition, and then after much effort, for the path of righteousness is long ('it is sometimes very difficult and painful to confront one's own sexuality'), you come into full realization of the depths of your man or woman being and enter from there into the kingdom of heavenly joy. Where once you had a soul, now you have a sex to save, and grace has become orgasm. The whole affair is called 'liberation', 'sexual liberation', yesterday's struggle and what we can all now thankfully benefit from (we have, remember, been 'catapulted out of the sexual dark ages into a glittering age of sexual enlightenment and pleasure'); an achievement that is set out and comes true for each of us in blessed moments of personal progress: 'As she lowered her head in the darkness and took his penis in her mouth, she felt not only love for him but a dramatic awakening of her own liberation.'

Where once we had a spiritual life and spiritual exercises, now we have a sex life and sexual exercises ('which, if followed carefully, honestly and, most importantly, in order, will enable you to develop your own good sex'). Everyone today understands that 'intimate story' means sex-life story, which means what you did and do with a

couple of organs and some bits of anatomy. 'When did you first
. . . ?' 'When did you last . . . ?', 'Was it good?', 'How's your sex life
these days?' Gay Talese, author of a best-selling celebratory chroni-
cle of the 'sex revolution' entitled *Thy Neighbour's Wife: Sex in the
World Today* (the world is the United States) and cast (how else?) in
the form of 'intimate stories (the penis-sucking liberation quotation
above is from one of them), greets people he meets with 'When did
you first masturbate?' ('a favourite opening gambit'). Good question, straight to the point, from the new religion, the new story of
life and lives. What's it all about? How can you ask! Penetrate,
agitate, ejaculate, and a few variants on the same. Don't worry if that
summary seems rather stark, the quality has improved ('It's not
going to be any of that three-minute stuff for me', says lovable
sexologist's son Michael) and women are included too (we like them
a lot and they have even bigger penises than men): equality reigns.

Equality of the orgasm, of course. The friends of the naked ape
have assured us that among all the primates only the human female
experiences orgasm (noting 'the immense behavioural reward it
brings to the act of sexual co-operation with the mated partner'). No
longer asked to be ashamed, she can now be grateful, she too is
touched with grace. Moreover, the women corresponds to the man,
is every bit his equal; as Cooper puts it, 'the female way of getting
pleasure . . . corresponds to the muscular dance of male ejaculation'.
Indeed, she ejaculates just the same as he does; according to *Playboy*
in 1980, Dr John Perry, a Vermont psychologist, has identified 'a
urethral discharge during sex' by women which is an 'ejaculation-
like emission'. Do not stop to ask why a totally different discharge,
assuming it exists, *has to be* described as an ejaculation-like emission,
simply be delighted, as delighted as *Playboy* is and as *My Secret Life*'s
Walter would have been: women are the same, man and woman
confirmed and together.* Orgasm is the goal of sex and the standard

---

* Naturally there is a directly complementary alternative representation. Either
women are woman the same or they are woman the different, man's difference
(both ways, men come out as man, established in his clear identity; untroubled by
the same and defined as not and against the different). Hence, as difference, and
psychoanalysis has been the main guarantor of this version, woman is a mystery
orgasm, an ineffable realm beyond language and man, a kind of absolute Other.
Since religion is what is at stake, woman ends up in a kind of dim equivalence with
God who, as her orgasm shows, 'has not yet made his exit': 'it is in as much as her
coming is radically other that the woman has more relation to God'. The same
psychoanalyst also manages to characterize God as 'woman made whole' – she is an
experience of God but incomplete, we can never forget the lack and the penis-
phallus, the latter the centre of this religious circle.

of sexuality, crucial to the representation of 'sexuality', to its production as thing (to be liberated), commodity (to be bought and
sold), religion (to be believed).

All of which adds up to the most formidable repression through sex.
As the sexual is held to sex, the sexes and the holy orgasm for
conversion into 'sexuality', so our society holds us into its usual
terms of commodity and exchange. There is a capitalism of the
sexual and we live under it: a whole investment in the sexual as sex
which allows its stable instrumentalization and manufacture and
circulation, with us as sexual agents as we are economic agents – that
is the imagination of ourselves in 'sexuality' and which we are incited
to buy in every sense of that word. Fetishism of commodities,
fetishism of sexes; economic relations, sexual relations; work, sex –
sex, two sexes, one thing, identify with that, be the man or the
woman, take your place, *fit.* Who can believe – but this is what the
representation of 'sexuality' requires, asks us to – that there is a
sexual *revolution*? Revolutions are about radical transformation but
the society we know and live in has not drastically changed in its
essential structures in response to orgasm and all the rest; on the
contrary, it has developed and consolidated a multi-million pound
or dollar industry, spread 'sexuality' like butter on all its products
and, exactly, constructed that representation. Talese's book is a
good indication in this respect: he gives not two hoots for women's
movements, gay movements, any form of movement and argument
that doesn't fit the general assumptions of 'sexuality' (reading the
book one would barely know that there had even ever been something called feminism); the 'sex revolution' is the capitalists of sex
from Hugh Hefner of the *Playboy* empire down to the local massage
parlour owner (not, of course, that Talese is interested in any
economic and ideological analysis; for him these are good guys,
working away for liberation*), plus individuals, ordinary people

*Here is Hefner in 1969 outlining in a secret memo why he and *Playboy* need an
article on the women's movement ('Talese insists that the only reason we fail to take
Hefner seriously is that we are captives of the old morality'): 'These chicks are our
natural enemy. . . . It is time we do battle with them. . . . What I want is a
devastating piece that takes the militant feminists apart. They are unalterably
opposed to the romantic boy–girl society that *Playboy* promotes. . . .' (*Playboy,* it
might be noted as indication of the tight web of 'sexuality' and its institution, has
contributed generously to the funding of Masters and Johnson's sexological
research.)

like you and me, going through the personal progress towards the proffered freedom ('a history of America through the bedroom').

The real problem and task is always one of social revolution. Privileging the sexual has nothing necessarily liberating about it at all; indeed, it functions only too easily as an instance by development of and reference to which society guarantees its order outside of any effective process of transformation, produces precisely a containing area and ideology of 'revolution' or 'liberation'. Hence the contemporary importance of 'sexuality', of the focus on the sexual as sex: keep everything to that, the province of 'the sexual act', the bed, penetrate and so on, our story; tell people again and again that that's where it's at, that's what they want, it's their freedom and their right and their opportunity and their glorious open university (Cooper: 'the dream and love laboratory of bed – one of the best universities I know'). And the fact and the propagation of sexology are fundamental in all this, a whole sexologization. Who can doubt these people, these sexologists with their titles and diplomas, their statistics and instruments, their evidently friendly (mostly) professionalism? The weight of science and its social image hangs heavily and to effect: the engineers of the body cannot be wrong, sexuality must be what they say, a matter of organs, anatomy, equipment, proper functioning of the apparatus; *and* they offer us orgasm, good orgasms, the 'Big O' . . .

Who can doubt . . . how can we say that sexuality is not equivalent to sex or the sexual act, that pleasure is not equivalent to orgasm, that orgasm is defined and limited in 'sexuality' and given to represent the exchange-value of our bodies and their pleasure in a circulation of normalized and interchangeable sexual agents, that the discourse on and representation from orgasm is an alienation, one more, a fix? That all of this is a way, yet again, of blotting out subjectivity and politics, the two together, not our story, wrapped up, sealed and certified conform, but our *history*? Repression through sex: anti-pleasure through the appeal to pleasure–orgasm; anti-difference through its hold to the difference, its man and woman identity; anti-freedom through its order of liberation, its overwhelming representation.

Go to a film, switch on the television, open a magazine, can we really think we are free, at liberty? For all its scientific image, sexology is locked into the general representation, informs and repeats it; .the 'neutrality' of sexology is as always a *system* of 'neutrality', full of assumptions and values. The international *Visual Encyclopedia of Sex* has the same photograph as the French Hachette *Encyclopédie de la vie sexuelle* to illustrate the family, the ideal sexually enlightened and open family (you didn't know that sexuality and the family go together like boy and girl?): father, mother, one son, one daughter, all naked, all white, all well-formed, all smiling. Why is this photo so popular, so transcultural, so universal (after all, there are lots of different families around to be photographed)? Why two children, one son, one daughter? Why is the wife blonde, of good height but just that little bit shorter to allow the father to look protectively down at her, possessing her as his wife? Aren't we reminded just slightly of the ideal contemporary Western capitalist advanced in-dustrial society middle-class family, just slightly? But if class comes into it, maybe the engineering approach has some limits, is a bit askew? And class does come into it, bet your sex life. Sexology and 'sexuality' are expensive: 'the average middle-class male is also the average male client at the sex therapy clinic', a sexologist reports, while the bread-and-orgasm Cooper adds as regards his practice that 'it is only unfortunate that the experiences were limited to middle-class intellectuals . . .'. Only unfortunate, all that is needed is to extend the same. The idea that, on the contrary, there might be some necessity to turn such statements into the basis for a critical analysis of the very terms of sexology is beyond the bounds of comprehen-sion: 'sexuality' goes without saying, is self-evident, we must accept without question.

The self-evidence is startling. The same French encyclopedia has a photograph of a naked little boy and girl, the former looking down towards his penis, the latter watching him, looking in the same direction; the caption reads: 'Pride, desire and anxiety are the most commonly observed emotional reactions in the child discovering the difference of the sexes. Without doubt the pride is in proportion to the penis envy shown by the little girl.' You think you see a picture of two children playing about in a garden, grass, sunshine, they seem pretty happy. Not at all, you see the difference of the sexes and penis envy; it's *self-evident*, you must see it, the photo shows you – penis envy is as natural as boys and girls or as mum and dad, the husband and wife we just saw in the photo of the normal family. . . . And the normal is central and constant. On the one hand, sexology (and the sexual revolution) says anything goes; on the other, since its whole conception is man, woman, organs, orgasm, sex, it can only actually present the norm and the deviations, the standard and the strange (to be *tolerated*). Thus the *Visual Encyclopedia*: the model family *and* the tatooed, penis-ringed man, how boys and girls grow up into man and woman *and* an introduction to the handkerchief language of gays, hetero *and* homo, and so on in a kind of confining vista of sex, everything surveyed from the one normal position, from the assumption of 'sexuality'. One might note here, moreover, the symptomatic way in which sexology takes and assimilates women's and gay movements as appendages to and demonstrations of itself, figments of its liberation, ties them to sex.

What if the questions raised by those movements had strictly nothing to do with sex, with our current 'sexuality', were a displacement of any such conception of the sexual, of the version of 'life' it supports? Certainly, women and gays may have had and have to talk from and against the sexual position assigned them, their fixing to that, to sex precisely (what are women? a sex, determined by and interested only in that; what are gays? homosexuals, a sexual quirk) but the force of their arguments and struggles has been quite beyond 'sexuality' which is a term of containment and oppression, has involved radical social and political analyses and actions. Liberation cannot be a question of bed or of bread and orgasm (an old programme, *panem et circenses*, bread and circuses, keeping the masses amused); it depends on social change. The end of oppression is a recasting of social relations that leaves men and women free, outside of any commodification of the sexual, removed from any of the violence and alienation of circulation and exchange as agents of sex and orgasm, away from any definition as a sexual identity, the identity of a sex, being fixed to this or that image, this or that norm, to this thing 'sexuality'.

We need to liberate sexuality from 'sexuality', the accepted construction, disengaging experience from the terms in which it is constrained, reworking ourselves, our lives. 'Homosexual', for instance, is still a term and a notion within the heterosexual system – sex, identity, the sexual act, and all the rest of it. Guy Hocquenghem, writer, film-maker, 'homosexual', puts this well: 'Homosexual desire: these terms don't go without saying. There

is no subdivision of desire as between homosexuality and hetero-
sexuality. Strictly speaking, there is no more homosexual desire
than there is heterosexual desire. Desire emerges in a multiple form,
the component elements of which are only separable *a posteriori*, in
respect of the manipulations to which we subject them.'

A matter of meaning and meanings. The sexological-'sexuality'-
capital myth of the body is that of a given natural unity, pure and
instrumental and with which we have – or can be liberated to have – a
free and direct relation. But this is to propose and hide a fundamental
abstraction of the body that is part and parcel of the commodification
of the sexual and the ideology of 'liberation'. The body is never
immediate, some kind of set-off thing with which we have this free
and direct relation; it is always immediately social, taken up in
meanings, ways of understanding, representations that define any
'relation', any 'freedom' and 'directness'. In a real sense, we should
jettison this talk of the body. Our society talks about and gives us
enough of it already. The body? Perfect. Occupy yourselves with
that, forget the social, forget the oppression in which you are
inscribed, inscribed as your body, forget. . . . What does it all come
down to? We are all bodies in the end, natures, inescapable
biologies.★ Believe that. Circulation assured. This myth of the
body, moreover, goes along with and contributes to a further
well-maintained and invested illusion, that of sexual relations. What
do you want? A good sexual relationship. We know at once what
that means: a man, a woman (if it comes to it, two men or even two
women; in any event it all comes down to the same), one lacks the
other (that's evident), they're complementary, two halves, together
they make a real one, a union (good title for a sexology magazine),
Adam and Eve, a man and a woman (good title for a film). All of
which is pure fiction, nothing to do with any nature: the story of the
other sex, feather in the cap of our hetero 'sexuality' – two sexes,
thesis, antithesis, synthesis, one, two, one again. No doubt it's
comforting at times to be a sex and have a relation with the other.
Suppose, though, that there was something like an interminable
plurality of sexes, that the notion of a sex with its obligation of an
identity wasn't much help (it helps oppression) . . . What does
Hocquenghem say? That there is no homosexual desire strictly

★ 'Sex without continuous awareness and amazement of each person's inescapable biology lacks a sense of wonder, which is the best turn-on of all.' Robert H.
Rimmer, author of 'the sex manifesto of the free love generation'.

speaking, that the hetero/homo system is a limiting identification, that there is just desire, multiple differences, possibilities, moments, that it is in the definitions assigned that desire turns out as 'homo' or 'hetero', that everything hinges on representations.

Desire is bound up with meaning, representation. The condition of sexuality, of the specifically human sexual, is the excess of the individual over the species function of reproduction and the condition in turn of the excess, of the individual, is language. We exist as individuals in relation to and in the relations of language, the systems of meaning and representation in which, precisely, we find ourselves – try to imagine the question of who you are and any answer outside of language, outside of those systems. Sexual relations are relations through language, not to a given other sex; the body is not a direct immediacy, it is tressed, marked out, intrinsically involved with meanings. Of course, we can shake our heads, appeal to the fact that *we know* the direct experience of the body, two bodies in love, making love. Yet 'direct experience', 'the body' and so on are themselves specific constructions, specific notions; the appeal to which is never natural but always part of a particular system, a particular representation – and with particular social effects. Look at almost any advertisement today. It tells us that there is the body, the ultimate authentic direct immediate body-to-body, man-to-woman relation – sun, surf, sex, the woman emerging glistening and heat-drenched from the water, nature before your eyes. All of which sells well, sells a beer, a perfume, anything you like; and what you like is the image, exactly that, an image: the nature, the body, the pure sexual state to be attained, attainment being – for this is an image, a myth not a reality – impossible; whence the necessity to buy the beer or the perfume or whatever, perhaps it will help to get us there.

It is this play of meaning and representation, the reality of that, which psychoanalysis can stress so powerfully. To know something about sexuality is not to fiddle around with organs and measure orgasms but to listen to individuals, to their histories, is to follow the process of their development as desiring beings. Sexuality is in consequence of the symbolic, of the relations of the sexual in the history of the individual, in his or her complex subjectivity, to patterns of meaning, terms of representation. The structure of my desire is the structure of my history, is from that, not from any nature. One of the great scandals and achievements of psychoanalysis is its elimination of all idea of sexuality as a content, as a kind of mission of nature with which we are invested at birth; sexuality is not a thing, a packet ready-wrapped, a nature, it is a movement, a process, a history. The problem is that psychoanalysis also went back on that elimination. Listening to individuals it heard stories, which came together, repeated one another, so many common places. No surprise. Individuals are socially realized, they have the meanings, the representations, the structures of their social existence. Sexuality is in consequence of the symbolic but the symbolic too is not itself some simple nature; it is *this* language, *this* set of systems, *these* terms of representation. Which is what psychoanalysis failed to take into its account, leading instead to the elaboration of another content of sexuality, so many supposed universal forms of the individual's development – the Oedipus complex and the penis–phallus and so on and so forth. It listened to the stories of individuals but missed too much in the end of their and its history, the particular social–historical context of those stories and of the terms of the descriptions and theory it produced in response to them. Consider penis envy. The stories heard from women touch on feelings of inferiority, the desire to be other than a woman, to change their position. Enter the concept of penis envy. There are two positions, man and woman, the latter different from the former, by virtue of the penis–phallus, her lack or deficiency; penis envy is 'a fundamental element of female sexuality', part of the normal process of sexual difference, the establishment of the opposite sexes: 'In girls, the discovery of the penis gives rise to envy for it, which later changes into the wish for a man as the possessor of a penis.' The trap is in the rapid ascension from particular stories to absolute terms of description: penis envy may well be a manifestation at certain moments in certain forms of society characterized by certain kinds of oppression and institution of the relations between men and women but to recognize and acknowledge this is a historical and social analysis quite distinct from – and in opposition to – any idea of it as an element in a normal process of being female. 'When a girl declares that "she would rather be a boy", we know what deficiency her wish is intended to put right'; we know because we know nothing of the social–historical, know only the individual and the universal and a basis of the first in the second via the fixed positions of man and woman, the penis–phallus and . . . 'sexuality'. For the paradox is there: psychoanalysis produces critical insights, gives radical directions, and simultaneously contributes – crucially – to the fix, comes back with a content, hears a 'sexuality', the specific construction, which it cannot analyze as such but can only accept and repeat and help to consolidate and define – a history of representations translated into a recognition of essence, a nature again.

That specific construction is ours today, we live in the reign of 'sexuality'. Which is why we need to pose again and urgently, after and despite all the rhetoric of the 'sexual revolution', 'the question of the place, proportion, *actual* importance of sexuality in our (now) longer-lived, more various, woman lives'. That formulation by the American writer Tillie Olsen goes, as regards the argument here, for men too, for us all. We need to pose the question, analyze, understand, refuse – refuse to be heterosexual and homosexual, the opposite sex and a sex at all. . . .

XI

' "The last chapter called *Consummation* is the best thing I have
ever read on the male-female relationship." "I agree," I said
fervently.'

dialogue between Stanley Cole and Sheila Anne Grove,
in Robert H. Rimmer, *The Harrad Experiment* (1966)

X So why did you write all this? It's not much fun in the end . . .

Y Against terrorism, the terrorism of 'sexuality' which I simply
wanted to set out and show up a little. No answers, just that,
almost like a series of quotations. I've suffered and suffer and I
think others must too – it's difficult not to in our society – from
'sexuality', the whole sexual fix. To the point of nausea. There's
a moment when you can realize that it's running through and
organizing your life, feelings, experience. And that realization
isn't easy, your identity's at stake. Time and time again we are
told – and in so many ways of which we often aren't even aware
– to 'confront our sexuality', 'find our own sex', and so on;
what's hard is when these orders snap and you grasp that your
sexuality, your own sex supposedly are figured out for you, that
you repeat those figures as yours, accepting all the rhetoric and
definition of 'your deepest self', 'the real you' . . . Let's face it,
there's a movement of fear here – the fear of not matching the
sex, sex life, sexuality you are supposed to be, of not being
normal, sexually ok and all the rest of it, flips over into the fear
now of what's left, where am I when that identity goes, when
that version of me is seen as such, a version a construction, a
matter of representations? So I wrote from there. Maybe it's not
much fun, I don't know, but I wanted to say that change is
possible, that we're not essentially this, that sexuality isn't some
immutable nature, some *thing* we have to be.

X Sexology *terrorist*?

Y Yes, I've tried to show how it is both limiting and coercive. For
example, you are told that if you learn masturbation, 'never
again need you experience sexual frustration'. Well, what is the

idea of sexuality that allows that kind of statement? That can put masturbation into an immediate equation with sexual fulfilment (no more frustration)? That . . .

X   You're against masturbation, it's the nineteenth century all over again, worse probably.

Y   On the contrary, I'm not against anything in that way. I simply want to object to the kind of abstractions with which sexology so readily works and which it justifies on the basis of the limiting conceptions that inform 'sexuality', conceptions that are often rooted in an appeal to some obvious and unarguable supposed physical fact or reality. Masturbation is 'physical relief' is the end of 'sexual frustration', nothing else to say, no problems. But precisely what is this abstract – abstract because merely referred to a purely physical level – sexual-fulfilment masturbation? Take it into the realm of the concrete, give it a particular content: men masturbating in private booths in a sex-shop cinema while watching films depicting people being beaten and tortured. All one has to say about this is 'never again need you experience sexual frustration', that's really all?

X   But when it comes down to it, sexology itself doesn't believe that that's all; it has a healthy notion of healthy sex, if you see what I mean.

Y   My point with the example, though, wasn't to label the behaviour described 'unhealthy'. 'Healthy' and 'unhealthy' are terms within the limits of sexology, part of the individual-medical-moral focus and understanding. What we need is analysis of the complex social-historical reality of sexuality for any individual, its institution for him or her, the forms in which it is determined and given. Sex shops, pornographic films and so on do not cater to natural needs, that is their alibi, a justification we are too willing to accept (too willing because of the belief in 'sexuality' we have learned); they are commercial operations at a certain stage of capitalist society and they are exploitations of individuals in relations of economic and ideological definition, a certain market of 'sex', a commodification and circulation of sexuality that permeates all areas, every aspect of social life. 'Sexual frustration' itself is a creation and function of that, not an absolute and unchanging facet of human being.

     As for what you say about sexology, its healthy notion of

healthy sex and the response it would make beyond that of merely 'that's all', there are several intertwining strands and emphases which are found in different patterns in different books and practices and which together make up a general sexological perspective and representation. Thus one emphasis is that anything goes, only provided – the glibly unthinking saving clause – that no one is forced or gets hurt (consideration of the various kinds of force and the manifold terms of hurt that might be involved is never attempted; the automatic assumption is that of abstractly free and equal individuals making purely independent decisions, with no conception that individuals exist only in social relations, that those relations may structure oppression, as for example between men and women, and so on): if it makes you happy, it must be good – bondage is as ok as boy kisses girl. Another emphasis, however, is resolutely directed towards a central paradigm: man, woman, 'normal' heterosexual sex with full fulfilment (='orgasm') and 'a loving relationship'. It is this that is 'healthy', the norm in respect of which there are a number of 'variations', more or less tolerable. But with a kind of reluctance to identify any practices straight out as vicious or degrading, as posing fundamental problems of social-sexual relations. The climate and the success of the ideas of 'the sexual revolution' have made it difficult to develop any criticism without at once being castigated as repressed and repressive. Everything's a question for individuals and individuals ought to be 'sexually adventurous', that's a standard of health too. And so the circle goes round and round, and turns into the coercion I mentioned and which is anyway part of the norm from the start.

Take the sexual exercises – the 'sexpieces' – you'll be told to do. 'Should any sexpiece not work for you, try to find the real reason for this. Just saying, "I don't like it" will not do.' In the sexological world you have no right not to like something – you're resisting, there's something wrong with you, something in you to be overcome, you need to find the *real* reason. . . . I think that's coercion, the terrorism of a 'sexuality' that you're supposed to fit and match, that you are taught – and by everything around you – to aspire to, and the creation of that aspiration is the fact of the economic and ideological return: the

sexual is produced as a commodity, a thing you have to have and
be. . . . It's a world of models and measurements and merchandise . . . .

X   There's something desperately obscurantist and reactionary
about all this. Sexology is first and foremost the diffusion of
information and advice about sexual matters; as such, it has
helped very large numbers of people, has brought them knowledge and relief. You do nothing but criticize.

Y   The criticism certainly isn't meant against the diffusion of
information and advice, against sex education. But to accept
unreservedly the need for information, advice, education is not
to accept that there is no necessity for critical discussion of the
terms in which it is given, the representations with which it is
made. My concern has been with that critical discussion, not
with any kind of attack on information. When one reads the
books, the manuals, what one finds, inevitably, is a mixture of
information and representation; the books, if you like, add up to
more than the information they give, they come out with a
certain idea of things, a certain version of how life is and should
be to which you are required to assent. This is what I've been
describing in the focus on 'sexuality', something of the history
and the terms of which I've tried to sketch out. In a way, what I
feel like saying practically about sexology is – read or listen but
don't *believe*, use any information you can but ask at every point
why, how, on what basis, in relation to what argument, position, general assumptions it is being given to you, proposed as
information. My sole ambition here is to help a little *against* the
belief demanded by sexology, *towards* the questioning of its
assumptions, of the general establishment of 'sexuality' today –
the one world in which Masters and Johnson and *Playboy* come
exactly together, in which Dr Robert Chartham, sexologist and
sexologist-author (*Sex Manners for Advanced Lovers*), also turns
up exactly in the commercialization of 'The Chartham Method
of Penis Development', which is then advertised in *Mayfair* and
equivalent magazines, 'order with complete confidence from
. . . . Ultranorm Ltd.' That world and sexology's major role in it
can and should be criticized.

X   Ok but what about liberation? There *has been* liberation and the
idea of liberation has informed movements that have and are

having real and vitally liberating effects – not just sexual liberation but equally women's liberation, gay liberation . . . .

Y I don't think women's and gay movements should be confused
with sexual liberation as though they were all one and the same
thing. One strategy of containment in our 'sexuality'-invested
society is to bring everything down to 'sex', its version of the
sexual as ultimate cause, nature, explanation. Thus women's
liberation, for example, is part of sexual liberation and everyone
can be happy: forget the social and political questions and
realities, all we need is love, good sex, male and female sexual
equals, we're all for it – take a 'freshly liberated wife' and a
'sensuous man' and what do you get? *The Love Explosion*,
'wildly uninhibited sexual adventure' and the title of Robert H.
Rimmer's very latest novel. If you'll allow a slight digression I
might mention just how well liberation works and sells in films
and novels, right down into the fiction pages of *Playboy* and
Mayfair and *Penthouse* and the others. Here's a bit from one of
their stories: 'The Baron was enchanted by Stephanie. "Are you
still a virgin?" he asked in real concern. "Not exactly," she said,
"But I'm still a novice." ' Baron and virgin are from an old style;
the new is in the 'not exactly' (saved again, though, by the 'But
I'm still a novice' which allows the structure of domination and
initiation to stand, having one's cake and eating it, getting sexual
experience and virginity all in one) and, especially, in the 'he
asked in real concern': women exist, we like them, we are really
genuinely concerned, they can be equals in our 'sexuality', and
that's liberation, theirs and ours.

   To come back more to your point, not only shouldn't different things be confused but it's also important to distinguish the
various emphases that the notion of liberation, sexual liberation,
can hold. Liberation *from* is one thing, liberation *of* is another, as
again is simple liberation, the term floating around in an entirely
abstract and self-confirming way, a kind of obvious and unques-
tionable goal and sphere of attainment like heaven. With liberation from, we are clearly involved in identifiable changes and
progress – significant transformations giving new possibilities,
new freedoms indeed. Developments in, information about and
availability of methods of contraception, for example, represent
a gain that is perfectly well describable as a liberation, liberation

from certain kinds of constraint which offers a control over the body and a different and easier patterning of sexual activity. Not that that is all there is to be said: the history of those developments is also and simultaneously analysable in regard to structures of male/female definition and domination, to the ways in which it has been ordered to fit in with 'sexuality' and to provide the conditions of circulation and exchange the latter demands; and there is a lot to say too in this connection about the role of medical authority, about the pharmaceutical industry, and so on; none of which is going to leave us in the end with a simple declaration of freedom won . . . Still I agree, of course, that there has been liberation from previous conditions, that that is real and good – 1980 is not 1880.

But liberation also brings liberation of, with the suggestion of 'of *what*?' We know the answer by now: 'sexuality', the thing, the nature to be freed, released into its own, precisely *liberated*. And so we're back into the fix and that's where the criticism is aimed, at that assumption of liberation, the 'sexual liberation' of which we've been made to hear so much. This is the point at which liberation becomes far removed from anything at all liberating, becomes on the contrary a command, the necessity of sex, what you should have, be and do, a whole programme, with orgasm as its pivot and goal.

X   No more orgasms either, I suppose – not one suspects that you ever had any anyway . . .

Y   It's a question of orgasm not orgasms, *the* orgasm, the Big O, the central fix and investment in that, the endless busying round that, the perpetual declaration that that's what it's all about, that that is and must be the actualization of desire, that that *is* the sexual. No surprise that above all other films it should have been *Deep Throat* that touched the contemporary imagination and emerged from the general anonymity of pornographic cinema. What is the premiss on which *Deep Throat* is based for its 'story'? A woman whose clitoris is located in her throat. Superb, the *ne plus ultra*, the acme of 'sexuality' today. Not only does the woman exist as the man's object, his sex, for him, reflecting his identity, not only does she have 'the orgasm', not only all that, *she has it where she speaks*, she can say it too, immediately, no gap between her sex – and so between mine – and what I want to hear, absolute proof that it all works. That's the role of the pants and cries and screams in pornographic cinema, they prove that she's having my orgasm and that therefore I am too. And the more women – and men – slip out of that identity, that visibility, that proof, the more violent the reaction. It's not by chance, for example, that the strength of the women's movement in the seventies was accompanied by considerable growth in the pornography industry and a trend towards ever-increasing violence, with *Snuff* in 1976 being a symptom, not an exception – *Snuff*, you remember, was the film said to record the actual murder of a woman, 'Bitch, now you're going to get what you want!'

X   And I know what's coming next, support for the anti-porn lobby – you're a kind of poorly disguised Lord Longford or worse.

Y   I don't see how from the left there can be anything but sustained political and ethical opposition to pornography. The arguments have been strongly made – quite outside of any appeal to some mystique of the purity of man and woman or to some traditional and repressive moral system – and I can only quote and repeat them. Pornography objectifies people as bodies in relations of instrumental exchange and usage that are exploitative and fundamentally violent. The major aspect of that violence is the degrading of women – women as the things exchanged and used – but men too suffer from that degradation and the standard it proposes for them. 'Pornography is the theory and rape the practice' – learning to understand the truth of that statement – and to understand it personally, with respect to one's own life – is a political-ethical necessity. Objections of the type porn-is-just-harmless-fantasy-nothing-to-do-with-reality-and-anyway-no-one-can-prove-its-effects are simply ways of covering up that truth which need to be fought. Violence is already in the pornography, in its representations. Few would doubt that direct social action should be taken in connection with magazines or films designed to show and approve and exploit the degradation of a particular racial group but so many of us live with a tacit or explicit acceptance of pornography. Let me quote: 'Is it really too much for reasonable women and men to recognize hate when they see it? If I were to see the picture of a Jew tied, spread-eagled, stripped, whipped, sucking cock, I think I would conclude rather quickly that the person who made the picture did not hold Jews in high esteem. But put a woman in that picture. . . .'

X So then it's censorship, goodbye to freedom of speech . . .

Y It's surely difficult to see how pornography today has anything
to do with freedom of speech. What's involved is not freedom
but money: pornography is commercial exploitation – how do
you and I have any freedom of speech in it? And again, we are –
most of us – ready to agree limits in other areas, that of
incitement to racial hatred being one, but put a woman in that
picture, but talk of sex. . . . One of the results of the sexual fix is
the intense reluctance we have to envisage that there are real
political–ethical problems in the area of sexuality, that we really
do need to develop a critical sexual politics. What we are
constantly told is that we have such a politics, we live in it,
happy us, the sexual revolution, good sexual functioning, all
problems dealable and dealt with, orgasm on. No. We live in
capitalist societies with specific modes of the organization and
definition of social relations, with the sexual constructed and
represented as 'sexuality' as part of that organization and definition. Political choice is always at stake, not abstract philosophi-
cal debate about once and for all universal terms. Thus tolerance,
for instance, is not some self-evident everyone-agrees unchanging entity: it has reality and force in specific contexts. And in the
context of discussions about pornography is often merely the
liberal alibi of the existing system, tolerance in fact as the
acceptance of the basic *in*tolerance of pornography itself.

   The challenge for a left practice, though, is to speak and act in
relation to all this without falling into the terms of the right-
wing moral opposition movements, the terms of Lord Longford
or Mary Whitehouse or David Holbrook. And those terms
include censorship. What we need, in the struggle within this
existing society, is to find new and original and educative ways
of protest and resistance.

X Resistance is a good word for your attitude. Throughout everything there's this refusal of the natural, one suspects a real dislike
of sex. Maybe you just never managed it very well, that's your
problem, but you should try to realize nevertheless that there are
feelings, sensations, depths, a whole reality of the natural that is
experienced in sex, experience which makes – in the words of
two of the sexological writers you are so fond of criticizing – 'the
following observation blindingly obvious: namely, that it is the
right of a healthy body to respond sexually and that the sexual

responses of our bodies are naturally pleasurable'. That's true, we know the truth of it in our lives, your limitation is that you won't . . . or can't.

Y   Of course I want in many ways to say yes to your emphasis on experience, to the words you quote, but. . . . Really the point is that an appeal to nature, a nature, is always dangerous, is quickly and almost inevitably part of an argument that essentializes cultural constructions and values. The problem is starting from a nature, say sex, whereas we have to start each time from culture, the precise constituted materiality – we would have as it were to subtract from that to find nature, which indicates the latter's difficulty, its impossibility, but without denying it, stressing simply that it can never be assumed as such, is never some pure and absolute given. The sexual is natural, if you like, but always already cultural, always constructed. The appeal to nature and the natural is part of the construction of today's 'sexuality', part of its strength and ideological hold. It supports, for example, the projection of men and women into the image of 'the man' and 'the woman', locked into the representation of their 'natures' in the 'naturality' of sex, this 'sexuality', 'a primal penis and vagina joined forever, uniting their separate bodies'.

X   I'm sorry but once again people do actually have exactly that experience, there is this experience of abandonment, of a kind of involvement and loss in the physical with an intensity that does really bring a feeling of something primal. That's what some of the passages from the novels you quote are saying. You criticize the Erica Jong passage, for example, and perhaps some of the points you make are right, but all the same that's a real experience, recognized and felt by many people. You just say everything's oppressive, which leaves nothing, ignores the fact that these novels, descriptions and so on are expressions of something lived and authentic. I'll go further, I think you think in some twisted way that making love is wrong, that it's all a fix and an oppression and a great mistake, you have no notion of the genuine relations, pleasures, sensations, feelings one can have.

Y   Look, take the following from a recent novel: 'Sitting naked on top of Tony, his penis deep and strong inside her, Karen had thrown back her head. . . .' Contrary to what you've been trying to suggest, I don't doubt that that corresponds to a common reality of making love, including the feeling 'his penis

deep and strong inside her'. And I suppose I have to add, given
your suggestions, that I don't believe that it is somehow
automatically wrong for women to have this feeling nor even
for men to want them to. The problem is in the fact of the
representation. We can read those words in just about any novel
we pick up today, they repeat and confirm a standard picture and
position: man, woman, 'sexuality', she from him, the spectacle
of that for us; 'his penis deep and strong inside her' is *our* position
in the picture, not Karen's, is the desire we must have and follow
in the scenario of 'sexuality', the scenario exactly of a primal
penis and a primal vagina that takes it, accepts.

X   But you keep saying anyway that the sexual is always bound
up with representations, always implicated in constructions,
meanings. . . .

Y   Yes, the terms that we have, that come back to us ceaselessly
on our bodies, in our actions, are those of this constructed 'sexuality'. Hence that effect of a tourniquet of recognition and
alienation, belief and refusal, we can have so often with the
descriptions we read and with the things we ourselves say in
love, the phrases we use, the feelings we know – it's that, but it's
not that, and what else can it be but that, where are the terms
for the difference?

X   I'm afraid you're going to give me a speech on love, mutual
respect, warm human beings and so on.

Y   Not at all. That's part and parcel of the discourse of sexology and
'sexuality' too: organs, the act, good functioning, orgasm *plus*
total loving, any and every stereotype you want. A common
trend is towards a there's-sex-and-sex notion: on the one hand,
sex as 'pleasuring', good healthy fun; on the other, the sex that's
'the real thing', the big thing, the primal union, your whole
being. It's strong in novels: adventures, affairs, casual stuff, and
then, end of the novel, the person who introduces you to
something else, sex-love, man and woman, the two of you in
your 'deeply sexual human selves'. And I don't disagree that
there is a reality of experience in all this, that we can and do feel
in that way. Simply, why should the endless variety of the
sexual and its relations in our lives from moment to moment in
the movement of our experience, why should that variety be
fitted into a casual/deep paradigm which denies it, fixes it, holds
us to 'sexuality' and the given terms of the investment in that?

It's the coercion again: either the casual, cool, like drinking a glass of water or – in fact *and*, the two hang together – the deep, real, ultimate, the 'primal penis and vagina joined forever'. Suppose neither of those versions fits all or any or some of my experience: am I ill, inadequate, lacking, not functioning properly, somehow not quite right? Yes I am, by the standard of 'sexuality'. And note how well those two versions match up with our society's requirement of circulation (exchange) and stability (the identities with which the exchange works): glass of water and primal penis/vagina, 'the man'/'the woman', Ultranorm Ltd. indeed.

X   You should see a sexologist or a psychoanalyst or both, I'm absolutely convinced of it. What credentials do you have to be going on about all this anyway?

Y   None, but then isn't the idea of credentials here part of 'sexuality' itself and its construction of the sexual? So that you have two kinds of authority: doctors–sexologists and those who are 'good in bed' (have had lots of 'experience'). The latter have either learnt from the former and so been initiated into the state of liberation or else they're just naturals, uncivilized and sexy (remember Reich and Cooper on the orgasmic character of the working classes and the third world). And as for the former, the sexologists themselves, they're generally also presented as being pretty hot – adventurous, sexually ok, always ready to join in a good thrash (I suppose the prize goes to Alex Comfort of *The Joy of Sex* fame as described by Gay Talese: 'Often the nude biologist Dr Alex Comfort, brandishing a cigar, traipsed through the room between the prone bodies with the professional air of a lepidopterist strolling through the fields waving a butterfly net, or an ornithologist tracking along the surf a rare species of tern. A gray-haired bespectacled owlish man with a well-preserved body, Dr Comfort was unabashedly drawn to the sight of sexually engaged couples and their concomitant cooing, considering such to be enchanting and endlessly instructive; and with the least amount of encouragement – after he had deposited his cigar in a safe place – he would join a friendly clutch of bodies and contribute to the merriment.'). But there isn't and shouldn't be any standard of life that guarantees sexuality, sexual being . . . whether you have ten thousand orgasms a year or none doesn't bring you nearer to or remove you further from sexuality, the fact of the human sexual, though it may from 'sexuality', the specific definition and construction of what that human sexual is. It's possible for me to 'go on', as you put it, without 'credentials', simply from an attempt to understand that historical definition and construction, to look at its terms, to speak indeed from the position of someone living today in relation to it, to that 'sexuality'. That's all, a small contribution to sexual politics, nothing more.

X   I knew you didn't have the faintest idea. I think maybe a good clinic. . . .

Y   We need to claim and realize against 'sexuality' the possibility of being as concrete individualities and not as identities, those identities of man and woman, the fictions of oppression. It's a political, social struggle – and one that we have to learn to carry through in every moment of our lives, our 'personal lives', at every point of our individual existence and experience, no matter how natural and primal and so on we are told to believe and end up believing it is. All I've done is to examine something of the fix, take up one or two of the major myths, try to weaken the thickness of the whole ideology. . . .

X   Enough! No more speeches, please! I'm going to say of you what you said of sexology, read but don't believe.

Y   That's what I want, that people *shouldn't believe.*

X   As for me, I'm going back to what I was reading before. You're not much fun, sexology's much more entertaining, let alone all these novels and films we have today, sex, passion, violence . . . Here, take sexology on fertilization. 'This process can be likened to imagining the whole population of London standing at one end of Lake Windermere ready, on a word of command, to plunge in and swim to the other end, the first one reaching there being like the sperm which meets the egg. It is a pretty crowded business with wholesale slaughter on the way.' That's my style, no nonsense and a good climax, fuck 'sexuality'!

Notes

I

page
1   'a sex-bomb . . .'
    New Man & Woman (London: Marshall Cavendish, 1980) part 21 p. 402.

    'If you're not sure . . .'
    ibid. p. 401.

    'We are all . . .'
    title of a book by French sexologist Michel Meignant, *Nous sommes tous des pervers sexuels persécutés* (Paris: Robert Laffont, 1980).

    'it is sometimes . . .'
    Michel Meignant, *Je t'aime: le livre rouge de la sexologie humaniste* (Paris: Buchet/Chastel, 1975) p. 222.

    'So let's . . .'
    'J' (Joan Terry Garrity), *Total Loving* (St Albans and London: Granada Publishing, 1978) p. 11.

    'magnificent work . . .' / 'terribly complicated . . .'
    ibid. pp. 74–5.

    'refuel in bed'
    Alayne Yates, *Sex Without Shame* (London: Futura Publications, 1980) p. 134.

    '*Your sexual equipment* . . .'
    'J', *Total Loving*, p. 96.

    'fabulous . . .' / 'contract . . .' / 'once . . .'
    ibid. p. 93

2   'those who ask . . .'
    Yates, *Sex Without Shame*, p. 8.

    Clearly you want . . .
    The books mentioned are: Paul Brown and Carolyn Faulder, *Treat Yourself to Sex* (Harmondsworth: Penguin Books, 1979); Iain Stewart, *Good Sex Guide* (London: Ocean Books, 1972); Alex Comfort, *The Joy of Sex: Gourmet Guide to Lovemaking* (London: Quartet Books, 1974) and *More Joy of Sex* (London: Quartet Books, 1977); Frank S. Caprio, *Your Right to Sex Happiness* (New York: Citadel Books, 1966); John E. Eichenlaub, *The Troubled Bed: The Obstacles to Sexual Happiness and What You Can Do About Them* (New York: Delacorte Press, 1971); Abraham I. Friedman, *How Sex Can Keep You Slim* (Englewood Cliffs, N.J.: Prentice-Hall, 1972); 'J', *Total Loving*; Rachel Moss (ed.), *God Says Yes to Sexuality* (London: Collins, 1981). It might be added that

the number of sex titles is enormous, something we know from experience of any bookstall. Many authors, including some of those just cited, are indefatigably prolific in all directions on the fix front. Frank S. Caprio, for example, is the author not only of the obligatory *The Sexually Adequate Female* (Greenwich, Conn.: Fawcett, 1953) but equally of *How to Heighten Your Sexual Pleasure Through Simple Mental Stimulation* (New York: Galahad Books, 1974) and *How to Solve Your Sex Problems With Self-Hypnosis* (Hollywood: Wilshire Book Co., 1972), plus many more . . .

2   'you are . . .'
'J', *Total Loving*, p. 98.

'melting erections . . .'
Yates, *Sex Without Shame*, p. 30.

'the natural state . . .'
Meignant, *Je t'aime*, p. 48.

'catapulted . . .'
'J', *Total Loving*, p. 74.

4   'the new understanding . . .' / 'The only rights . . .'
Brown and Faulder, *Treat Yourself to Sex*, pp. 7, 23.

'sex is . . .'
David Holbrook, *The Masks of Hate* (Oxford: Pergamon Press, 1972) p. 73.

a book entitled . . .
Mary Whitehouse, *Whatever Happened to Sex?* (London: Hodder & Stoughton, 1978).

II

page

7   'It was a moment . . .'
Thomas Hardy, *Tess of the d'Urbervilles* (1891) (London: Pan Books, 1978) p. 192.

9   whose novel *Sons and Lovers* . . .
The quotation is: 'the sex instinct that Miriam had over-refined for so long now grew particularly strong'
D. H. Lawrence, *Sons and Lovers* (1913) (Harmondsworth: Penguin Books, 1966) p. 308.

'The Woman's Question'
Pearson's essay is included in his volume *The Ethics of Freethought* (London, 1888); quotations are from p. 371.

10   'Socialism and Sex'
in Pearson, *The Ethics of Freethought*; quotation from p. 445.

10   'But I want to return . . .'
William Morris, *News From Nowhere* (1891), in *Three Works by William Morris*
(London: Lawrence & Wishart, 1968) pp. 240–1; the reference to 'English and
Jutish blood' is on p. 244.

12   the medical journal . . .
The Lancet 7 November 1857, p. 478.

Arthur Munby . . .
On Munby, see Michael Hiley, *Victorian Working Women: Portraits From Life*
(London: Gordon Fraser, 1979); Munby's photographs and papers are in the
library of Trinity College, Cambridge.

13   'infamous conduct . . .'
cit. Norman E. Hines, *Medical History of Contraception* (Baltimore: Williams &
Wilkins Co., 1936) p. 251; on birth control in this period, see Angus McLaren,
Birth Control in Nineteenth Century England (London: Croom Helm, 1978).

14   'adding shilling . . .'
'Walter', *My Secret Life*, abridged version edited by Phyllis and Eberhard
Kronhausen as (inevitably) *Walter the English Casanova* (London: Polybooks,
1967) p. 238.

17   'most women . . .'
William Acton, *The Functions and Disorders of the Reproductive Organs* (1857) 3rd
edn (London, 1862) p. 101; for the 'society' slip, see 5th edn (London, 1871)
p. 115.

'the best mothers . . .'
ibid. (3rd edn) p. 102.

III

page

19   'Debate in Congregation . . .'
C. L. Dodgson, diary entry for 11 March 1884, *The Diaries of Lewis Carroll*
ed. R. L. Green (London: Cassell, 1953) vol. II p. 424.

'The first is . . .'
Harold Merskey, *The Analysis of Hysteria* (London: Baillière Tindall, 1979)
p. 131.

'the great similitude' / 'the difference . . .'
Thomas Sydenham (writing in 1681), *The Entire Works of Dr Thomas Sydenham*
(London, 1742) p. 368.

'upon the whole . . .'
Robert Whytt, *Observations on the Nature, Causes and Cure of those disorders
which have been commonly called Nervous, Hypochondriac or Hysteric* (Edinburgh,
1765) p. 107.

20 'hypochondria usually . . .'
E. F. Dubois, *Histoire philosophique de l'hypochondrie et de l'hystérie* (Paris, 1833) p. 22.

'physicians have . . .'
Whytt, *Observations*, p. iii.

21 Lallemand
Claude-François Lallemand, *Des Pertes séminales involontaires* (Paris 1836–42).

'the battle . . .'
J. L. Milton, *On the Pathology and Treatment of Spermatorrhoea* 12th edn (London, 1887) p. 5.

'the present state . . .'
ibid. p. 6.

'seminal emissions . . .'
ibid. p. 14.

'in men . . .'
ibid. p. 16.

'lads . . .'
ibid. p. 19.

'an emission . . .' / 'a very dangerous tenet'
ibid. pp. 12–13.

'I am putting . . .'
ibid. p. 30.

'will grapple . . .'
ibid. p. 30.

'epilepsy . . .'
ibid. p. 33.

22 'it is useless . . .'
ibid. p. 161.

'urethral ring' / 'electric alarum'
Laws Milton provides drawings of these two appliances (pp. 129 and 132), together with the name and address of a supplier. Nor is he alone in his various suggested remedies. Acton, for example, shows much of the same detailed obsessiveness and rigour: 'I advise an early riser to take lodgings at St John's Wood and attend the Public Gymnasium at Primrose Hill from six to eight AM. After that hour the place is beset by small boys. . . .' *The Functions and Disorders* 1st edn (London, 1857) p. 80; 'walk four or six miles, in flannel waistcoat and drawers, two pairs of trousers, comforter, and two coats; then come home, lay under a feather-bed for an hour, and sponge over', ibid. p. 81. He is perhaps less inclined, however, to some of the more extreme mechanical treatments: 'Trouseau . . . recommends an instrument to pass up the rectum to press on the vesiculae, and mechanically prevent the emissions. I have tried the plan on one or two patients, but was obliged to leave it off, as I found that it produced considerable irritation', ibid. p. 80.

22   '*connexion has . . .*'
Laws Milton, *On the Pathology*, p. 174.

'He will go on . . .'
ibid. p. 29.

'the frame still . . .'
ibid. p. 174.

23   'barristers . . .'
ibid. p. 173.

24   'Ch. I . . .' / 'Ch. III . . .'
John Davenport, *Curiositates Eroticae Physiologiae* (London, 1875) pp. ix, xii. The French epitaph mentioned, roughly translated, is as follows: 'I died of love undertaken between the legs of a lady, happy to have lost my life in the same place where I was given it'; Davenport then goes on to add the appropriate Victorian gloss, 'the unfortunate story of a young man whose hand had been amputated, and who, when the cure was nearly, but not quite, effected, having wished to embrace his wife, and being forbidden by the surgeon, had recourse to masturbation, and died four days afterwards', pp. 69–70.

25   'this supreme . . .'
'Walter', *My Secret Life*, p. 234.

'his positive . . .'
ibid. p. 236 (comment by editors Phyllis and Eberhard Kronhausen).

'we must steer clear . . .'
Charles Kingsley, letter to J. S. Mill (1870), *Charles Kingsley: His Letters and Memories of His Life edited by His Wife* (London, 1877) vol. II p. 247.

26   'I was ready . . .' / 'If you won't . . .' / 'I was so . . .' / 'The hysterical passion . . .' / '*Then* . . .'
Wilkie Collins, *The Moonstone* (1868), Penguin English Library edition (Harmondsworth: Penguin Books, 1978) pp. 130, 253, 280, 403, 422.

27   'a green woman . . .'
Cf. N. P. Davies, *The Life of Wilkie Collins* (Urbana: University of Illinois Press, 1956) p. 4.

'As she laughed . . .'
T. S. Eliot, 'Hysteria', *Collected Poems 1909–1962* (London: Faber & Faber, 1963) p. 34.

a very long history
For an account of the history, see Ilza Veith, *Hysteria: The History of a Disease* (Chicago and London: University of Chicago Press, 1965).

28   'failure to recognize . . .'
E. M. Thornton, *Hypnotism, Hysteria and Epilepsy: An Historical Synthesis* (London: Heinemann, 1976) p. 115.

'a vigorous entity . . .'
Merskey, *The Analysis of Hysteria*, p. 234.

28 'Hysteria: a condition . . .'
Brain Injuries Committee (Medical Research Council), War Memorandum No. 4: *A Glossary of Psychological Terms Commonly Used in Cases of Head Injury* (1941), cit. Merskey, *The Analysis of Hysteria* p. 258.

29 'the matrix or womb . . .'
Plato, *Timaeus* § 91, *Timaeus and Critias* (Harmondsworth: Penguin Books, 1971) p. 120.

'an affect of the Mother . . .'
Edward Jorden, *A Briefe Discourse of a Disease called the Suffocation of the Mother* (London, 1603) pp. 5–6.

'the Vapours . . .'
Joseph Addison, *The Spectator* no. 115 (12 July 1711), *The Spectator* ed. D. F. Bond (Oxford: Clarendon Press, 1965) vol. I p. 473. Earlier that year (3 March), the journal had carried an advertisement for Bernard de Mandeville's 'just published' *Treatise of the Hypochondriack and Hysteric Passions, vulgarly called the Hypo in Men and Vapours in Women.*

30 'hysteria, male and female'
Kingsley, letter to J. S. Mill, p. 270.

'emotion is . . .'
Robert Brudenell Carter, *On the Pathology and Treatment of Hysteria* (London, 1853) p. 25.

'that protean disease . . .'
The Lancet 3 January 1891, p. 2; the lecture by Dr Robert Saundby was on 'Toxic Hysteria'. It can be noted that Sydenham in 1681 was already lamenting the difficulty of comprehending hysteria 'under any uniform appearance', it confronting the physician with 'a kind of disorderly train of symptoms; so that 'tis a difficult task to write the history of this disease', *The Entire Works* p. 375.

31 'the first cunt-knight . . .'
cit. Lawrence Stone, *The Family, Sex and Marriage in England 1500–1800* (London: Weidenfeld & Nicolson, 1977) p. 73.

32 'notwithstanding . . .'
Merskey, *The Analysis of Hysteria*, p. 233.

IV

page

33
'He seems to have . . .'
S. Freud, letter to C. G. Jung (19 September 1907), *The Freud/Jung Letters* ed. William McGuire (London: Hogarth and Routledge & Kegan Paul, 1974) p. 89

(the fellow psychoanalyst in question was Max Eitingon, who was to become a Charter member of the Berlin Psychoanalytic Society and who later founded the Palestine Psychoanalytic Society).

34   'the strange practices . . .'
A full discovery of the strange practices of Dr Elliotson . . . , pamphlet (London, no date). Dickens was greatly interested in the hypnotic demonstrations and took up Elliotson's cause when the latter was forced to resign from University College Hospital. The two men became friends, Elliotson acting as godfather to Dickens's fourth child and as the Dickens family doctor. Elliotson was also quoted in Wilkie Collins's *The Moonstone* in connection with a complicated experiment involving laudanum and the acting out of past occurrences. Thackeray dedicated his novel *The History of Pendennis* to Elliotson.

35   'the result of ideas . . .'
Freud, 'Charcot' (1893), *The Standard Edition of the Complete Psychological Works of Sigmund Freud* 24 vols (London: Hogarth, 1953–74) vol. III p. 22.

'authors, journalists . . .'
Axel Munthe, *The Story of San Michele* (1929) (London: John Murray, 1975) p. 214; Munthe attended Charcot's Tuesday lessons and gives a vivid account in a chapter entitled 'La Salpêtrière' (pp. 214–26).

36   can report having seen . . . and cite . . .
Merskey, *The Analysis of Hysteria*, p. 21.

a three-volume 'iconography' . . .
D. Bourneville and P. Regnard, *Iconographie photographique de la Salpêtrière* 3 vols (Paris, 1876–80).

37   'it is obvious . . .'
Freud, letter to Jung (11 December 1908), *The Freud/Jung Letters*, p. 187.

'the genital thing'
Freud, 'On the History of the Psycho-Analytic Movement' (1914), *Standard Edition* vol. XIV p. 14 ('Charcot suddenly broke out with great animation: Mais, dans des cas pareils c'est toujours la chose génitale, toujours . . . toujours . . . toujours [But in this sort of case it's always a question of the genitals – always, always, always]; and he crossed his arms over his stomach, hugging himself and jumping up and down on his toes several times in his own characteristically lively way.').

38   'Mummy!' / 'someone with . . .'
J. M. Charcot, Salpêtrière lessons 1887–8, *L'Hystérie* texts edited by E. Trillat (Toulouse: Privat, 1971) pp. 119, 113.

39   'the genuineness . . .' / 'an old surgeon . . .'
Freud, *An Autobiographical Study* (1924), *Standard Edition* vol. XX pp. 13, 15.

40   'when this had been . . .'
Joseph Breuer, *Studies on Hysteria* (1893–5, in collaboration with Freud), *Standard Edition* vol. II p. 35.

40   '*hysterics suffer* . . . '
Breuer and Freud, ibid. p. 7.

'*by means of* . . . '
Freud, ibid. p. 268.

41   'no one . . . '
Freud, 'Fragment of an Analysis of a Case of Hysteria' (1901), *Standard Edition* vol. VII p.113.

'the indispensable . . . '
Freud, letter to Jung (19 April 1908), *The Freud/Jung Letters*, pp. 140–1.

'Sexual motive forces . . . '
Freud, 'The Aetiology of Hysteria' (1896), *Standard Edition* vol. III p. 200.

42   'It is not . . . '
Freud, 'Further Remarks on the Neuro-Psychoses of Defence' (1896), *Standard Edition* vol. III p. 164.

'I have learned . . . '
Freud, 'My Views on the Part Played by Sexuality in the Aetiology of the Neuroses' (1905), *Standard Edition* vol. VII p. 274.

43   'Fortunately, for our therapy . . . '
Freud, letter to Jung (14 June 1907), *The Freud/Jung Letters*, p. 64.

Charcot . . . Breuer . . . Chrobak . . .
Freud, 'On the History of the Psycho-Analytic Movement', pp. 13-15.

44   'assign chemical processes . . . '
Freud, *An Autobiographical Study*, p. 25.

45   'aberration . . . ' / 'an instance . . . '
Freud, *Three Essays on the Theory of Sexuality* (1905), *Standard Edition* vol. VII p. 231.

'the royal road . . . '
Freud, *The Interpretation of Dreams* (1900), *Standard Edition* vol. V p. 608.

46   'I was going back . . . '
Freud, *An Autobiographical Study*, p. 24.

'all women play on . . . '
Michèle Montrelay, *L' Ombre et le nom: sur la féminité* (Paris: Minuit, 1977) p. 28.

'has stemmed . . . '
cit. Max Schur, *Freud: Living and Dying* (New York: International Universities Press, 1972) p. 546; the poem, one of the very few poems Freud ever wrote, was sent in a letter to Fliess dated 29 December 1898.

'the hysterical position . . . '
Irène Diamantis, 'Recherches sur la féminité', *Ornicar? – Analytica* vol. 5 (July 1977) p. 27.

46   'pressed her dress . . .'
Freud, 'Hysterical Phantasies and their Relation to Bisexuality' (1908), *Standard Edition* vol. IX p. 166.

47   'the polar character . . .'
Freud, 'My Views on the Part Played by Sexuality in the Aetiology of the Neuroses', p. 272.

'we have been in the habit . . .'
Freud, 'Some Psychical Consequences of the Anatomical Distinction between the Sexes' (1925), *Standard Edition* vol. XIX p. 249.

'we need not feel . . .'
Freud, *The Question of Lay Analysis* (1926), *Standard Edition* vol. XX p. 212.

48   'God . . .'
Jacques Lacan, *Encore, le séminaire livre XX* (Paris: Seuil, 1975) p. 78.

'Queen Victoria . . .'
Lacan, seminar 11 February 1975, *Ornicar?* no. 4 p. 94.

'I have a woman friend . . .'
Moustapha Safouan, *L'Echec du principe du plaisir* (Paris: Seuil, 1979) p. 43; an English version of this incident can be found in Safouan's paper 'Representation and Pleasure', in *The Talking Cure* ed. C. MacCabe (London: Macmillan, 1981) pp. 85–6.

V

page

51   'There were . . .'
Erica Jong, *Fear of Flying* (1973) (St Albans: Panther Books, 1979) p. 11 (this is the novel's opening sentence).

'Sexuality became . . .'
Wilhelm Reich, *Reich Speaks of Freud* (Harmondsworth: Penguin Books, 1975) p. 105n.

'They regard me . . .'
Freud, letter to Fliess (21 May 1894), *The Origins of Psycho-Analysis* (London: Imago, 1954) p. 83.

52   'every bedroom . . .'
Brown and Faulder, *Treat Yourself to Sex*, p. 17.

52–3 'something effectively incurable . . .'
Jacques-Alain Miller (leading disciple of Lacan), radio interview with Y. Levai, Europe I, 11 January 1980.

53   'we refuse . . .' / 'the real symptom'
Claude van Ruth, 'La demande d'orgasme', in *Psychologie et sexualité* ed. J. P. Birouste and J. P. Martineau (Toulouse: Privat, 1976) pp. 213, 215.

54   'He is big chief . . .'
      Jung, letter to Freud (18 May 1911), *The Freud/Jung Letters*, p. 423.

      'Magnus Hirschfeld . . .'
      Freud, letter to Jung (2 November 1911) ibid. pp. 453–4.

      'a disposition to . . .'
      Freud, *Three Essays on the Theory of Sexuality*, p. 231.

56   'observations of . . .' / 'Recorded and observed . . .'
      William H. Masters and Virginia E. Johnson, *Human Sexual Response* (New
      York: Bantam Books, 1980) pp. 9, 20.

57   'this book is intended . . .'
      Alfred C. Kinsey, Wardell B. Pomeroy and Clyde E. Martin, *Sexual Behaviour
      in the Human Male* (Philadelphia and London: W. B. Saunders Co., 1948),
      publisher's note.

57–8 'this man and woman . . .' / 'subject C . . .'
      Masters and Johnson, *Human Sexual Response*, pp. 305, 307.

58   'Psychoanalysis is bound down . . .' / 'Freud succeeded . . .'
      Reich, *Reich Speaks of Freud*, pp. 21, 38–9.

      'The "talking cure" . . .'
      David Cooper, *Grammar of Living* (Harmondsworth: Penguin Books, 1976) p.
      122.

59   'we have to . . .' / 'Contact at Sandstone . . .'
      cit. Gay Talese, *Thy Neighbour's Wife: Sex in the World Today* (London: Collins,
      1980) pp. 194, 332.

60   'very much dissatisfied . . .' / '*most psychoanalysts* . . .'
      Reich, *Reich Speaks of Freud*, pp. 33, 31.

VI

page

61   'The Erotic Path . . .'
      'J', *Total Loving*, p. 76.

      'I'm always very apprehensive . . .'
      Meignant, *Je t'aime*, p. 122.

62   'vivid orgasm . . .'
      William Howitt, *Homes and Haunts of the Most Eminent British Poets* (London,
      1847) vol. I p. 425.

      'for 30 years . . .'
      The Lancet 22 November 1862, p. 570; Tilt is reported as making this comment
      in a monograph under review entitled *Uterine and Ovarian Inflammation*.

      'Nature intends . . .' / 'with orgasms . . .'
      'J', *Total Loving*, pp. 102, 90.

63   'the naked ape . . .' / 'By making . . .'
        Desmond Morris, *The Naked Ape* (1967) (St Albans and London: Triad/
        Panther Books, 1979) pp. 56, 73.

64   'is limited to . . .'
        Masters and Johnson, *Human Sexual Response*, p. 6.

        'of rapid return to . . .' / 'of maintaining . . .'
        ibid. p. 131.

65   'Other female primates . . .' / 'a "borrowed" male pattern'
        ibid. pp. 49, 70.

        'blind beakishness'
        D. H. Lawrence, *Lady Chatterley's Lover* (1928) (Harmondsworth: Penguin
        Books, 1960) p. 210 ('They talk about men's selfishness, but I doubt if it can
        ever touch a woman's blind beakishness, once she's gone that way. Like an old
        trull!'; in *The Plumed Serpent* (1926), Lawrence had already talked of 'beak-like
        friction', 'the seething electric female ecstasy', and brought his heroine Kate to
        'realize the worthlessness of this foam-effervescence' (Harmondsworth: Pen-
        guin Books, 1971) p. 439.

        'the uterine orgasm'
        'Female Orgasm, Where Are You?', *Playboy* vol. 27 no. 7 (July 1980) p. 264.

        'IT HAPPENS . . .'
        'J', *Total Loving*, p. 78.

66   six possible sources
        Kinsey *et al.*, *The Sexual Behaviour of the Human Male*, p. 159.

        'It's not just to fuck . . .'
        Reich, *Reich Speaks of Freud*, p. 37.

        '*the repression . . .*'
        Cooper, *The Grammar of Living*, p. 40.

        'partial releases . . .' / 'ultimate vegetatively involuntary surrender'
        Reich, *The Function of the Orgasm* (1942) (St Albans and London: Panther
        Books, 1968) pp. 119, 120.

        '*phallic-pornographic-clitoral . . .*'
        Reich, *Reich Speaks of Freud*, p. 241.

        'clitoral genitality . . .' / 'there are human beings . . .'
        Reich, *The Function of the Orgasm*, p. 201.

67   'in the first-world bourgeoisie . . .'
        Cooper, *The Grammar of Living*, p. 44.

        'In the sexual act . . .'
        Lawrence Lipton, *The Holy Barbarians* (New York: Julian Messner, 1959)
        p. 158.

        'Orgastically potent individuals . . .' / 'the healthy woman . . .'
        Reich, *The Function of the Orgasm*, pp. 116–17, 118.

67   'it is so essential . . .'
        Cooper, *The Grammar of Living*, p. 42.

        'Looking an individual . . .'
        Kinsey *et al.*, *The Sexual Behaviour of the Human Male*, p. 54.

68   'orgasm is a matter . . .' / 'One can always . . .'
        Cooper, *The Grammar of Living*, pp. 44, 41.

        '*Keep that erotic stimulation . . .*'
        'J', *Total Loving*, p. 91.

        human male and female 'cycles'
        Cf. Masters and Johnson, *Human Sexual Response*, pp. 4–7.

69   a kind of orgasm model
        Cf. Reich, *The Function of the Orgasm*, pp. 114–21.

        'normally . . .'
        ibid. p. 120.

        'It starts . . .'
        'J', *Total Loving*, p. 76.

70   'It's . . .' / 'oblivious to . . .' / 'And then . . .' / 'You slide down . . .'
        ibid. pp. 76–8.

        'A pale light . . .'
        Yates, *Sex Without Shame*, p. 3.

        'the equipment . . .'
        Masters and Johnson, *Human Sexual Response*, p. 21.

        'his whole body . . .'
        Yates, *Sex Without Shame*, p. 3.

        'the fabulous love muscle' / 'those fabulous orgasmic sensations' / 'you are
        quivering . . .' / 'a delicious swelling . . .'
        'J', *Total Loving*, pp. 93, 91, 77, 76.

71   'hands . . .' / 'legs . . .'
        New Man & Woman, p. 403.

        'you have . . .'
        Meignant, *Je t'aime*, p. 47.

        'Verily . . .'
        'Walter', *My Secret Life*, p. 188.

        'ERASE . . .'
        'J', *Total Loving*, pp. 104–9

        'Rinse yourself down . . .'
        Meignant, *Je t'aime*, pp. 49–50.

        'On the subject . . .'
        ibid. p. 108.

71   'a moistened middle finger'
      Brown and Faulder, *Treat Yourself*, p. 61.

      Gerald Zwang
      Lettre ouverte aux mal-baisants (Paris: Albin Michel, 1975).

      'In a recent questionnaire . . .'
      Cooper, *The Grammar of Living*, p. 115 n.

72–3 'A medical student . . .' / 'One lady . . .' / 'Walter intimated . . .'
      Yates, *Sex Without Shame*, pp. 12, 65, 26.

74–5 'Just imagine . . .' / 'for most of the time . . .' / 'If a man selling . . .' / 'What
      if . . .' / 'it is like having . . .' / 'It may be helpful . . .'
      Brown and Faulder, *Treat Yourself*, pp. 16, 93, 17–18, 22, 35, 141.

75   'Hélène: "François is . . ."' / 'I am . . .'
      Meignant, *Je t'aime*, pp. 17, 42.

      'while it is . . .'
      'J', *Total Loving*, p. 78.

      'put their fingers . . .'
      Reich, *Reich Speaks of Freud*, p. 95.

      'When the relationship . . .'
      ibid. pp. 94–5.

      'She wanted . . .' / 'her orgasms . . .'
      Cooper, *The Grammar of Living*, p. 114.

76   'Fellatio . . .'
      Meignant, *Je t'aime*, p. 98.

      'the advantage . . .'
      ibid. p. 46.

      'the natural . . .'
      ibid. p. 48.

      'natural sexuality' / 'natural emotional life expression' / 'natural (orgastic)
      sexual gratification' / 'surrender to . . .' / 'armouring . . .'
      Reich, *The Function of the Orgasm*, pp. 29, 30, 114.

76–7 'a time-less moment . . .' / For the sake of . . .' / 'as a dream . . .'
      Cooper, *The Grammar of Living*, pp. 41, 52–3, 105.

77   'good sex . . .'
      Brown and Faulder, *Treat Yourself*, p. 15.

      I Love You
      Translation of the title of the book already referred to by Michel Meignant, *Je
      t'aime: le livre rouge de la sexologie humaniste*.

      'sexuality is . . .'
      Bernard Muldworf, 'Irruption de la politique', *La Nef* no. 58 (1975) (special
      number devoted to 'love and sexuality') p. 38.

78   Robert T. Francoeur . . . outlines
      Francoeur gives this outline in his book *Eve's New Rib: Twenty Faces of Sex,
      Marriage and Family* (London: MacGibbon & Kee, 1972); Harrad College is first
      presented much as it is by Rimmer himself in his original novel *The Harrad
      Experiment* (1966), fiction as fact, and then taken over into discussion of
      proposals for educational developments, courses, etc. Rimmer's Harrad is said
      by Francoeur to represent 'a common if informal reality in many colleges and
      universities throughout the country', p. 48.

      'a long-time . . .' / 'after some . . .' / 'movies of . . .' / 'Rimmer suggests . . .'
      Francoeur, *Eve's New Rib*, pp. 43, 46, 193.

79   'if a girl . . .' / 'although . . .' / 'In one such party . . .'
      Yates, *Sex Without Shame*, pp. 146, 168.

      'we assume . . .' / 'Sheila Anne . . .' / 'Stanley Cole . . .' / 'show that . . .'
      Francoeur, *Eve's New Rib*, pp. 46, 44,

80   'You don't have to . . .' / 'for a badly . . .' / 'One glance . . .' / 'Realize. . . .' /
      '*Tell* him . . .' / 'your wanting . . .' / 'The modern . . .'
      'J', *Total Loving*, pp. 31, 31, 32-3, 125, 12, 9.

81   'the glorified body'
      Marielle David, *Lettres de l'École Freudienne* no. 19 (July 1976) p. 134.

      'the alpha . . .'
      Serge Leclaire, *Psychanalyser* (Paris: Seuil, 1968) p. 163.

      'An extinction . . .'
      Moustapha Safouan, *La Sexualité féminine* (Paris: Seuil, 1976) pp. 16–17.

82   'These young women . . .' / 'After having . . .'
      Meignant, *Je t'aime*, pp. 43, 153–4.

      'the woman's whole . . .' / '*women have* . . .' / 'Big Fuck' / '*mutual* penetration
      . . .' / 'today we recognize . . .' / 'the feeling quality . . .' / 'the beautiful . . .'
      Cooper, *The Grammar of Living*, pp. 44–9.

VII

page

85   'while Millicent . . .'
      J. J. Scott, 'The end-away justifies the means', *Mayfair* vol. 15 no. 7 (July 1980)
      p. 35.

      'Man is . . .' / 'the various forms . . .'
      Karl Marx, *A Contribution to the Critique of Political Economy* (1857) (Moscow:
      Progress Publications, 1977) p. 189.

87   Nancy Friday
My Secret Garden: Women's Sexual Fantasies (New York: Trident Press, 1973);
Forbidden Flowers: More Women's Sexual Fantasies (New York: Pocket Books,
1975); *Men in Love: Men's Sexual Fantasies: The Triumph of Love over Rage*
(London: Hutchinson, 1980).

'private papers . . .'
Gay Talese, *Thy Neighbour's Wife*, p. 548.

'Receptionist . . .'
'Quest: The Laboratory of Human Response', *Mayfair* vol. 15 no. 7 (July 1980)
pp. 92–3.

88   'The first time . . .'
Lynda Schor, 'Some Perspectives on the Penis' ('a leading erotic writer takes a
long hard look at one of the tools of her trade'), *Playboy* vol. 27 no.7 (July 1980)
p. 151 ('the kind of penis I like for sex is a well-rounded one that enjoys
everything', p. 184).

Get a number of personalities . . .
Karl and Anne Fleming (eds), *The First Time* (New York: Medallion Books,
1973).

television and Sunday newspaper performer
Clive James, *Unreliable Memoirs* (London: Cape, 1980).

'I had sex . . .'
Playgirl vol. VII no.11 (April 1980) p. 8 ('His erect cock sprang loose from its
fabric prison and stood out throbbing from his body').

'one might wish' / 'women are possessed . . .' / 'Better than . . .'
John Philip Lundin, *Women* (1963) (London: New English Library, 1980)
pp. 10, 221, 11.

89   'an entirely new . . .'
back cover blurb for James Jones, *Go to the Widow-Maker* (1968) (New York:
Dell, 1978).

90–1 'the heiress . . .' / 'the illimitable caprice . . .' / this was not . . .' / 'What was the
captain . . .' / 'such a pretty . . .'
Thomas Hardy, *A Laodicean* (1881) (London: Macmillan, 1975) pp. 354, 48,
124, 196–7, 193.

92   'Independent . . .'
Havelock Ellis, 'The Novels of Thomas Hardy', *Westminster Review* no. CXXVI
(April 1883).

'Jim knows nothing . . .'
cit. Richard Ellmann, *James Joyce* (New York: Oxford University Press, 1959)
p. 642.

93   'wildly, ribaldly funny . . .'
front cover blurb for Lisa Alther, *Kinflicks* (1976) (Harmondsworth: Penguin
Books, 1977).

93   'the Free Farm . . .' / 'locked in . . .' / 'Laverne was . . .' / where the woman . . .'
     / 'I knew that . . .' / 'Faster! . . .' / 'My nipples . . .' / 'The doctor held . . .'
     ibid. pp. 352, 353, 354, 356, 356, 326, 326, 377.

94   'Praxis, meaning . . .'
     Fay Weldon, *Praxis* (1978) (London: Coronet Books, 1980) p. 9.

     'this was . . .' / 'a breathtaking . . .' / 'one that outdid . . .' / 'If you have . . .'
     Alther, *Kinflicks*, pp. 53, 304, 438, 513.

96   'She was beautiful . . .' / 'one of those . . .' / 'While I fix up . . .' / 'Poor little
     bitch . . .' / 'I never met . . .' / 'All you need . . .'
     Ian Fleming, *Goldfinger* (London: Pan Books, 1961) pp. 161, 189, 128, 205, 223,
     223.

97   'it took me . . .' / 'She studied herself . . .'
     H. B. Gilmour, *Eyes of Laura Mars* (London: Corgi Books, 1978) pp. 171,
     169–70.

98–9 'Yet she looked . . .' / 'deft body . . .' / 'Why had nobody . . .' / 'as she reached
     . . .' / 'My husband . . .' / 'I've never seen . . .'
     A. Alvarez, *Hers* (1974) (Harmondsworth: Penguin Books, 1977) pp. 9, 10,
     176, 218, 16.

99   'But this time . . .'
     Henry James, *The American* (1877): 1877 version – *The American* (London:
     Macmillan, 1879) p. 177; revision for 1907 New York Edition – *The American:
     The Version of 1877 revised in Autograph and Typescript for the New York Edition of
     1907* (facsimile) (London: Scolar, 1976) p. 226; final 1907 version – *The
     American* (New York: Charles Scribner's Sons, 1907) p. 272.

101 'Do you ever . . .' / 'we should have . . .'
     Peter Benchley, *Jaws* (1974) (London: Pan Books, 1975) pp. 156, 160.

     'Simon, have you never . . .'
     Kingsley Amis, *I Want It Now* (1968) (London: Panther Books, 1970) p. 93.

     'And then they both . . .'
     Erica Jong, *How To Save Your Own Life* (1977) (New York: Signet, 1978)
     pp. 285–6.

     'Then suddenly . . .'
     Jilly Cooper, *Octavia* (1977) (London: Corgi Books, 1978) p. 187.

     'Jerry and Sally . . .'
     John Updike, *Marry Me* (Greenwich, Conn.: Fawcett Crest, 1976) pp. 36–7.

102 'and she thought . . .'
     Jong, *How To Save Your Own Life*, p. 285.

     'through the . . .'
     Updike, *Marry Me*, p. 71.

     'Lawrence knew about . . .'
     Frieda Lawrence, letter to Frederick J. Hoffman (1942), cit. Frederick J.
     Hoffman and Harry T. Moore eds., *The Achievement of D. H. Lawrence*
     (Norman: University of Oklahoma Press, 1953) p. 109.

103 'the phallic hunting out' / 'to the very heart . . .' / 'to the real bedrock . . .' / 'the phallus alone . . .'
D. H. Lawrence, *Lady Chatterley's Lover*, pp. 258–9.

'She was withstanding him . . .'
D. H. Lawrence, *Aaron's Rod* (1922) (Harmondsworth: Penguin Books, 1972) p. 303.

Kate Millett . . . Norman Mailer . . . Carol Dix . . .
Kate Millett, *Sexual Politics* (New York: Doubleday, 1970); Norman Mailer, *The Prisoner of Sex* (Boston: Little, Brown & Co, 1971); Carol Dix, *D. H. Lawrence and Women* (London: Macmillan, 1980).

'far from treating . . .' / 'Recalling his . . .'
Dix, *D. H. Lawrence and Women*, pp. x, 76.

104 'Handicapped . . .' / 'her body went into . . .' / 'We're making . . .' / 'Then he took hold of . . .'
Amis, *I Want It Now*, pp. 94, 65, 93, 167.

106 'An Argument . . .'
Sir C. B., 'The Dreame', manuscript in the library of Harvard University; cit. Roger Thompson, *Unfit for Modest Ears* (London: Macmillan, 1979) p. 49.

'I to my chamber . . .'
The Diary of Samuel Pepys vol. IX, ed. R. Latham and W. Matthews (London: G. Bell, 1976) p. 59.

107 'when the stream . . .'
C. L. Dodgson, cit. Helmut Gernsheim, *Lewis Carroll Photographer* (New York: Dover, 1969) p. 18 ('About nine out of ten, I think, of my child friendships get shipwrecked at the critical point "when the stream and river meet", and the child friends, once so affectionate, become uninteresting acquaintances whom I have no wish to set eyes on again.').

'he had imagined . . .'
Effie Gray, letter to her parents (7 March 1854), in Mary Lutyens, *Millais and the Ruskins* (London: John Murray, 1967) p. 156.

108 'I *know* it is . . .'
D. H. Lawrence, *John Thomas and Lady Jane* (1927, = the second draft of *Lady Chatterley's Lover*) (Harmondsworth: Penguin Books, 1973) p. 312.

'The concept phallus . . .'
anonymous review, *Scilicet* no. 5 (1977) p. 115.

'the penis is . . .'
Lawrence, *John Thomas*, p. 238.

110 'deep inside . . .' / 'she went into . . .'
Lundin, *Women* pp. 26–7, 109.

'I know the penis . . .'
Lawrence, *John Thomas*, p. 312.

VIII

page

111   'I allow . . .'
      Madeleine Smith, letter to Émile L'Angelier (*circa* 1885), cit. P. Hunt, *The Madeleine Smith Affair* (London: Carrol & Nicholson, 1950) pp. 83–4.

      What does . . .
      Freud's question, *Was will das Weib?*, occurs in a letter to Marie Bonaparte: 'The great question that has never been answered and which I have not yet been able to answer, despite my thirty years of research into the feminine soul, is "What does a woman want?"'; cit. E. Jones, *Sigmund Freud: Life and Work* (London: Hogarth, 1953–7) vol. II, p. 468. Or as Erica Jong puts it in the mouth of her heroine Isadora Wing: 'What do you women want? Freud puzzled this and never came up with much.' *Fear of Flying*, p. 30.

      'give her . . .'
      D. H. Lawrence, 'Give Her a Pattern' (first appeared in the *Daily Express*, 19 June 1929, as 'The Real Trouble About Women'), in *Phoenix* vol II, ed. Warren Roberts and Harry T. Moore (London: Heinemann, 1968) pp. 535–8.

      'What Marsha . . .'
      Lundin, *Women*, p. 144.

      'For me the question . . .'
      Hélène Cixous, *La jeune née* (in collaboration with Catherine Clément) (Paris: Union Générale d'Éditions, 1975) p. 151.

112   'Let the woman . . .' / 'And Adam . . .'
      1 Timothy 2: 11–12, 14.

113   'Even so . . .'
      Virginia Woolf, *A Room of One's Own* (1929) (St Albans and London: Granada, 1977) p. 99.

115   'He had performed . . .'
      Lawrence, *Aaron's Rod*, p. 300.

116   'watch . . .'
      F. Nietzsche, *Beyond Good and Evil* (1886) (Harmondsworth: Penguin Books, 1978) p. 165.

      'Woman's desire . . .'
      Luce Irigaray, *Ce Sexe qui n'en est pas un* (Paris: Seuil, 1977) p. 25.

      'it is the woman . . .'
      Eugénie Lemoine-Luccioni, 'Ecrire', *Sorcières* no. 7 p. 14.

      'female pleasure . . .'
      Michèle Montrelay, *L'Ombre et le nom*, pp. 80–1.

      'it is obvious . . .'
      Hélène Cixous, 'Quelques questions à Hélène Cixous', *Les Cahiers du GRIF* no. 13 (October 1976) p. 20.

116   'a feminine textual body . . .'
H. Cixous, 'Le sexe ou la tête', *Les Cahiers du GRIF* no. 13 (October 1976) p. 14.

117   'the "I" . . .'
Mary Daly, *Gyn/Ecology* (London: The Women's Press, 1979) p. 327.

'cannot describe itself . . .'
Luce Irigaray, 'Woman's Exile', *Ideology and Consciousness* no. 1 (May 1977) p. 65.

'auto-affection' / 'two lips'
Irigaray, *Ce Sexe*, p. 130 ('I'm trying to say that the female sex would be, above all, made up of *"two lips"* . . . *these "two lips" are always joined in an embrace*' 'Woman's Exile', pp. 64–5).

'neither subject nor object'
ibid. p. 132. Translations of French feminist texts, including one or two pieces by Irigaray, can be found in *New French Feminisms* ed. Elaine Marks and Isabelle de Courtivron (Amherst: University of Massachusetts Press, 1980).

'the eschewing . . .'
Gillian Beer, 'Beyond Determinism: George Eliot and Virginia Woolf', in *Women Writing and Writing About Women* (London: Croom Helm, 1979) p. 95.

'the psychological sentence . . .' / 'of a more elastic . . .'
Virginia Woolf, 'Romance and the Heart' (1923), *Contemporary Writers* (London: Hogarth, 1965) pp. 124–5.

'the female . . .'
Ezra Pound, Canto XXIX, *The Cantos of Ezra Pound* (London: Faber & Faber, 1968) p. 149.

118   'But women . . .'
D. H. Lawrence, 'Do Women Change?' (1929), *Phoenix* II, p. 541.

'full self-responsibility . . .'
D. H. Lawrence, 'Matriarchy' (1928), *Phoenix* II, p. 552.

'If the male orgasm . . .'
Jean-Louis Tristani, *Le Stade du respir* (Paris: Minuit, 1978) p. 36.

'Feminine in its . . .'
Arnold Bennett, *The Journals of Arnold Bennett* ed. Newman Flower (London: Cassell, 1932) vol. I p. 6.

'feminine forgetfulness . . .'
Walter Pater, *Plato and Platonism* (1893) (London: Macmillan, 1920) p. 281.

'the female elements . . .'
Holbrook, *The Masks of Hate*, p. 237.

'the lovely henny surety . . .'
D. H. Lawrence, 'Cocksure Women and Hensure Men' (1929), *Phoenix* II, p. 555.

120   'women are women'
      Lawrence, 'Do Women Change?' (1929), *Phoenix* II, p. 538 (the title of the
      article on its original publication in the *Sunday Dispatch* answered the question:
      'Women Don't Change').

121   'She looked . . .' / 'Gustave was . . .'
      Margaret Anson, *The Merry Order of St Bridget: Personal Recollections of the Use of
      the Rod* ('York, 1857'; the true author was James G. Bertram, the place of
      publication London, the date 1868).

122   'Not a human being . . .'
      Hardy, *Tess of the d' Urbervilles*, pp. 191–2.

124   'After three verses . . .'
      Lawrence, *Aaron's Rod*, pp. 298–300.

      'the magic feeling . . .'
      ibid. p. 317.

      'the personality must . . .'
      Lawrence, *John Thomas*, p. 238.

126   'He took her . . .'
      Lawrence, *Lady Chatterley's Lover*, pp. 180–1.

128   'In the bedroom . . .'
      Cooper, *Octavia*, pp. 186–7.

129   'It was no good . . .'
      Jong, *How To Save Your Own Life*, pp. 285–6.

131   'But Nancy appealed . . .'
      Brigid Brophy, *Flesh* (1962) (London: Allison & Busby, 1979) pp. 44–6.

133   'Study sensation . . .'
      Kate Millett, *Flying* (1974) (St Albans: Paladin, 1976) pp. 539–40.

135   'If they ask me . . .'
      Adrienne Rich, 'The Stranger', *Diving into the Wreck: Poems 1971–1972* (New
      York: W. W. Norton, 1973) p. 19.

IX

page
137   'sexual in the sense . . .'
      Jones, *Go to the Widow-Maker*, p. 504.

      'The concepts . . .'
      S. Freud, cit. Frank J. Sulloway, *Freud: Biologist of the Mind* (London: Burnett
      Books, 1979) p. 431. Sulloway's book is a major study of the intellectual history
      of Freud's work and confirmed and helped much of the account given here.

      '"Masculine" . . .'
      Freud, *Three Essays on the Theory of Sexuality*, pp. 219–20.

139 'We are faced . . .'
Freud, 'An Outline of Psycho-Analysis' (1938), *Standard Edition* vol. XXIII, p. 188.

140 'in both sexes . . .'
Freud, 'The Psychogenesis of a Case of Homosexuality in a Woman' (1920), *Standard Edition* vol. XVIII, p. 154.

'the reactions . . .' / 'pure masculinity . . .'
Freud, 'Some Psychical Consequences of the Anatomical Distinction between the Sexes' (1925), *Standard Edition* vol. XIX, pp. 255, 258.

'the morphological distinction . . .'
Freud, 'The Dissolution of the Oedipus Complex' (1924); *Standard Edition* vol. XIX, p. 178.

141 'every man . . .'
D. H. Lawrence, *Study of Thomas Hardy* (1932), *Phoenix* I ed. Edward D. McDonald (London: Heinemann, 1961) p. 481.

'the man is . . .'
D. H. Lawrence, *Women in Love* (1921) (Harmondsworth: Penguin Books, 1961) p. 225.

143 'then the embryo . . .' / 'to masculinize . . .'
John Money and Anke A. Ehrhardt, *Man & Woman, Boy & Girl* (Baltimore and London: Johns Hopkins U.P., 1972) pp. 7, 8.

'Biological bisexuality . . .'
André Green, 'Le genre neutre', *Nouvelle Revue de la Psychanalyse* no. 7 (1973) pp. 251–2.

144 'modern genetic theory . . .'
Money and Ehrhardt, *Man & Woman*, p. 1.

145 'Sex, in so far as . . .'
Ezra Pound, 'Rémy de Gourmont' (1919), *Literary Essays of Ezra Pound* ed. T. S. Eliot (London: Faber & Faber, 1960) p. 341.

'Because . . .'
Jong, *Fear of Flying*, p. 40.

146 'bread *and* orgasm'
Cooper, *The Grammar of Living*, p. 40.

X

page

147 'But say you have . . .'
John Maynard Smith, cit. in 'The Bashed-in Cars Theory of Sex', *Sunday Times Magazine* 20 August 1978, p. 39.

147 'As she lowered . . .'
Talese, *Thy Neighbour's Wife*, p. 37.

'which, if followed carefully . . .'
Brown and Faulder, *Treat Yourself*, p. 8.

148 'When did you first . . .'
Cf. Stephen Fay, 'Gay Talese's Sexual Odyssey', *Sunday Times Magazine* 29 June 1980, p. 24.

'the immense behavioural reward . . .'
Morris, *The Naked Ape*, p. 69

'the female way . . .'
Cooper, *The Grammar of Living*, p. 41.

according to *Playboy*
article cited, 'Female Orgasm, Where Are You?'

'it is in as much . . .'
J. Lacan, *Encore*, p. 77.

'woman made whole'
Lacan, seminar 11 March 1975.

149 'Talese insists . . .'
Fay, 'Gay Talese's Sexual Odyssey', p. 29.

'These chicks . . .'
Hugh Hefner, internal *Playboy* memo 1969, cit. Susan Braudy, 'The Article I Wrote on Women That *Playboy* Wouldn't Publish', *Glamour* May 1971, p. 202.

150 'the dream and love laboratory . . .'
Cooper, *The Grammar of Living*, p. 2.

151 'the average middle-class male . . .'
Yates, *Sex Without Shame*, p. 66.

'it is only unfortunate . . .'
Cooper, *The Grammar of Living*, p. 127.

'Pride, desire and anxiety . . .'
Gilbert Tordjman, *Réalités et problèmes de la vie sexuelle* (Paris: Hachette, 1978) p. 42.

152 'Homosexual desire . . .'
Guy Hocquenghem, *Le Désir homosexuel* (Paris: Éditions Universitaires, 1972) p. 12.

153 'Sex without . . .'
Robert H. Rimmer, *The Harrad Experiment* (1966) (New York: Bantam Books, 1978) p. 334 (the front cover of this edition describes the book as 'the sex manifesto of the free love generation').

155 'In girls . . .'
S. Freud, 'On Transformations of Instinct as Exemplified in Anal Erotism' (1917), *Standard Edition* vol. XVII p. 132.

155 'When a girl . . .'
Freud, 'On the Sexual Theories of Children' (1908), *Standard Edition* vol. IX p. 218.

156 'the question . . .'
Tillie Olsen, *Silences* (1978) (London: Virago, 1980) p. 255.

XI

page

157 'The last chapter . . .'
Rimmer, *The Harrad Experiment*, p. 197.

'never again . . .'
Brown and Faulder, *Treat Yourself*, p. 54.

159 'Should any sexpiece . . .'
ibid. p. 9.

161 'freshly liberated wife' / 'sensuous man' / 'wildly uninhibited . . .'
Robert H. Rimmer, *The Love Explosion* (New York: Signet Books, 1980) front and back cover blurb.

'The Baron . . .'
Scott, 'The end-away justifies the means', p. 16.

163 'Pornography is . . .'
Robin Morgan, 'Theory and Practice: Pornography and Rape', in *Take Back the Night* ed. Laura Lederer (New York: William Morrow Co., 1980) p. 139.

'Is it really . . .'
Ann Jones, 'A Little Knowledge', in *Take Back the Night*, p. 181.

164 'the following observation . . .'
Brown and Faulder, *Treat Yourself*, p. 94.

165-6 'a primal penis . . .' / 'Sitting naked . . .' / 'deeply sexual . . .'
Rimmer, *The Love Explosion*, pp. 30, 41, 70.

167 'Often the nude biologist . . .'
Talese, *Thy Neighbour's Wife*, p. 349. Another classic credentials description is provided by Rimmer eulogizing Vern L. Bullough, author of a book entitled *Sexual Variance in Society and History*: 'Vern is a history professor who knows more about human sexuality, past, present, and future, than any man alive . . . and he gets a lot of help from his wife, Bonnie', *The Love Explosion*, p. 202.

168 'This process . . .'
Brown and Faulder, *Treat Yourself*, p. 65.